Hebrew and Aramaic Dictionary
of the Old Testament

Hebrew and Aramaic Dictionary
of the Old Testament

Edited by Georg Fohrer

in cooperation with
Hans Werner Hoffmann · Friedrich Huber
Jochen Vollmer · Gunther Wanke

English version by
W. Johnstone

Walter de Gruyter · Berlin · New York
1973

Translated from the German
Hebräisches und aramäisches Wörterbuch zum Alten Testament
© 1971 by Walter de Gruyter · Berlin · New York

ISBN 3 11 00 4572 9
Translation © SCM Press Ltd 1973

Printed in England

CONTENTS

INTRODUCTION

1. The *Hebrew and Aramaic Dictionary of the Old Testament* is intended to fill a long-standing gap. There are large lexica, with a comprehensive technical apparatus, which will continue to be used in Old Testament scholarship. But there is need for a convenient and inexpensive dictionary for everyday use, especially for reading and translating Old Testament texts. Here is such a dictionary which seeks, not to make the large lexica dispensable or superfluous, but to stand alongside and complement them.

2. This dictionary contains the complete Hebrew and Aramaic vocabulary of the Old Testament, including the names. For these latter entries, as for the others, an English rendering is offered. Thus forms of names which are differentiated in Hebrew are correspondingly differentiated in the English rendering, since historical or geographical identification cannot be the task of a dictionary.

In addition, the dictionary notes, with references to the passages concerned, significant special meanings and, in clear cases, also includes conjectures. It makes use of results of recent research, but not, of course, in such a way as to coin a new Hebrew vocabulary by means of an uncritical use of Ugaritic or another Semitic language.

3. The dictionary presupposes a knowledge of Hebrew grammar. For most purposes the standard text-books suffice, but in particular instances such grammars as that of W. Gesenius–E. Kautzsch must be consulted. On this presupposition, the citing of all the various forms of the words, especially the verbs, has been dispensed with. A reproduction of the complete list of forms would have made the dictionary too bulky; a mere selection of them would have been too subjective.

In addition, to avoid any pre-judgments, all material is excluded which belongs more appropriately to the task of exegesis. This is especially the case in the matter of the identification of names.

4. Combinations of two or more Hebrew words are, for the purposes of listing, treated as single, composite words.

The form in which the entries are listed is based on the Massoretic Text; thus, where they are regularly or exclusively used, mixed Kethib and Qere forms which occur in the Massoretic Text are reproduced as such in the dictionary.

The rendering of the names usually follows the practice of the *Revised Standard Version*. Feminine names are marked *f.*; those not marked are to be taken as masculine.

Italics are used for explanatory and periphrastic notes.

FORMS OF THE HEBREW VERB

Representation:	for:
aph	aphel
hi	hiphil
hitp	hitpael
hitpal	hitpalel
hitpalp	hitpalpel
hitpo	hitpoel
hitpol	hitpolel
ho	hophal
hotpaal	hotpaal
iphtael	iphtael
itpa	itpaal
ni	niphal
nitp	nitpael
pal	palel
pealal	pealal
pi	piel
pil	pilel
pilp	pilpel
poal	poal
poalal	poalal
poel	poel
pol	polel
polal	polal
polp	polpal
pu	pual
pul	pulal
q	qal
tiphal	tiphal

FORMS OF THE ARAMAIC VERB

Representation:	for:
aph	aphel
ha	haphel
hišt	hištaphal
hitpa	hitpaal
hitpe	hitpeel
hitpol	hitpolel
itpa	itpaal
itpe	itpeel
itpol	itpole/al
pa	pael
pe	peal, peil
po	poe/al
pol	polel
sa	saphel
ša	šaphel

ABBREVIATIONS AND SYMBOLS

abs.	absolute
adv.	adverb
alw.	always
Aram.	Aramaic, Aramaizing; → also the symbol °.
Assyr.	Assyrian
Bab.	Babylonian
c.	circa
cm	centimetre
coll.	collective
cond.	conditional
conj.	conjunction
cstr.	construct
du.	dual
dub.	dubious
Eg.	Egyptian
f.	feminine, following
fig.	figurative(ly)
fut.	future
g	gram
gent.	gentilic
impf.	imperfect
imv.	imperative
inf.	infinitive
intrans.	intransitive
K	Kethib
kg	kilogram
l	litre
m.	masculine
n.	name of
part.	particle
pass.	passive
peop.	people, inhabitants of towns, etc.

pers.	person
Pers.	Persian
pf.	perfect
pl.	plural
prep.	preposition
pt.	participle
Q	Qere
rd.	read (suggested emendation)
refl.	reflexive
sg.	singular
subst.	substantive, substantival
terr.	territory
text corr.	text corrupt
tog.	together
trans.	transitive
w.	with
usu.	usually
>	symbol for development: becomes
<	symbol for development: is derived from
→	symbol for reference: see
?	uncertain meaning, uncertain
*	A word so marked is not attested in the (basic) form given. (The asterisk is not put in when the basic form is attested in pause or with the article or with a preposition, or if the construct is identical with the absolute state. The other principal omission of the asterisk is in cross-reference.)
○	Aramaism. (The symbol is used to identify an entry in the Hebrew Part as an Aramaism in its entire use and meaning; otherwise → *Aram.*)

Books of the Bible

Gen.	II Kings	Nahum	Cant.
Ex.	Isa.	Hab.	Eccles.
Lev.	Jer.	Zeph.	Lam.
Num.	Ezek.	Hag.	Esther
Deut.	Hos.	Zech.	Dan.
Josh.	Joel	Mal.	Ezra
Judg.	Amos	Ps.	Neh.
I Sam.	Obad.	Job	I Chron.
II Sam.	Jonah	Prov.	II Chron.
I Kings	Micah	Ruth	

Hebrew Part

א

אָב   father, ancestor *(also in the broadest sense)*; *II Chron. 2.12;*
    4.16 title of respect?

אֵב*   shoot, bud.

אֹב   → אוֹב.

אֲבַגְתָא   *n. pers.* Abagtha.

אבד   *q* be lost, wander, stray, perish.
    pi lose, let stray, destroy, exterminate.
    hi annihilate, exterminate.

אֹבֵד   destruction > עֲדֵי אֹבֵד for ever.

אֲבֵדָה   lost property.

אֲבַדֹּה   underworld.

אֲבַדּוֹן   destruction, place of destruction *(of the abode of the dead)*.

אָבְדָן°,   destruction.

אָבְדָן°*

אבה   *q* want, be willing.

אֵבֶה   reed.

אֲבוֹי   desire > misery.

אֵבוּס   trough, manger.

אִבְחָה*   *rd.* מֶבַח הַ' *(Ezek. 21.20).*

אֲבַטִּחִים   water-melons.

אָבִי   if only!

אֲבִי   *n. pers. f.* Abi < אֲבִיָּה.

אֲבִיאֵל   *n. pers.* Abiel.

אֲבִיאָסָף   *n. pers.* Abiasaph.

אָבִיב   *coll.* ears of corn; Abib *(name of a month, March/April).*

אֲבִיגַיִל   *n. pers. f.* Abigail *(also* אֲבִינַל*).*

אֲבִידָן   *n. pers.* Abidan.

אֲבִידָע   *n. pers.* Abida.

אֲבִיָּה   *n. pers. m. and f.* Abijah.

אֲבִיָּהוּ   *n. pers.* Abijah.

אֲבִיהוּא   *n. pers.* Abihu.

אֲבִיהוּד   *n. pers.* Abihud.

אֲבִיהַיִל   *n. pers. f.* Abihail.

אֲבִי הָעֶזְרִי   *gent.* Abiezrite.

אֶבְיוֹן   poor, wretched.

אֲבִיּוֹנָה   caper.

אֲבִיחַיִל   *n. pers.* Abihail.

אֲבִיטוּב   *n. pers.* Abitub.

אֲבִיטַל   *n. pers. f.* Abital.

אֲבִיָּם   *n. pers.* Abijam.

אֲבִימָאֵל   *n. pers.* Abimael.

אֲבִימֶלֶךְ   *n. pers.* Abimelech.

אֲבִינָדָב   *n. pers.* Abinadab.

אֲבִינֹעַם   *n. pers.* Abinoam.

אֲבִינֵר   *n. pers.* Abner.

אֶבְיָסָף   *n. pers.* Ebiasaph.

אֲבִיעֶזֶר   *n. pers.* Abiezer.

אֲבִי־עַלְבוֹן   *n. pers.* Abialbon.

אָבִיר*   strong one; *w.* יַעֲקֹב *or* יִשְׂרָאֵל the Strong One of Jacob/Israel?, Defender of Jacob/Israel? *(title of a God).*

אַבִּיר   strong, mighty, eminent; *subst.* strong one; *fig. for* celestial being, stallion, bull.

אֲבִירָם   *n. pers.* Abiram.

אֲבִישַׁג   *n. pers. f.* Abishag.

אֲבִישׁוּעַ   *n. pers.* Abishua.

אֲבִישׁוּר   *n. pers.* Abishur.

אֲבִישַׁי   *n. pers.* Abishai.

אֲבִישָׁלוֹם   *n. pers.* Abishalom.

אֶבְיָתָר   *n. pers.* Abiathar.

אבך   *hitp* whirl upwards.

אבל   *q* lament, observe mourning rites; *fig. applied to nature* dry up. *hi* cause to observe mourning rites.
hitp mourn.

I אָבֵל   observing mourning rites, mourning.

II אָבֵל   *element of n. place* Abel (watercourse, stream?).

אֵבֶל   mourning rites, mourning.

אֲבָל   surely, truly; *adversative part.* no, but, however.

אֻבָל   watercourse, channel.

אֶבֶן *f.* stone, (stone)weight; *Gen. 49.24* rock.

אָבֶן* *du.* potter's wheel; *Ex. 1.16* delivery stones *?*

אֲבָנָה *n. river* Abana.

אֶבֶן הָעֵזֶר *n. place* Ebenezer.

אַבְנֵט sash.

אַבְנֵר *n. pers.* Abner.

אבס *q pt. pass.* fattened.

אֲבַעְבֻּעֹת sores.

אֶבֶץ *n. place* Ebez.

אִבְצָן *n. pers.* Ibzan.

אבק *ni* wrestle.

אָבָק dust *(whirled up)*; *Ex. 9.9* soot.

אֲבָקָה* powdered spices.

אבר *hi* soar up.

אֵבֶר pinion, wing.

אֶבְרָה pinion, wing.

אַבְרָהָם *n. pers.* Abraham.

אַבְרֵךְ *unexplained acclamation.*

אַבְרָם *n. pers.* Abram.

אֲבִשַׁי *n. pers.* Abishai.

אַבְשָׁל(וֹ)ם *n. pers.* Absalom.

אֹבֹת *n. place* Oboth.

אָגֵא *n. pers.* Agee.

אֲגָג, אֲגַג *n. pers.* Agag.

אֲגָגִי *gent.* Agagite.

אֲגֻדָּה *Ex. 12.22* bunch; *II Sam. 2.25* band; *Isa. 58.6* rope; *Amos 9.6* vault.

אֱגוֹז nut.

אָגוּר *n. pers.* Agur.

אֲגוֹרָה* payment.

אֶגֶל* drop.

אֶגְלַיִם *n. place* Eglaim.

אֲגַם reedy pool; *Jer. 51.32* redoubt *?*

אָגֵם* distressed.

אַגְמוֹן, אַגְמֹן reed; *Job 41.12 rd.* אָגֵם glowing.

אַגָּן* bowl, basin.

אֲגַף* band, army.

אגר *q* gather in *(crop).*

אֲנַרְטָל* basin.

אֶגְרֹף fist.

אִגֶּרֶת letter.

אֵד stream?, underground water?, mist?

אדב hi *I Sam. 2.33* < לְהַאֲדִיב cause to languish.

אַדְבְּאֵל *n. pers.* Adbeel.

אֲדַד *n. pers.* Hadad.

אִדּוֹ *n. pers.* Iddo.

אֱדוֹם *n. pers., n. peop., n. terr.* Edom.

אֱדוֹמִי* *gent.* Edomite.

אָדוֹן lord; אֲדֹנָי Lord *(only used of God).*

אַדּוֹן *n. place* Addon.

אֲדוֹרַיִם *n. place* Adoraim.

אֲדוֹת → אוֹדֹת.

אַדִּיר mighty, glorious.

אֲדַלְיָא *n. pers.* Adalia.

אדם *q* be red.

    pu pt. dyed red.

    hi be/become red.

    hitp gleam red.

I אָדָם *coll.* mankind, humanity, people; human being *(frequently* בֶּן־אָדָם *or similar)*; *Eccles. 7.28* man.

II אָדָם *n. pers.* Adam; *n. place Josh. 3.16* Adam; *Hos. 6.7 rd.* בְּאָדָם.

אָדֹם red, reddish-brown.

אֹדֶם *red precious stone* ruby?

אֲדַמְדָּם reddish.

I אֲדָמָה cultivable ground *(also* landed property, earth *as material substance).*

II אֲדָמָה *n. place* Adamah.

אַדְמָה *n. place* Admah.

אַדְמוֹנִי red, ruddy.

אַדֹמִי *gent.* Edomite.

אֲדָמִי הַנֶּקֶב *n. place* Adami-nekeb.

אֲדֻמִּים *n. place* Adummim.

אַדְמֹנִי → אַדְמוֹנִי.

אַדְמָתָא *n. pers.* Admatha.

אֶדֶן pedestal; *Job 38.6* base.

אַדָּן *n. place* Addan.

אַדֹנָי → אָדוֹן.

אֲדֹנִי בֶזֶק, *n. pers.* Adoni-bezek.
אֲדֹנִי־בֶזֶק

אֲדֹנִיָּה(וּ) *n. pers.* Adonijah.

אֲדֹנִי־צֶדֶק *n. pers.* Adoni-zedek.

אֲדֹנִיקָם *n. pers.* Adonikam.

אֲדֹנִירָם *n. pers.* Adoniram.

אדר *ni* show oneself mighty.
hi make mighty, glorious.

אֶדֶר might, glory.

אֲדָר Adar *(name of a month, February/March)*.

אַדָּר *n. pers., n. place* Addar.

אֲדַרְכּוֹן* daric *(Pers. gold coin)*.

אֲדֹרָם *n. pers.* Adoram.

אַדְרַמֶּלֶךְ *n. pers.* Adrammelech.

אֶדְרֶעִי *n. place* Edrei.

אַדֶּרֶת splendour, glory; fine garment, robe of state.

אדש *q* thresh.

אהב *q* like, love; *pt. also* friend.
ni pt. worthy of love.
pi pt. lover.

אֹהַב* enjoyment of love.

אַהַב* loving gift; loveliness.

אַהֲבָה love.

אֹהַד *n. pers.* Ohad.

אֲהָהּ alas! *(apotropaic cry of alarm)*.

אַהֲוָא *n. river* Ahava.

אֵהוּד *n. pers.* Ehud.

אֱהִי *rd.* אַיֵּה *(Hos. 13.10, 14)*.

I אהל *hi Job 25.5* be bright.

II אהל *q* move camp, live as nomad.
pi pitch a tent.

I אֹהֶל tent.

II אֹהֶל *n. pers.* Ohel.

אׇהֳלָה *n. pers. f.* Oholah.

אֲהָלוֹת aloes.

אׇהֳלִיאָב *n. pers.* Oholiab.

אׇהֳלִיבָה *n. pers. f.* Oholibah.

אָהֳלִיבָמָה *n. pers. f., n. peop.?* Oholibamah.

אֲהָלִים aloes; *Num. 24.6 dub.*

אַהֲרֹן *n. pers.* Aaron.

אוֹ or; or rather, or if; אוֹ—אוֹ whether—or.

אוֹ *Prov. 31.4 text corr.*

אוּאֵל *n. pers.* Uel.

I ‏אוֹב* *Job 32.19* wine-skin.

II אוֹב spirit of the dead.

אוֹבִיל *n. pers.* Obil.

אוּבָל → אָבָל.

אוּד piece of firewood.

אוֹדֹת cause; *alw. w.* עַל because of.

אוה *ni?* be lovely, fair; be fitting.

    pi wish, desire.

    hitp show oneself desirous.

אַוָּה* desire, longing.

אוּזַי *n. pers.* Uzai.

אוּזָל *n. pers.* Uzal.

אֱוִי *n. pers.* Evi.

אוֹי alas! *(cry of anguish)*.

אוֹיָה alas!

אֱוִיל foolish, uninstructed; fool *(frequently with the secondary meaning of impiety)*.

אֱוִיל מְרֹדַךְ *n. pers.* Evil-merodach *(Bab.* Amel Marduk).

אוּל* *Ps. 73.4* body?

אוּלַי *rd. Q (II Kings 24.15).*

אֱוִלִי incompetent.

I אוּלַי perhaps.

II אוּלַי *n. river* Ulai.

I אוּלָם on the other hand, on the contrary.

II אוּלָם *n. pers.* Ulam.

III אוּלָם porch; *properly* → אֵילָם.

אִוֶּלֶת folly *(frequently with the secondary meaning of impiety)*.

אוֹמֶר matter.

אוֹמָר *n. pers.* Omar.

אָוֶן evil, sinister thing; trouble; wrong, wickedness, deception, emptiness.

I אוֹן   procreative power, strength; wealth, abundance.

II אוֹן   n. pers. On; n. place Gen. 41.45, 50; 46.20 (Ezek. 30.17) On, Heliopolis.

אוֹנוֹ   n. place Ono.

אוֹנִים   pl. of אוֹן or אֹנֶה.

אוֹנָם   n. pers. Onam.

אוֹנָן   n. pers. Onan.

אוּפָז   n. terr. Uphaz.

אוֹפִיר   n. pers. Gen. 10.29; I Chron. 1.23 Ophir; n. terr. Ophir; Job 22.24 gold of Ophir.

אוֹפַן   wheel.

אוֹפָר   → אוֹפִיר.

אוץ   q urge, be in a hurry, hasten; Josh. 17.15 be too confined.
hi urge someone.

אוֹצָר   store, treasure.

אור   q be/become light, shine.
ni? be lit up.
hi make shine, illuminate, light; spread light, shine.

אוֹר   light.

I אוּר   glow (of light), fire.

II *אוּר   only pl., usually occurring with תֻּמִּים, lot for oracular consultation (decision in the negative).

III אוּר   n. place Ur (of the Chaldeans); n. pers. Ur.

אוֹרֵב   → אֹרֵב.

אוֹרָה   light, happiness; II Kings 4.39 (Isa. 26.19?) mallow.

אֲוֵרוֹת   stalls.

אוּרִי   n. pers. Uri.

אוּרִיאֵל   n. pers. Uriel.

אוּרִיָּה(וּ)   n. pers. Uriah.

אֲוַרְנָה   rd. Q (II Sam. 24.16).

אוּת   q agree.

אוֹת   sign, token, ensign; miracle.

אָז   at that time; then (fut. and cond.).

אֵזוֹב   → אֵזוֹב.

אֶזְבַּי   n. pers. Ezbai.

אֵזוֹב   hyssop.

אֵזוֹר   loin-cloth.

אֲזַי° *parallel form of* אָז then.

אַזְכָּרָה *that part of the meal-offering which is burnt; the incense accompanying the shewbread.*

אזל° *q* go away, disappear.

אֲזֵל *rd.* הַלָּאו *(I Sam. 20.19)* that one.

I אזן *hi* listen to.

II אזן *pi* weigh up.

אֹזֶן *f.* ear.

אָזֵן* *equipment.

אַזְנוֹת תָּבוֹר *n. place* Aznoth-tabor.

אזנח *hi of* I זנח.

אָזְנִי *n. pers.* Ozni; *gent.* Oznite.

אֲזַנְיָה *n. pers.* Azaniah.

אֶזֶן שֶׁאֱרָה *n. place* Uzzen-sheerah.

אֲזִקִּים manacles.

אזר *q* put on a loin-cloth, gird (oneself).

         ni be girded.

         pi gird someone.

         hitp gird oneself, arm.

אֶזְרוֹעַ *f.* arm.

אֶזְרָח a native.

אֶזְרָחִי *gent.* Ezrahite.

אֶזְרֹעַ → אֶזְרוֹעַ.

I אָח brother *(also in the broadest sense).*

II אָח *ah!* alas!

אָח brazier.

אֹחַ* owl?, hyena?

אַחְאָב *n. pers.* Ahab.

אֶחָב *n. pers.* Ahab.

אַחְבָּן *n. pers.* Ahban.

אחד *Ezek. 21.21 dub.*

אֶחָד one, sole, single, first, anyone, once; *pl.* some, a few; כְּאֶחָד *(Aram.)* together, at the same time.

אָחוּ reeds.

אֵחוּד *n. pers.* Ehud.

I אַחְוָה°* statement.

II אַחֲוָה brotherhood.

אֲחוֹחַ *n. pers.* Ahoah.

אֲחוֹחִי *gent.* Ahohite.

אֲחוּמַי *n. pers.* Ahumai.

אָחוֹר behind, the west; afterwards, future; *pl.* back, hindquarters.

אָחוֹת sister *(also in the broadest sense)*.

אחז *q* seize, grasp, take hold; insert, join *(architectural)*; *Esther 1.6* fasten; *Neh. 7.3* bar *(Aram.)*.

ni be seized, held; be settled.

pi close.

ho II Chron. 9.18 dub.

אָחָז *n. pers.* Ahaz.

אָחֻזֿ holding.

אֲחֻזָּה landed property.

אַחְזַי *n. pers.* Ahzai.

אֲחַזְיָה(וּ) *n. pers.* Ahaziah.

אֲחֻזָּם *n. pers.* Ahuzzam.

אֲחֻזַּת *n. pers.* Ahuzzath.

אֲחֹחִי → אֲחוֹחִי

אֵחִי *n. pers.* Ehi.

אֲחִי *n. pers.* Ahi.

אֲחִיאָם *n. pers.* Ahiam.

אֲחִיָּה(וּ) *n. pers.* Ahijah.

אֲחִיהוּד *n. pers.* Ahihud.

אַחְיוֹ *n. pers.* Ahio.

אֲחִיחֻד *n. pers.* Ahihud.

אֲחִיטוּב *n. pers.* Ahitub.

אֲחִילוּד *n. pers.* Ahilud.

אֲחִימוֹת *n. pers.* Ahimoth.

אֲחִימֶלֶךְ *n. pers.* Ahimelech.

אֲחִימַן *n. pers.* Ahiman.

אֲחִימַעַץ *n. pers.* Ahimaaz.

אַחְיָן *n. pers.* Ahian.

אֲחִינָדָב *n. pers.* Ahinadab.

אֲחִינֹעַם *n. pers. f.* Ahinoam.

אֲחִיסָמָךְ *n. pers.* Ahisamach.

אֲחִיעֶזֶר *n. pers.* Ahiezer.

אֲחִיקָם *n. pers.* Ahikam.

אֲחִירָם *n. pers.* Ahiram.

אֲחִירָמִי *gent.* Ahiramite.

אֲחִירַע *n. pers.* Ahira.

אֲחִישַׁחַר *n. pers.* Ahishahar.

אֲחִישָׁר *n. pers.* Ahishar.

אֲחִיתֹפֶל *n. pers.* Ahithophel.

אַחְלָב *n. place* Ahlab.

אַחֲלַי, אַחֲלֵי O if only!

אַחְלָי *n. pers.* Ahlai.

אַחְלָמָה jasper.

אֲחַסְבַּי *n. pers.* Ahasbai.

אחר *q* stay.

   pi detain; be late; delay, linger; *Ex. 22.28* hold back.
   hi be late.

I אַחֵר following, next, another.

II אַחֵר *n. pers.* Aher.

אַחַר *sg.* behind, in the rear, after, afterwards; *pl.* end, behind, after *(prep. and conj.)*.

אַחֲרוֹן rear, the west, last; later, future; *f.* last, in the end.

אַחְרַח *n. pers.* Aharah.

אֲחַרְחֵל *n. pers.* Aharhel.

אַחֲרִית issue, end *(in space, time, quality)*; remnant, posterity.

אֲחֹרַנִּית back, backwards.

אֲחַשְׁדַּרְפְּנִים satraps, governors.

אֲחַשְׁוֵר(וֹ)שׁ *n. pers.* Xerxes.

אֲחַשְׁרֵשׁ *rd. Q (Esther 10.1)*.

אֲחַשְׁתָּרִי *gent.* Ahashtarite.

אֲחַשְׁתְּרָנִים belonging to the king's service, royal.

אַט, אִט* gently, softly; *Gen. 33.14* convenience.

אָטָד *thorn-bush* boxthorn?

אֵטוּן linen.

אִטִּים exorcists.

אטם *q* stop up, close; *I Kings 6.4; Ezek. 40.16; 41.16, 26* close with lattice-work? frame?

אטר *q* close.

אָטֵר *n. pers.* Ater.

אִטֵּר restricted on the right > left-handed *or* ambidextrous.

אֵי where?; אֵי־זֶה which?, where?

I אִי coast, island.

II *אִי demon?, jackal?

III אִי alas!; *Job 22.30 dub.*

אִיב q be hostile towards; *pt. also* enemy.

אֵיבָה enmity, hostility.

אֵיד disaster.

I אַיָּה hawk, kite.

II אַיָּה *n. pers.* Aiah.

אַיֵּה where?

אַיֵּו *rd. Q (Jer. 37.19)*.

אִיּוֹב *n. pers.* Job.

אִיזֶבֶל *n. pers. f.* Jezebel.

אֵיךְ how?; how!

אִי(־)כָבוֹד *n. pers.* Ichabod.

אֵיכָה how?; how!; *Cant. 1.7* where? *(Aram.)*.

°אֵיכֹה where?

אֵיכָכָה how?

אַיִל ram; mighty one, leader; large tree; pillar, post.

°אֱיָל strength.

אַיָּל deer.

אַיָּלָה doe, hind.

אִילוֹ *rd.* אִי לוֹ *(Eccles. 4.10)*.

אַיָּלוֹן *n. place* Aijalon.

אֵילוֹן *n. pers., n. place* Elon.

אֵילוֹת *n. place* Eloth.

°*אֱיָלוּת strength.

*אֵילָם porch.

אֵילִם *n. place* Elim.

אֵילָן → אַיָּלוֹן.

אֵיל פָּארָן *n. place* El-paran.

אֵילַת *n. place* Elath.

אַיֶּלֶת doe, hind.

אָיֹם terrible.

אֵימָה terror; *Jer. 50.38* apparition > idol.

אֵימִים   *n. peop.* Emim.

I אַיִן   non-existence > not, no, without, -less.

II אַיִן   where?, *always* מֵאַיִן whence?

אִין   *rd.* אַיִן *(I Sam. 21.9).*

אִיעֶזֶר   *n. pers.* Iezer.

אִיעֶזְרִי   *gent.* Iezrite.

אֵיפָה   *grain-measure* ephah *(between 22 and 45 l).*

אֵיפֹה   where?

אִישׁ   man, human being; one, anyone, each one; *pl.* people.

אִישׁ(־)בֹּשֶׁת   *n. pers. derogatory form of* אֶשְׁבַּעַל Ishbosheth.

אִישְׁהוֹד   *n. pers.* Ishhod.

אִישׁוֹן   pupil.

אִישׁוּן   time.

אִישׁ טוֹב,   *n. pers.* Ish-tob.
אִישׁ־טוֹב

אִישַׁי°   *n. pers.* Jesse.

אִיתַי   *n. pers.* Ithai.

אִיתִיאֵל   *n. pers.* Ithiel.

אִיתָמָר   *n. pers.* Ithamar.

I אֵיתָן   ever-flowing; enduring; *pl.* Ethanim *(name of a month, September/October).*

II אֵיתָן   *n. pers.* Ethan.

אַךְ   only; surely, certainly; however.

אַכַּד   *n. place* Accad.

אַכְזָב   deceitful.

אַכְזִיב   *n. place* Achzib.

אַכְזָר   cruel.

אַכְזָרִי   cruel.

אַכְזְרִיּוּת   cruelty.

אֲכִילָה   food.
אָכִישׁ

אכל   *q* eat, devour; taste, enjoy.

ni be eaten, consumed.

pu be devoured, consumed.

hi feed, make to enjoy.

אֹכֶל   food, nourishment.

אָכָל   *n. pers?*

אָכְלָה   food, nourishment.

אָכֵן surely; but, however.

אכף °q press someone.

אֶכֶף °* pressure.

אִכָּר farmer, farm-worker.

אַכְשָׁף n. place Achshaph.

אַל not; I Sam. 27.10 rd. אָן or אֶל־מִי.

I אֵל cstr. of אַיִל.

II אֵל power.

III אֵל god, God.

IV אֵל these.

אֶל towards, up to, against, with regard to; at, on; *frequently for* עַל.

אֶלָא n. pers. Ela.

אֶלְגָּבִישׁ ice crystals, hail.

אַלְגוּמִּים rd. אַלְמֻגִּים.

אֶלְדָּד n. pers. Eldad.

אֶלְדָּעָה n. pers. Eldaah.

I אלה q swear.

hi curse, place under oath (hypothetical curse).

II אלה °q lament.

III אלה q be unable.

אָלָה oath, curse.

I אֵלָה large tree.

II אֵלָה n. pers., n. peop.? Elah.

אַלָּה large tree.

אֵלֶּה these.

אֱלָהּ, אֱלַהּ, אֱלָהּ → אֱלוֹהַּ.

אֱלֹהִים God, gods.

אִלּוּ °if.

אֱלוֹהַּ God.

אֱלוּל Elul (name of a month, August/September).

I אֵלוֹן large tree.

II אֵלוֹן → אַיָּלוֹן.

I אַלּוֹן large tree.

II אַלּוֹן n. pers. Allon.

I אַלּוּף friendly, tame; *subst.* intimate; Ps. 144.14 cow?

II אַלּוּף chief.

אָלוּשׁ *n. place* Alush.

אָלוֹת → אֵילוֹת.

אֶלְזָבָד *n. pers.* Elzabad.

אלח *ni* be corrupt.

אֶלְחָנָן *n. pers.* Elhanan.

אֱלַי → I אוּלַי.

אֱלִיאָב *n. pers.* Eliab.

אֱלִיאֵל *n. pers.* Eliel.

אֱלִיאָתָה° *n. pers.* Eliathah.

אֱלִידָד *n. pers.* Elidad.

אֶלְיָדָע *n. pers.* Eliada.

אַלְיָה fat tail *(of sheep)*.

אֵלִיָּה(וּ) *n. pers.* Elijah.

אֱלִיהוּ *n. pers.* Elihu.

אֱלִיהוּא *n. pers.* Elihu.

אֶלְיְהוֹעֵינַי *n. pers.* Eliehoenai.

אֶלְיוֹעֵינַי *n. pers.* Elioenai.

אֶלְיַחְבָּא *n. pers.* Eliahba.

אֶלִיחֹרֶף *n. pers.* Elihoreph.

אֱלִיל gods *(alw. used contemptuously)*, idol; nothing, futile.

אֱלִימֶלֶךְ *n. pers.* Elimelech.

אֶלְיָסָף *n. pers.* Eliasaph.

אֱלִיעֶזֶר *n. pers.* Eliezer.

אֱלִיעָם *n. pers.* Eliam.

אֱלִיעֵנַי *n. pers.* Elienai.

אֱלִיפַז *n. pers.* Eliphaz.

אֱלִיפָל *n. pers.* Eliphal.

אֱלִיפְלֵהוּ *n. pers.* Eliphelehu.

אֱלִיפֶלֶט *n. pers.* Eliphelet.

אֱלִיצוּר *n. pers.* Elizur.

אֱלִיצָפָן *n. pers.* Elizaphan.

אֱלִיקָא *n. pers.* Elika.

אֶלְיָקִים *n. pers.* Eliakim.

אֱלִישֶׁבַע *n. pers. f.* Elisheba.

אֱלִישָׁה *n. terr.* Elishah.

אֱלִישׁוּעַ *n. pers.* Elishua.

אֶלְיָשִׁיב *n. pers.* Eliashib.

אֱלִישָׁמָע *n. pers.* Elishama.

אֱלִישָׁע   *n. pers.* Elisha.

אֱלִישָׁפָט   *n. pers.* Elishaphat.

אֱלִיָּתָה   *n. pers.* Eliathah.

אֱלָל   → אֱלִיל.

אַלְלַי   alas!

אלם   *pi* bind *(sheaves).*

    ni be/become bound, dumb.

אֵלֶם   silence?

אִלֵּם   dumb.

אֵלָם   → אֵילָם.

אֵלָם   → III אוּלָם.

אַלְמֻגִּים   almug wood *(species of wood from Lebanon).*

אֲלֻמָּה*   sheaf.

אַלְמוֹדָד   *n. pers.* Almodad.

אַלַּמֶּלֶךְ   *n. place* Allammelech.

אַלְמָן   widower.

אַלְמֹן   widowhood.

אַלְמָנָה   widow; *pl. also* widowhood.

אַלְמָנוּת*   widowhood.

אַלְמֹנִי   a particular, a certain.

אֵלֹנִי   *gent.* Elonite.

אֶלְנַעַם   *n. pers.* Elnaam.

אֶלְנָתָן   *n. pers.* Elnathan.

אֶלָּסָר   *n. place* Ellasar, Larsa.

אֶלְעָד   *n. pers.* Elead.

אֶלְעָדָה   *n. pers.* Eleadah.

אֶלְעוּזַי   *n. pers.* Eluzai.

אֶלְעָזָר   *n. pers.* Eleazar.

אֶלְעָלֵא, אֶלְעָלֵה   *n. place* Elealeh.

אֶלְעָשָׂה   *n. pers.* Eleasah.

I אלף   *q* become familiar with.

    pi (Aram.) teach, instruct.

II אלף   *hi* produce in thousands.

I אֶלֶף   cattle.

II אֶלֶף   thousand; company of a thousand > clan, tribe, district.

III אֶלֶף   *n. place* Eleph.

אֶלְפֶּלֶט   *n. pers.* Elpelet.

אֶלְפַּעַל   *n. pers.* Elpaal.

אֱלִיץ *pi* pester, press hard.

אֶלְצָפָן *n. pers.* Elzaphan.

אַלְקוּם *dub.* (troops?).

אֶלְקָנָה *n. pers.* Elkanah.

אֶלְקשִׁי *gent.* Elkoshite.

אֶלְתּוֹלַד *n. place* Eltolad.

אֶלְתְּקֵה, אֶלְתְּקָא *n. place* Elteke.

אֶלְתְּקֹן *n. place* Eltekon.

אִם if, though, even if, if only, when; whether; הַ—אִם whether—or; אִם—אִם whether it be—or; אִם *introduces an oath to be translated in the negative*, אִם לֹא *an oath to be translated in the affirmative.*

אִם mother *(also in the broadest sense)*; Ezek. 21.26 אֵם הַדֶּרֶךְ parting of the ways.

אָמָה female slave.

I אַמָּה cubit *(c. 45 cm, on the old standard c. 53 cm)*; Isa. 6.4 pivot *of leaf of door.*

II אַמָּה *II Sam. 8.1 dub.*

III אַמָּה *n. place* Ammah.

אֻמָּה → אֵימָה.

אֻמָּה* clan, tribe.

I אָמוֹן artisan; *Prov. 8.30* fondling?, darling?

II אָמוֹן *n. pers.* Amon *(also the name of an Eg. god).*

אָמוּן* sincere one; honesty.

אֱמוּנָה firmness, faithfulness, constancy.

אָמוֹץ *n. pers.* Amoz.

אַמּוֹת rd. מֵאוֹת *(Ezek. 42.16).*

אָמִי *n. pers.* Ami.

אֵמִים → אֵימִים.

אֲמִינוֹן *n. pers.* Aminon.

אַמִּיץ strong.

אָמִיר branch.

אמל *pul* dry up, wither, become feeble.

אֲמֵלַל* languishing?

אֻמְלַל feeble.

אֲמֵלָל* feeble, wretched.

אָמָם *n. place* Amam.

אמן *q* → אָמֵן; *pt. pass. Lam. 4.5* supported, carried.

ni prove firm, faithful; be faithful, reliable, true; last, remain, endure; *pt. also* entrusted, appointed; *Isa. 60.4* be carried.

hi feel confidence, consider faithful, believe, trust, rely on.

אָמָן craftsman.

אָמֵן surely!

אֹמֵן tutor, foster-father; *f.* nurse.

אֹמֶן faithfulness.

אֹמֶן faithfulness.

אֲמֵנָה → אֲמוּנָה.

I אֲמָנָה firm agreement, fixed arrangement.

II אֲמָנָה *n. place* Amana.

I אָמְנָה in fact, indeed.

II אָמְנָה upbringing, fostering.

אֹמְנָה* door-post?, plate?

אַמְנוֹן *n. pers.* Amnon.

אָמְנָם surely, indeed.

אֻמְנָם surely, indeed.

אַמְנוֹן → אֲמָנוֹן.

אמץ *q* be strong.

pi strengthen; harden; *Ps 80.16, 18* rear; *II Chron. 24.13* repair.

hi feel strong.

hitp show strength; *Ruth 1.18* be firmly resolved.

אַמֵּץ → אַמִּיץ.

אָמֹץ* dappled?

אֹמֶץ strength.

אַמְצָה strength.

אַמְצִי *n. pers.* Amzi.

אֲמַצְיָה(וּ) *n. pers.* Amaziah.

I אמר *q* say, speak; call; think.

ni be said, spoken; it is said, told; be called.

hi make to declare.

II אמר *hitp* boast.

אֹמֶר speech, information; *Job 22.28* → אוֹמֶר.

18

I* אֵמֶר speech, word.

II* אֵמֶר antler.

אִמֵּר *n. pers., n. place?* Immer.

אִמְרָה*, word, saying.
אִמְרָה*

אֱמֹרִי *gent.* Amorite.

אִמְרִי *n. pers.* Imri.

אֲמַרְיָה(וּ) *n. pers.* Amariah.

אַמְרָפֶל *n. pers.* Amraphel.

אֶמֶשׁ last night.

אֱמֶת firmness, faithfulness, stability, constancy, truth.

אַמְתַּחַת sack.

אֲמִתַּי *n. pers.* Amittai.

אָן where?, whither?; *w.* עַד how long?

אֹן אָן → אָוֶן.

אָנָּא, אָנָּה ah now!

I אנה *q* mourn.

II אנה *pi* cause to fall.

pu befall.

hitp pick a quarrel.

אֹנֶה* time of mourning, mourning.

אָנָה, אָנֶה where?, whither?; *w.* עַד how long?

אַנּוּ *rd.* Q *(Jer. 42.6).*

אָנוּשׁ incurable, desperate, disastrous.

I° אֱנוֹשׁ mankind, man.

II° אֱנוֹשׁ *n. pers.* Enosh.

אנח *ni* sigh, groan.

אֲנָחָה sighing, groaning.

אֲנַחְנוּ we.

אֲנָחֲרַת *n. place* Anaharath.

אֲנִי I.

אֳנִי *m. and f.* fleet, ships.

אֳנִיָּה ship.

אֲנִיָּה mourning, lamentation.

אֲנִיעָם *n. pers.* Aniam.

אֲנָךְ plumb-line?, plummet?

אָנֹכִי I.

אָנַן *hitpo* indulge in complaints.

אָנַס° *q* compel.

אָנַף *q* be angry.

     hitp be angry.

אֲנָפָה heron?

אָנַק *q* groan.

     ni groan.

I אֲנָקָה groaning.

II אֲנָקָה gecko *(species of lizard)*.

אָנַשׁ *ni* be taken ill.

אָסָא *n. pers.* Asa.

אָסוּךְ small oil-jar.

אָסוֹן accident *(frequently fatal)*.

אֵסוּר fetter.

אָסִיף ingathering, harvest.

אָסִיר prisoner.

I אַסִּיר prisoner.

II אַסִּיר *n. pers.* Assir.

אָסָם* store.

אַסְנָה *n. pers.* Asnah.

אָסְנַת *n. pers. f.* Asenath.

אָסַף *q* gather, gather in, gather together; receive, remove; *Isa. 58.8*

     bring up the rear.

     ni gather together *(refl.)*; be gathered; be removed, perish.

     pi gather in, receive; bring up the rear.

     pu be gathered, be removed.

     hitp gather together *(refl.)*.

אָסָף *n. pers.* Asaph.

אָסֶף → אָסִיף.

אֹסֶף* store, storehouse.

אֹסֶף ingathering.

אֲסֵפָה incarceration.

אֲסֻפָּה* collection.

אֲסַפְסֻף rabble.

אַסְפָּתָא *n. pers.* Aspatha.

אֶסַּק   *impf. q of* סלק.

אסר   *q* fetter, bind, yoke; *Num. 30.3ff.* place oneself under obligation.
ni be fettered.
pu be captured.

אִסָּר°   vow of abstinence.

אַסִּיר   אַסִּיר I → .

אֵסַר־חַדֹּן,   *n. pers.* Esarhaddon.
אֵסַר חַדֹּן

אֶסְתֵּר   *n. pers. f.* Esther.

אַף I   also, besides, even; אַף כִּי even if, yes and what is more, how much more, how much less, let alone.

אַף II   nose; anger; *du. also* face.

אפד   *q* tie on.

אֵפֹד I   אֵפוֹד → .

אֵפֹד II   *n. pers.* Ephod.

אֻפְדָּה*   covering.

אַפֶּדֶן*   palace.

אפה   *q* bake.
ni be baked.

אֵפָה   אֵיפָה → .

אֵפוֹ, אֵפוֹא   then, so.

אֵפוֹד   ephod (*priestly garment, cult object, oracular instrument*).

אֲפִיחַ   *n. pers.* Aphiah.

אָפִיל*   late.

אַפַּיִם   *n. pers.* Appaim.

אָפִיק I   stream-bed, channel; *Job 40.18* tube; *Job 41.7* furrow.

אָפִיק* II   strong.

אֲפִיק   *n. place* Aphik.

אֹפִיר   *n. terr. I Kings 10.11* Ophir; → *also* אוֹפִיר.

אֹפֶל   darkness.

אָפֵל   darkness.

אֲפֵלָה   darkness.

אֶפְלָל   *n. pers.* Ephlal.

אֹפֶן*   in time?

אפס   *q* be at an end, cease to be.

אֶפֶס   end, non-existence, nothing; no longer, not, only; אֶפֶס כִּי except that, but, yet.

אֶפֶס דַּמִּים   *n. place* Ephes-dammim.

אֲפָסַיִם ankles.

אֶפַע *rd.* אֶפֶס *(Isa. 41.24).*

אֶפְעֶה *species of snake* viper?

אפף *q* encompass.

אפק *hitp* summon one's strength, control oneself.

אֲפֵק *n. place* Aphek.

אֲפֵקָה *n. place* Aphekah.

אֵפֶר *f.* loose soil, dust; *Num. 19.9f.; Ezek. 28.18* ash.

אֲפֵר bandage.

אֶפְרֹחַ* young *(of birds).*

אַפִּרְיוֹן litter.

אֶפְרַיִם *n. pers., n. peop., n. terr., n. place* Ephraim.

אֶפְרָת *n. pers. f.* Ephrath.

אֶפְרָתָה *n. place* Ephrathah.

אֶפְרָתִי *gent.* Ephrathite.

אֶצְבּוֹן, אֶצְבֹּן *n. pers.* Ezbon.

אֶצְבַּע *f.* finger; toe.

I אָצִיל* remote part.

II אָצִיל* eminent.

אַצִּיל*, אַצִּילָה *Jer. 38.12* armpit; *Ezek. 13.18* wrist; *Ezek. 41.8* in height?

אצל *q* lay aside, remove.

ni be recessed *(architectural).*

אֵצֶל side; beside.

אָצֵל *n. pers.* Azel.

אָצַל *Zech. 14.5 text corr.*

אֲצַלְיָהוּ *n. pers.* Azaliah.

אֹצֶם *n. pers.* Ozem.

אֶצְעָדָה step-chain; armlet.

אצר *q* store up.

ni be stored up.

hi make to store.

אֵצֶר *n. pers.* Ezer.

אֶקְדָּח beryl?

אַקּוֹ wild goat.

אֹר *rd.* יְאֹר *(Amos 8.8).*

אֲרָא *n. pers.* Ara.

אֲרִאֵל, אֲרִיאֵל → I אֲרִיאֵל.

אֲראֵל → II אֲרִיאֵל.

אַראֵלִי *n. pers.* Areli; *gent.* Arelite.

אֶרְאֶלָּם *rd.* אֲרְאֶלִים *(Isa. 33.7)* people of Ariel.

ארב *q* lie in wait, ambush.

    pi ambush.

    hi set an ambush.

אֲרָב *n. place* Arab.

אֶרֶב ambush, lurking-place.

אֹרֶב* ambush.

אֹרֶב ambush.

אַרְבֵאל → בֵּית אַרְבֵאל.

אַרְבֶּה migratory locust.

אָרְבֶּה* *dub.*

אֲרֻבָּה opening, window.

אֲרֻבּוֹת *n. place* Arubboth.

אַרְבִּי *gent.* Arbite.

I אַרְבַּע four; *du.* four-fold; *pl.* forty.

II אַרְבַּע *n. pers.* Arba.

ארג *q* weave.

אֶרֶג shuttle.

אַרְגֹּב *n. terr.* Argob; *II Kings 15.25 dub.*

אַרְגָּוָן wool dyed with red purple.

אַרְגָּז container.

אַרְגָּמָן wool dyed with red purple.

אַרְדְּ *n. pers.* Ard.

אַרְדּוֹן *n. pers.* Ardon.

אַרְדִּי *gent.* Ardite.

אֲרִדַי *n. pers.* Aridai.

ארה *q* pluck.

אֲרוֹד *n. pers.* Arod.

אַרְוַד *n. place* Arvad *(island and city).*

אֲרוֹדִי *n. pers.* Arodi; *gent.* Arodite.

אַרְוָדִי *gent.* Arvadite.

אֻרְוָה* stabling.

אָרוּז* tight.

אֲרוּכָה healing; restoration.

אֲרוּמָה *n. place* Arumah.

אֲרוֹן chest, ark; *Gen. 50.26* coffin.

אֲרַוְנָה   *n. pers.* Araunah.

אֶרֶז   cedar.

אַרְזָה   cedar-panelling.

ארח   *q* journey, travel.

אָרַח   *n. pers.* Arah.

אֹרַח   way *(also in the broadest sense).*

אֹרְחָה*   caravan.

אֲרֻחָה   provisions for the journey, allowance.

אֲרִי   lion.

אֲרִי   → אוּרִי.

I אֲרִיאֵל   hearth for sacrifice > *name for Jerusalem.*

II אֲרִיאֵל   *n. pers.* Ariel.

אֲרִידָתָא   *n. pers.* Aridatha.

I° אַרְיֵה   lion.

II אַרְיֵה   *II Kings 15.25 dub.*

אֻרְיָה*   stabling.

אַרְיוֹךְ   *n. pers.* Arioch.

אֲרָיִם   *pl. of* I אוּר.

אֲרִיסַי   *n. pers.* Arisai.

ארך   *q* be/become long.
     hi lengthen, prolong.

אָרֵךְ*   long; אֶרֶךְ אַפַּיִם long-suffering.

אֹרֶךְ   length; אֹרֶךְ אַפַּיִם patience.

אָרֹךְ*   long, lasting.

אֶרֶךְ   *n. place* Erech, Uruk.

אֲרֻכָה   → אֲרוּכָה.

אַרְכִּי   *gent.* Archite.

אֲרָם   *n. pers., n. terr.* Aram.

אַרְמוֹן   fortified dwelling, dwelling-tower.

אֲרַמִּי   *gent.* Aramaean.

אֲרָמִית   in Aramaic.

אֲרַם נַהֲרַיִם   *n. terr.* Aram-naharaim *(region on the middle Euphrates).*

אַרְמֹנִי   *n. pers.* Armoni.

אֲרָן   *n. pers.* Aran.

I אֹרֶן   laurel.

II אֹרֶן   *n. pers.* Oren.

אַרְנֶבֶת   hare.

אַרְנוֹן *n. river* Arnon.

אֲרַנְיָה *n. pers.* Araniah.

אַרְנָן *n. pers.* Arnan.

אָרְנָן *n. pers.* Ornan.

אַרְנֹן → אַרְנוֹן.

אַרְפַּד *n. place* Arpad.

אַרְפַּכְשַׁד *n. pers.* Arpachshad.

אֶרֶץ piece of land, land, earth.

אַרְצָא *n. pers.* Arza.

ארר *q* curse.

    ni be cursed.

    pi curse, bring a curse.

    ho be laid under curse.

אֲרָרַט *n. terr.* Ararat.

אֲרָרִי *gent.* Ararite.

ארש *pi* be betrothed.

    pu be betrothed.

אֲרֶשֶׁת request.

אַרְתַּחְשַׁסְתָּא, *n. pers.* Artaxerxes.
אַרְתַּחְשַׁשְׁתָּא,
אַרְתַּחְשַׁשְׂתָּא

אֲשַׂרְאֵל *n. pers.* Asarel.

אֲשַׂרְאֵלָה *n. pers.* Asarelah.

אַשְׂרִאֵלִי *gent.* Asrielite.

אַשְׂרִיאֵל *n. pers.* Asriel.

אֵשׁ fire.

אֵשׁ° existence; there is.

אַשְׁבֵּל *n. pers.* Ashbel.

אַשְׁבֵּלִי *gent.* Ashbelite.

אֶשְׁבָּן *n. pers.* Eshban.

אַשְׁבֵּעַ *n. pers.* Ashbea.

אֶשְׁבַּעַל *n. pers.* Eshbaal.

אֲשֵׁד* slope.

אַשְׁדּוֹד *n. place* Ashdod.

אַשְׁדּוֹדִי *gent.* Ashdodite.

אַשְׁדּוֹדִית in the language of Ashdod.

אֶשְׁדַּת *Deut. 33.2 text corr.*

אֶשֶׁה* *Jer. 6.29 text corr.*

אִשָּׁה   woman; each.

אִשֶּׁה   offering made by fire, offering.

אֶשְׁוָיָה*   rd. Q *(Jer. 50.15)* buttress; tower.

אַשּׁוּר   n. pers. Asshur; n. peop. Assyrians; n. terr. Assyria.

אַשּׁוּרִי   gent. Ashurite.

אַשּׁוּרִים   n. peop. Asshurim.

אַשְׁחוּר   n. pers. Ashhur.

אֲשִׁימָא   n. deity Ashima *(name of a Syrian god).*

אֲשֵׁירָה   → אֲשֵׁרָה.

אֲשִׁישָׁה   cake of raisins *(made from dried, compressed grapes).*

אֶשֶׁךְ   testicle.

אֶשְׁכּוֹל, I   bunch of grapes.
אֶשְׁכֹּל I

אֶשְׁכּוֹל, II   n. pers., n. place Eshcol.
אֶשְׁכֹּל II

אַשְׁכְּנַז,   n. pers., n. peop. Ashkenaz.
אַשְׁכְּנַז

אֶשְׁכָּר   tax, tribute.

אֶשֶׁל   tamarisk.

אשם   q commit an offence, suffer punishment for guilt.

    ni perish.

    hi bring punishment upon.

אָשָׁם   guilt, liability incurred, guilt-offering, gift in atonement, compensation.

אָשֵׁם   guilty.

אַשְׁמָה   guilt, offence.

אַשְׁמוּרָה   night-watch.

אֲשְׁמַנִּים   Isa. 59.10 dub.

אַשְׁמֹרֶת   night-watch.

אֶשְׁנָב   window-lattice.

אַשְׁנָה   n. place Ashnah.

אֶשְׁעָן   n. place Eshan.

אַשָּׁף*   exorcist.

אַשְׁפָּה   quiver.

אַשְׁפּוֹת   → אַשְׁפֹּת.

אַשְׁפְּנַז   n. pers. Ashpenaz.

אֶשְׁפָּר   cake of dates.

אַשְׁפֹּת ash-pit; rubbish-dump.

אַשְׁקְלוֹן *n. place* Ashkelon.

אֶשְׁקְלוֹנִי *gent.* Ashkelonite.

I אשׁר *q* advance.

    pi advance; lead, correct.

    pu be led.

II אשׁר *pi* call happy.

    pu be called happy.

אָשֵׁר *n. pers., n. peop.* Asher.

אֲשֶׁר *relative particle; conjunction* that, so that, because, in order that, if, when, as.

*אֹשֶׁר happiness.

*אָשֻׁר *f.* step.

I *אָשֻׁר *f.* step.

II אַשֻּׁר → אַשּׁוּר.

אֲשֵׁרָה asherah *(sacred pole)*, Asherah *(name of a goddess)*.

אֲשֵׁרִי *gent.* Asherite.

אַשְׁרֵי happy! *(introductory word of blessings)*.

אשׁשׁ *hitpo dub., rd.* הִתְבּוֹשָׁשׁוּ *(Isa. 46.8)*.

אֶשְׁתָּאוֹל, *n. place* Eshtaol.
אֶשְׁתָּאֹל

אֶשְׁתָּאֻלִי *gent.* Eshtaolite.

אֶשְׁתּוֹן *n. pers.* Eshton.

אֶשְׁתְּמֹה *n. place* Eshtemoh.

אֶשְׁתְּמֹעַ *n. place* Eshtemoa.

אַתְּ → אַתָּה.

אַתְּ *f. sg.* you.

I אֵת *sign of the accusative.*

II אֵת together with, with, beside; מֵאֵת away from.

III *אֵת ploughshare *or* mattock.

אֵת → אוֹת.

אתא → אתה.

אֶתְבַּעַל *n. pers.* Ethbaal.

°אתה *q* come.

    hi bring.

אַתָּה *m. sg.* you.

אָתוֹן *f.* female donkey.

*אַתּוּק *rd. Q (Ezek. 41.15)*.

אַתִּי   *rd. Q.*

אִתַּי   *n. pers.* Ittai.

אַתִּיק   gallery?

אַתֶּם   *m. pl.* you.

אֵתָם   *n. place* Etham.

אֶתְמוֹל, אֶתְמוּל, אִתְּמוֹל   yesterday, long ago.

אֵתָן   → I אֵיתָן.

אַתֵּן, אַתֵּנָה   *f. pl.* you.

אֶתְנָה   gift.

אֶתְנִי   *n. pers.* Ethni.

אֲתָנִים   → I אֵיתָן.

I אֶתְנַן   gift.

II אֶתְנַן   *n. pers.* Ethnan.

אֲתָרִים   *n. place?* Atharim.

ב

בְּ   in; among, upon, into; on, by, with; on account of; *w. inf.* as, when, while.

בְּאָה   entrance.

באר   *pi* make clear; *Hab. 2.2* inscribe.

I בְּאֵר   well; pit.

II בְּאֵר   *n. place* Beer.

בֹּאר   → בּוֹר.

בְּאֵרָא   *n. pers.* Beera.

בְּאֵר אֵילִים   *n. place* Beer-elim.

בְּאֵרָה   *n. pers.* Beerah.

בְּאֵרוֹת   *n. place* Beeroth.

בְּאֵרִי   *n. pers.* Beeri.

בְּאֵר לַחַי רֹאִי   *n. place* Beer-lahai-roi.

בְּאֵר שֶׁבַע   *n. place* Beersheba.

בְּאֵרֹת בְּנֵי־יַעֲקָן   *n. place* Beeroth-bene-jaakan.

בְּאֵרֹתִי   *gent.* Beerothite.

באש   *q* putrefy, stink.

ni make oneself odious.

hi cause to stink, make odious; stink, be odious.

hitp make oneself odious.

בָּאְשׁ stench.

*בָּאֻשׁ rotting berry.

בָּאְשָׁה darnel *(noxious weed)*.

בַּאֲשֶׁר because.

*בָּבָה בָּבַת הָעַיִן eyeball.

בֵּבַי *n. pers.* Bebai.

בָּבֶל *n. place* Babel; *n. terr.* Babylonia.

בַּג *rd. Q (Ezek. 25.7)*.

בגד *q* act treacherously.

I בֶּגֶד treachery.

II בֶּגֶד garment, covering.

בֹּגְדוֹת treachery.

*בָּגוֹד treacherous.

בִּגְוַי *n. pers.* Bigvai.

בִּגְלַל on account of.

בִּגְתָא *n. pers.* Bigtha.

בִּגְתָן, בִּגְתָנָא *n. pers.* Bigthan, Bigthana.

I בַּד part, piece; piece > piece of cloth, linen; לְבַד alone, apart, by oneself, *w.* מִן besides, apart from; *pl.* poles, carrying-poles, shoots.

II °*בַּד empty talk.

III *בַּד oracular priest.

°ברא *q* devise.

בדד *q* be solitary.

בָּדָד alone.

בְּדַד *n. pers.* Bedad.

בִּדְי → דַּי.

בְּדָיָה *n. pers.* Bedeiah.

בְּדִיל tin.

*בָּדִיל dross.

בדל *ni* separate oneself, go over to; be set apart.

hi separate, divide, distinguish; set apart, choose.

*בָּדָל part, piece.

בְּדֹלַח bdellium-gum.

בְּדָן   *n. pers.* Bedan.

בדק   *q* repair.

בֶּדֶק   breach, seam.

בִּדְקַר   *n. pers.* Bidkar.

בֹּהוּ   emptiness, waste.

*בְּהוֹן   thumb, big toe.

בַּהַט   *precious stone.*

°בָּהִיר   brilliant?, obscured?

בהל   *ni* be/become frightened, dismayed; hasten *(Aram.)*.
    pi frighten, dismay someone; hasten *(Aram.)*.
    pu pt. hastened, hastily acquired *(Aram.)*.
    hi frighten, dismay someone; hurry; *II Chron. 26.20* remove
    quickly *(Aram.)*.

בֶּהָלָה   dismay, terror.

בְּהֵמָה   cattle, animals; *Job 40.15* בְּהֵמוֹת hippopotamus.

בֹּהֶן   thumb.

בֹּהַן   *n. pers.* Bohan.

בֹּהַק   *harmless eruption on the skin.*

בַּהֶרֶת   blotch *(symptom of a skin-disease)*.

בוא   *q* enter, come; set *(sun)*.
    hi bring in, bring.
    ho be brought in, brought.

בוז   *q* treat contemptuously, despise.

I בּוּז   contempt, scorn.

II בּוּז   *n. pers., n. peop., n. terr.* Buz.

בּוּזָה   contempt, scorn.

בּוּזִי   *n. pers.* Buzi; *gent.* Buzite.

בַּוַּי   *n. pers.* Bavvai.

בוּךְ   *ni* be stirred up, wander about.

I בּוּל   dry wood.

II בּוּל   Bul *(name of a month, October/November)*.

בון   → בין.

בּוּנָה   *n. pers.* Bunah.

בּוּנִּי   *n. pers.* Bunni.

בום   *q* trample down, trample under foot.
    pol trample down > desecrate.
    ho pt. trodden down.
    hitpol kick about.

בּוּץ byssus *(fine white cloth)*.

בֹּצֵץ *n. place* Bozez.

בּוּקָה waste, emptiness.

בּוֹקֵר cowherd.

בּוֹר cistern, pit; grave; prison.

בֹּאֵר *rd. Q (Jer. 6.7)* well.

בּוֹר הַסִּרָה → סִרָה.

בּוֹר־עָשָׁן *n. place* Borashan.

בּוֹשׁ *q* feel shame, be ashamed; *Ezra 8.22* hesitate.
pol delay.
hi put to shame, treat shamefully, be ashamed.
hitpol be ashamed before one another.

בּוּשָׁה confusion, shame.

בַּז plundering, plunder.

בּוֹא *q* wash away.

בּוּה *q* despise.
ni be despised, scorned.
hi make despised.

בִּזָּה plundering, plunder.

בּזז *q* plunder, strip, take as booty.
ni be plundered.
pu be plundered.

בִּזָּיוֹן contempt, scorn.

בִּזְיוֹתְיָה *rd.* בְּנוֹתֶיהָ *(Josh. 15.28)*.

בָּזָק lightning flash.

בֶּזֶק *n. place* Bezek.

בזר° *q* scatter, distribute.
pi disperse.

בִּזְתָא *n. pers.* Biztha.

בָּחוֹן assayer.

בָּחוּר young man *(adult, vigorous, still unmarried)*.

בְּחוּרוֹת* time of life, age, condition of a young man.

בַּחוּרִים → בַּחֻרִים.

בַּחִין* *rd. Q (Isa. 23.13)* siege-tower?

בָּחִיר* chosen.

בחל *q* feel loathing.
pu rd. Q (Prov. 20.21).

בָּחַן‎ *q* try, put to the test.

    ni be tried, put to the test.

    pu Ezek. 21.18 text corr.

בַּחַן‎ watch-tower.

בֹּחַן‎ testing?; אֶבֶן בֹּחַן‎ hard stone? (schistose gneiss?).

בחר‎ *q* select, choose; prefer; try *(Aram.)*.

    ni be chosen, preferred; be tried *(Aram.)*.

    pu rd. Q (Eccles. 9.4).

בַּחֲרוּמִי‎ *gent.* Baharumite.

*בְּחֻרִים‎ time of life, age, condition of a young man.

בַּחֻרִים‎ *n. place* Bahurim.

בטא, בטה‎ *q* speak rashly.

    pi speak rashly.

בָּטוּחַ‎ trusting.

בטח‎ *q* feel safe, trust, rely on.

    hi instil trust.

I בֶּטַח‎ security, trust; *usu. adv.* securely, carefree.

II בֶּטַח‎ *n. place* Betah.

בָּטַח‎ → בָּטוּחַ‎.

בִּטְחָה‎ trust.

בִּטָּחוֹן‎ trust.

בַּטֻּחוֹת‎ security.

°בטל‎ *q* be idle.

I בֶּטֶן‎ belly, body, womb, innermost part; *I Kings 7.20* swelling? *(architectural).*

II בֶּטֶן‎ *n. place* Beten.

בָּטְנִים‎ pistachio nuts.

בְּטֹנִים‎ *n. place* Betonim.

בִּי‎ if you please *(at start of a conversation).*

בין‎ *q* distinguish, perceive, pay attention, consider, understand, discern.

    ni be discerning, skilled.

    pol be attentive.

    hi be able to distinguish, have discernment; lead to discernment, discrimination, instruct.

    hitpol act with discernment, pay attention.

*בַּיִן‎ interval; *cstr. predominantly used as prep.* between.

בִּינָה ability to discriminate, discernment, understanding.

בֵּיצִים eggs.

בִּירָה citadel; *I Chron. 29.1, 19 of temple.*

בִּירָנָה* fortified place.

בַּיִת house, abode, interior; household, family; property.

בֵּית אָוֶן *n. place* Beth-aven.

בֵּית(־)אֵל *n. place* Bethel.

בֵּית אַרְבֵּאל *n. place* Beth-arbel.

בֵּית אַשְׁבֵּעַ *n. place?* Beth-ashbea.

בֵּית בַּעַל מְעוֹן *n. place* Beth-baal-meon.

בֵּית בִּרְאִי *n. place* Beth-birei.

בֵּית בָּרָה *n. place* Beth-barah.

בֵּית־גָּדֵר *n. place* Beth-gader.

בֵּית גָּמוּל *n. place* Beth-gamul.

בֵּית דִּבְלָתַיִם *n. place* Beth-diblathaim.

בֵּית־דָּגוֹן, *n. place* Beth-dagon.

בֵּית דָּגֹן

בֵּית הָאֱלִי *gent.* Bethelite.

בֵּית הָאָצֵל *n. place* Beth-ezel.

בֵּית הַגִּלְגָּל *n. place* Beth-gilgal.

בֵּית הַגָּן *n. place* Beth-haggan.

בֵּית הַיְשִׁ(י)מֹת, *n. place* Beth-jeshimoth.

בֵּית הַיְשִׁמוֹת

בֵּית הַכֶּרֶם *n. place* Beth-haccherem.

בֵּית הַלַּחְמִי *gent.* Bethlehemite.

בֵּית הַמַּרְכָּבוֹת *n. place* Beth-marcaboth.

בֵּית הָעֵמֶק *n. place* Beth-emek.

בֵּית הָעֲרָבָה *n. place* Beth-arabah.

בֵּית הָרָם *n. place* Beth-haram.

בֵּית הָרָן *n. place* Beth-haran.

בֵּית הַשִּׁטָּה *n. place* Beth-shittah.

בֵּית הַשִּׁמְשִׁי *gent.* of Beth-shemesh.

בֵּית(־)חָגְלָה *n. place* Beth-hoglah.

בֵּית(־)חֹר(וֹ)ן → .בֵּית(־)חֹר(וֹ)ן

בֵּית חָנָן *n. place* Beth-hanan.

בֵּית(־)חֹר(וֹ)ן *n. place* Beth-horon.

בֵּית יוֹאָב *n. place?* Beth-joab.

בֵּית כַּר *n. place* Beth-car.

בֵּית לְבָאוֹת *n. place* Beth-lebaoth.

בֵּית לֶחֶם *n. place* Bethlehem.

בֵּית לְעַפְרָה *n. place* Beth-le-aphrah.

בֵּית מִלּ(וֹ)א *n. place?* Beth-millo.

בֵּית מְעוֹן *n. place* Beth-meon.

בֵּית מַעֲכָה *n. place* Beth-maacah.

בֵּית מַרְכָּבוֹת *n. place* Beth-marcaboth.

פִּיתָן palace.

בֵּית נִמְרָה *n. place* Beth-nimrah.

בֵּית עֶדֶן *n. place* Beth-eden.

בֵּית עַזְמָוֶת *n. place* Beth-azmaveth.

בֵּית־עֲנוֹת *n. place* Beth-anoth.

בֵּית־עֲנָת *n. place* Beth-anath.

בֵּית־עֵקֶד *n. place* Beth-eked (-roim)
(הָרֹעִים)

בֵּית פֶּלֶט *n. place* Beth-pelet.

בֵּית פְּעוֹר *n. place* Beth-peor.

בֵּית פַּצֵּץ *n. place* Beth-pazzez.

בֵּית־צוּר *n. place* Beth-zur.

בֵּית רְחוֹב *n. place* Beth-rehob.

בֵּית־רֶכֶב ← רֶכֶב.

בֵּית־רִמּוֹן *n. place* Beth-rimmon.

בֵּית רָפָא ← רָפָא.

בֵּית־שְׁאָן *n. place* Beth-shean.

בֵּית(־)שֶׁמֶשׁ *n. place* Beth-shemesh.

בֵּית(־)שָׁן *n. place* Beth-shan.

בֵּית תּוֹגַרְמָה ← תּוֹגַרְמָה.

בֵּית־תַּפּוּחַ *n. place* Beth-tappuah.

בָּכָא baca-shrub.

בכה *q* weep.
pi bewail.

בֶּכֶה weeping.

בְּכוֹר ← בְּכֹר.

בִּפּוּרָה early fig.

בִּכּוּרִים early fruits, first-fruits.

בְּכוֹרַת *n. pers.* Becorath.

בָּכוּת weeping.

בְּכִי   weeping; *Job 28.11* trickling.

בֹּכִים   *n. place* Bochim.

בְּכִירָה   the older (woman).

בְּכִית*   mourning.

בכר   *pi* bear early fruits; treat as first-born.

    pu be destined as first-born.

    hi give birth to first child.

בֶּכֶר*   young male camel.

בֶּכֶר   *n. pers.* Becher.

בְּכֹר   first-born; *periphrasis for superlative.*

בְּכֹרָה   rights as first-born.

בִּכְרָה   young female camel.

בֹּכְרוּ   *n. pers.* Bocheru.

בַּכְרִי   *gent.* Becherite.

בִּכְרִי   *n. pers.* Bichri; *gent.* Bichrite.

בַּל   wearing out, non-existence > not.

בֵּל   Bel *(name of the god Marduk).*

בַּלְאֲדָן   *n. pers.* Baladan.

בֵּלְאשַׁצַּר   → בֵּלְשַׁאצַּר.

בלג   *hi* become cheerful; *Amos 5.9* flash.

בִּלְגָּה   *n. pers.* Bilgah.

בִּלְגַּי   *n. pers.* Bilgai.

בִּלְדַּד   *n. pers.* Bildad.

בלה   *q* be worn out, done; wear out, fall in pieces.

    pi wear out, enjoy the use of; make to waste away; oppress.

בָּלֶה*   worn out, done.

בָּלָה   *n. place* Balah.

בלה   *pi* discourage.

בַּלָּהָה   terror.

בִּלְהָה   *n. pers. f., n. place* Bilhah.

בִּלְהָן   *n. pers.* Bilhan.

בְּלוֹא*, בְּלוֹי*   worn out clothes, rags.

בֵּלְטְשַׁאצַּר   *n. pers.* Belteshazzar.

בְּלִי   *Isa. 38.17* wearing out, destruction; *negation* not, un-, -less, without.

בְּלִיל   mixed fodder.

בְּלִימָה   nothingness.

בְּלִיַּעַל worthlessness, destruction; good-for-nothing; wicked, worthless person.

בלל *q* mix, confuse; *Judg. 19.21* give fodder.

hitpo intermingle.

Isa. 64.5 rd. וַתְּבֶּל.

בלם *q* restrain?, curb?

בלם *q* nip sycamore figs.

I בלע *q* swallow, gulp down.

ni be swallowed.

pi swallow, destroy.

II בלע *pi* inform, spread abroad.

pu be informed.

III בלע *ni* be confused.

pi confuse.

pu pt. confused.

hitp appear confused.

I *בֶּלַע thing swallowed.

II בֶּלַע confusion.

III בֶּלַע *n. pers., n. place* Bela.

בִּלְעֲדֵי, בַּלְעֲדֵי without, apart from, besides.

בַּלְעִי *gent.* Belaite.

בִּלְעָם *n. pers.* Balaam; *n. place* Bileam.

בלק *q* lay waste.

pu pt. laid waste.

בָּלָק *n. pers.* Balak.

בֵּלְשַׁאצַּר *n. pers.* Belshazzar.

בִּלְשָׁן *n. pers.* Bilshan.

בִּלְתִּי cessation of existence, non-existence > un-, except, without, not; לְבִלְתִּי *w. inf. negates subordinate clauses.*

בָּמָה high ground, high place for worship.

בִּמְהָל *n. pers.* Bimhal.

בְּמוֹ *synonymous with* בְּ.

בָּמוֹת *n. place* Bamoth.

I בֵּן son *(also in the broadest sense);* expresses membership in the broadest sense.

II בֵּן *n. pers.* Ben.

בֶּן־אוֹנִי *n. pers.* Ben-oni.

בנה   *q* build, construct, build up, rebuild.

     ni be built, rebuilt; *fig.* obtain a child, live on *(in the children)*.

בֶּן־הֲדַד   *n. pers.* Ben-hadad.

בִּנּוּי   *n. pers.* Binnui.

בֶּן־זוֹחֵת   *I Chron. 4.20 n. pers.? text corr.?*

בֶּן־חַיִל   *n. pers.* Ben-hayil.

בֶּן־חָנָן   *n. pers.* Ben-hanan.

בָּנִי   *n. pers.* Bani.

בֻּנִּי   *n. pers.* Bunni.

בְּנֵי־בְרַק   *n. place* Bene-berak.

בִּנְיָה   building.

בְּנָיָה(וּ)   *n. pers.* Benaiah.

בְּנֵי יַעֲקָן   *n. place* Bene-jaakan.

בֵּנַיִם   אִישׁ הַבֵּנַיִם champion, single combatant *(between two battle lines)*.

בִּנְיָמִ(י)ן, בֶּן־יָמִין   *n. pers., n. peop.* Benjamin.

בֶּן־יְמִינִי   *gent.* Benjaminite.

בִּנְיָן   building.

בְּנִינוּ   *n. pers.* Beninu.

בִּנְעָא   *n. pers.* Binea.

בְּסוֹדְיָה   *n. pers.* Besodeiah.

בֵּסַי   *n. pers.* Besai.

בֹּסֶר   unripe, sour grapes/fruit.

בַּעַד   distance; *prep.* in through, out through, behind, around, on behalf of, for; *Prov. 6.26 dub.*

בעה   *q Isa. 21.12* inquire; *Isa. 64.1* bring to the boil.

     ni Obad. 6 be searched out; *Isa. 30.13* bulge out.

בְּעוֹר   *n. pers.* Beor.

בְּעוּת*   terror.

בֹּעַז   *n. pers.* Boaz *(also the name of the left-hand pillar in front of the temple in Jerusalem)*.

בעט   *q* lash out; *I Sam. 2.29* despise.

בְּעָיָם   *rd.* בְּעֹצֶם *(Isa. 11.15)*.

בְּעִיר*   cattle, property.

בעל   *q* possess, rule; take possession of *(as a wife)*, marry.

     ni be taken possession of *(as a wife)*, married.

בַּעַל I owner, citizen *(as owner of land)*, husband; *expression for the power to make use of, or have a share in, something; frequent designation of deity;* Baal *(name of a Canaanite god)*.

בַּעַל II *n. pers.* Baal.

בַּעַל־גָּד *n. place* Baal-gad.

בַּעֲלָה I* *f.* owner.

בַּעֲלָה II *n. place* Baalah.

בַּעַל הָמוֹן *n. place* Baal-hamon.

בְּעָלוֹת *n. place* Bealoth.

בַּעַל חָנָן *n. pers.* Baal-hanan.

בַּעַל חָצוֹר *n. place* Baal-hazor.

בַּעַל חֶרְמוֹן *n. place* Baal-hermon.

בְּעֶלְיָדָע *n. pers.* Beeliada.

בְּעַלְיָה *n. pers.* Bealiah.

בַּעֲלֵי יְהוּדָה *rd.* בַּעֲלַת יְהוּדָה *(II Sam. 6.2).*

בַּעֲלִים *n. pers.* Baalis.

בַּעַל מְעוֹן *n. place* Baal-meon.

בַּעַל(־)פְּרָצִים *n. place* Baal-perazim.

בַּעַל צְפ(וֹ)ן *n. place* Baal-zephon.

בַּעַל שָׁלִשָׁה *n. place* Baal-shalishah.

בַּעֲלַת *n. place* Baalath.

בַּעֲלַת בְּאֵר *n. place* Baalath-beer.

בַּעַל תָּמָר *n. place* Baal-tamar.

בְּעֹן *n. place* Beon.

בַּעֲנָא, בַּעֲנָה *n. pers.* Baanah.

בער I *q* be on fire, burn, consume.
pi set on fire, kindle, burn down.
pu be kindled.
hi set on fire, reduce to ashes.

בער II *pi* remove; lay waste.
hi clear away?

בער III *q* be brutish, stupid.
ni behave in a brutish, stupid manner.

בַּעַר brutish, stupid.

בַּעֲרָא *n. pers. f.* Baara.

בְּעֵרָה burning.

בַּעֲשֵׂיָה *n. pers.* Baaseiah.

בַּעְשָׁא *n. pers.* Baasha.

בְּעֶשְׁתְּרָה *n. place* Be-eshterah.

בעת *ni* be overcome with terror.
pi terrify.

בְּעָתָה terror.

בֹּץ mud.

בֵּץ → בּוּץ.

בִּצָּה marsh.

בָּצוּר* fortified, inaccessible; *Jer. 33.3* inconceivable thing.

בָּצוּר *rd.* K *(Zech. 11.2)*.

בֵּצָי *n. pers.* Bezai.

בָּצִיר vintage.

בָּצָל* onion.

בְּצַלְאֵל *n. pers.* Bezalel.

בַּצְלוּת *n. pers.* Bazluth.

בַּצְלִית *n. pers.* Bazlith.

בצע *q* cut off; make gain.
pi cut off, finish, fulfil; defraud.

בֶּצַע cut > gain.

בְּצַעֲנַיִם *rd.* Q *(Judg. 4.11)*.

בצק *q* swell up.

בָּצֵק dough.

בָּצְקַת *n. place* Bozkath.

I בצר *q* gather grapes.

II בצר *q* humble.

III בצר *ni* be inaccessible, impossible.
pi make inaccessible.

I בֶּצֶר gold ore.

II בֶּצֶר *n. pers., n. place* Bezer.

I בָּצְרָה *Micah 2.12* fold?

II בָּצְרָה *n. place* Bozrah.

בַּצֹּרֶה lack of rain, drought.

בִּצָּרוֹן *Zech. 9.12* stronghold? *text corr.*

בַּצֹּרֶת lack of rain, drought.

בַּקְבּוּק *n. pers.* Bakbuk.

בַּקְבֻּק flask.

בַּקְבֻּקְיָה *n. pers.* Bakbukiah.

בַּקְבַּקַּר *n. pers.* Bakbakkar.

בֻּקִּי *n. pers.* Bukki.

בֻּקִּיָּהוּ *n. pers.* Bukkiah.

בָּקִיעַ* breach, fragment.

בקע *q* split, divide; break through, break in; *Isa. 34.15* hatch; *Amos 1.13* slit open; *Ps. 74.15* break open.

ni split, break open, break through, be conquered; *Isa. 59.5* be hatched.

pi split, slit open, make to break through; break in pieces; *Isa. 59.5* hatch; *Job 28.10* cut out.

pu Josh. 9.4 be split; *Ezek. 26.10* be conquered; *Hos. 14.1* be slit open.

hi II Kings 3.26 break through; *Isa. 7.6* conquer.

ho be conquered.

hitp split, break apart.

בֶּקַע *unit of weight* beka *(half-shekel, 5.712 g)*.

בִּקְעָה valley with flat bottom.

בִּקְעַת־אָוֶן *n. place* valley of Aven.

I בקק *q* ravage, bring to nothing.

ni be ravaged, disturbed.

po ravage.

II בקק *q Hos. 10.1* be luxuriant.

בקר° *pi* care for, concern oneself about; *Ps. 27.4* take delight.

בָּקָר *coll.* cattle, herd of cattle.

בֹּקֶר morning.

בַּקָּרָה* care.

בִּקֹּרֶת reparation.

בקש *pi* seek, seek to obtain; seek out, consult; demand, require.

pu be sought.

בַּקָּשָׁה* request, desire.

בֵּר* *rd.* בִּכְרִים *(II Sam. 20.14)*.

I° בֵּר son.

II בֵּר pure, clear, unsullied.

III בֵּר grain, wheat.

IV° בֵּר open country.

I בֹּר purity; potash, lye *(purifying agent)*.

II בֹּר → בּוֹר.

בּרא I   *q* create *(only used of God)*.
     ni be created.

בּרא II   *hi* make oneself fat.

בּרא III   *pi* cut down the trees, clear; *fig.* cut in pieces.

בּרא IV   *II Sam. 12.17* → בּרה I.

בָּרָא   → בָּרִיא.

בְּרֹאדַך   *n. pers.* Berodach.

בִּרְאִי   → בֵּית בִּרְאִי.

בְּרָאיָה   *n. pers.* Beraiah.

בַּרְבֻּר*   cuckoo.

בּרד   *q* hail.

בָּרָד   hail.

בָּרֹד*   dappled.

בֶּרֶד   *n. pers., n. place* Bered.

בּרה I   *q* eat, fortify oneself.
     hi feed, fortify someone.

בּרה II   *q* choose?

בָּרוּך   *n. pers.* Baruch.

בָּרוּר   pure, clear.

בְּרוֹשׁ   juniper.

בְּרוֹת*°   juniper.

בָּרוֹת, בָּרוּת*   food, refreshment.

בֵּרוֹתָה   *n. place* Berotha.

בִּרְזַוִת   *n. pers.* Birzavith.

בַּרְזֶל   iron.

בַּרְזִלַּי   *n. pers.* Barzillai.

בּרח   *q* run away, flee; *Ex. 36.33* pass through, slide.
     hi drive away, put to flight; *Ex. 26.28* pass through, slide;
       I Chron. 12.16 render impassable.

בָּרַח   gliding, fleeing.

בַּרְחֻמִי   *gent.* Barhumite.

בֵּרִי   *n. pers.* Beri.

בָּרִיא   fattened, fat.

בְּרִיאָה   act of creation.

בִּרְיָה   food, refreshment.

בָּרִיחַ   *n. pers.* Bariah.

בְּרִיחַ   bar.

בְּרִיעָה   *n. pers.* Beriah.

בְּרִיעִי *gent.* Beriite.

בְּרִית promise, obligation.

בֹּרִית soda.

I בֹּרֵךְ *q* kneel down.

hi make to kneel down.

II בֹּרֵךְ *q* praise, bless.

ni wish blessing for oneself.

pi bless, praise; *euphemism for* blaspheme, curse.

pu be/become blessed, praised.

hitp wish blessing for oneself, consider oneself fortunate.

בֶּרֶךְ *f.* knee.

בַּרַכְאֵל *n. pers.* Barachel.

I בְּרָכָה blessing; benediction, wish for blessing, blessing formula; gift *(accompanied by a wish for blessing)*; II Kings *18.31*; Isa. *36.16* capitulation.

II בְּרָכָה *n. pers.* Beracah.

בְּרֵכָה pool.

(וּ)בֶּרֶכְיָה *n. pers.* Berechiah.

בַּרֹמִים cloth of two colours.

בֹּרְנֶעַ → קָדֵשׁ בַּרְנֵעַ.

בֶּרַע *n. pers.* Bera.

בִּרְעָה → בְּרִיעָה.

בָּרַק *q* flash.

I בָּרָק lightning.

II בָּרָק *n. pers.* Barak.

בָּרָק → בְּנֵי־בְרָק.

בַּרְקֹוס *n. pers.* Barkos.

בַּרְקָנִים thorns?, threshing-sledges?

בָּרֶקֶת, בָּרְקַת *green precious stone* beryl *or* emerald.

I בָּרַר *q* separate, purge out; test.

ni keep oneself pure; be pure, undefiled.

pi sift.

hi purify.

hitp show oneself pure.

II בָּרַר *q* sharpen.

hi sharpen.

בִּרְשַׁע *n. pers.* Birsha.

בֵּרֹתַי *n. pers.* Berothai.

בֵּרֹתִי   *gent.* Berothite.

בְּשׂוֹר   *n. river* Besor.

בְּשׂוֹרָה   → בְּשׂרָה.

בֹּשֶׂם, בֶּשֶׂם   balsam-tree, balsam-oil; perfume.

בָּשָׂם*

בָּשְׂמַת   *n. pers. f.* Basemath.

בשׂר   *pi* announce, inform, proclaim.

     hitp receive news.

בָּשָׂר   flesh; body; *euphemism for* genitals; *Isa. 58.7* relatives.

בְּשׂרָה   message, news; messenger's reward.

בְּשַׁגַּם   since (< גַּם, שֶׁ, בְּ).

בשׁל   *q* ripen, boil.

     pi cook.

     pu be boiled.

     hi ripen.

בָּשֵׁל   boiled.

בִּשְׁלָם°   *n. pers.* Bishlam.

בָּשָׁן   *n. terr.* Bashan.

בָּשְׁנָה   shame.

בשׁס   *po?* levy farm-rent.

בֹּשֶׁת   feeling of shame, shame; disgrace *(also as derogatory substitute for Baal).*

I בַּת   daughter *(also in the broadest sense)*; *expresses membership in the broadest sense*; population; *Ps. 17.8* בַּת־עָיִן eyeball.

II בַּת   *liquid measure* bath *(between 22 and 45 l).*

בָּתָה   waste.

בֹּתָה*   *II Chron. 34.6 text corr.*

בַּתָּה*   ravine.

בְּתוּאֵל   *n. pers., n. place* Bethuel.

בְּתוּל   *n. place* Bethul.

בְּתוּלָה   virgin.

בְּתוּלִים   time of life, state of a virgin; proof of virginity.

בִּתְיָה   *n. pers. f.* Bithiah.

בתק   *pi* cut down.

בתר   *q* cut up.

     pi cut up.

I בֶּתֶר* piece, part.

II בֶּתֶר *Cant. 2.17* clefts in the rock?, perfume?

בִּתְרוֹן *II Sam. 2.29* ravine?, half a day?

בַּת־שֶׁבַע *n. pers. f.* Bathsheba.

בַּת־שׁוּעַ *n. pers. f.* Bathshua.

נ

גֵּא proud.

נאה *q* be/become high; be exalted, be arrogant.

גֵּאָה pride.

גֵּאֶה high, exalted; proud.

גְּאוּאֵל *n. pers.* Geuel.

גַּאֲוָה majesty; pride; *Ps. 46.4* raging.

גְּאוּלִים* release?, duty as avenger?

גָּאוֹן height; thicket; majesty; pride.

גֵּאוּת rising up; majesty; pride.

גַּאֲיוֹן* *Ps. 123.4* proud.

גֵּאָיוֹת, גֵּאָיֹת *pl. of* גַּיְא.

I גאל *q* redeem, release; ransom; claim back; גֹּאֵל הַדָּם > גֹּאֵל avenger of blood.

    ni be redeemed, bought back.

II גאל *ni* be defiled *(cultically)*.

    pi defile.

    pu be pronounced unclean.

    aph stain.

    hitp defile oneself.

גֹּאֱל* *pl.* defilement.

גְּאֻלָּה redemption; right, duty of redemption.

גַּב torus, elevation; boss, back; rim.

I גֵּב* ditch.

II גֵּב* *I Kings 6.9* beam.

III גֵּב* swarm.

גֵּבֶא pool.

נבה *q* be high, exalted; be proud.

    hi make high.

גָּבֵהַּ* high; haughty.

גָּבֹהַּ high, exalted; proud.

גֹּבַהּ height, majesty; pride.

גַּבְהוּת pride.

גְּבוֹל rd. Q (Josh. 15.47).

גְּבוּל boundary, territory.

גְּבוּלָה* boundary, territory.

גִּבּוֹר valiant, powerful; warrior, champion; I Chron. 9.26 chief.

גְּבוּרָה strength, might; pl. mighty deeds.

גִּבֵּחַ bald on the forehead.

גַּבַּחַת baldness on the forehead; bareness.

גוֹבַי swarm of locusts.

גַּבַּי n. pers. Gabbai.

גֵּבִים n. place Gebim.

גָּבִיעַ goblet, cup.

גְּבִיר lord, ruler.

גְּבִירָה lady, mistress (also title of the queen-mother).

גָּבִישׁ rock crystal.

גבל q bound; border upon.

    hi set bounds for.

גְּבַל° n. place Byblos.

גְּבָל n. terr. Gebal.

גֶּבֶל → גְּבוּל.

גִּבְלִי gent. of Byblos.

גַּבְלֻת twisting.

גִּבֵּן hunchbacked.

גְּבִנָּה cheese.

גַּבְנֹן* (mountain) peak.

גֶּבַע n. place Geba.

גָּבַע → גָּבִיעַ.

גִּבְעָא n. pers. Gibea.

גִּבְעָה I hill.

גִּבְעָה II n. place Gibeah.

גִּבְעוֹן n. place Gibeon.

גִּבְעֹנִי gent. Gibeonite.

גַּבְעֹל bud?, seed-pod?

גִּבְעֹנִי → גִּבְעֹנִי.

גִּבְעַת   *n. place* Gibeah.

גִּבְעָתִי   *gent.* Gibeathite.

גבר   *q* prevail, be strong; increase; succeed.

     pi make prevail; exert.

     hi prevail.

     hitp assert superiority.

I גֶּבֶר   young, strong man; man > each.

II גֶּבֶר   *n. pers.* Geber.

גִּבָּר   *n. place* Gibbar.

גְּבֹר   → גְּבוֹר.

גַּבְרִיאֵל   *n. pers.* Gabriel.

גִּבֶרֶת   *cstr. of* גְּבִירָה.

גִּבְּתוֹן   *n. place* Gibbethon.

גַּג   flat roof, covering slab.

I גַּד   coriander.

II גַּד   good fortune; *Isa. 65.11* god.

III גָּד, גַּד   *n. pers., n. peop.* Gad.

גֻּדְגֹּד   → חֹר הַגִּדְגָּד.

גֻּדְגֹּדָה   *n. place* Gudgodah.

גדד   *q* band together.

     hitpo administer cuts to oneself.

גְּדֻדָה*   cut.

I גְּדוּד*   soil *thrown up by the plough.*

II גְּדוּד   raid, plundering expedition; host, horde, band of robbers.

גָּדוֹל   great *(in the broadest sense).*

גְּדוּלָּה, גְּדוּלָה   greatness; great deeds.

גִּדּוּף* °   reviling, abuse.

גִּדּוּפָה°, גִּדּוּפָה* °   reviling, abuse.

גְּדוֹר   → גָּדֹר.

גְּדֹרֹת*   *pl. of* גְּדֵרָה.

גְּדִי   kid *(m).*

גָּדִי   *gent.* Gadite; *n. pers. II Kings 15.14, 17* Gadi.

גַּדִּי   *n. pers.* Gaddi.

גַּדִּיאֵל   *n. pers.* Gaddiel.

גְּדִיָּה*   kid *(f).*

גָּדָה*   river-bank.

גָּדִישׁ   stack of sheaves; *Job 21.32* burial-mound.

גדל *q* be/become great *(also in the broader sense)*.

pi make great, grow; magnify, extol, praise; bring up.

pu pt. grown up.

hi make great; display greatness; magnify oneself, do great things.

hitp magnify oneself, show oneself great.

גֹּדֶל greatness; glory, praise; *w.* לֵבָב pride.

גָּדֵל growing, becoming great, great.

גָּדִל* tassel, twisted ornamentation.

גִּדֵּל *n. pers.* Giddel.

גָּדֹל → גָּדוֹל.

גְּדָלָה → גְּדוּלָּה.

גְּדַלְיָה(וּ) *n. pers.* Gedaliah.

גִּדַּלְתִּי *n. pers.* Giddalti.

גדע *q* hew off, fell, break in pieces, cut off.

ni be hewn off, broken in pieces.

pi strike off, shatter.

pu be felled.

גִּדְעוֹן *n. pers.* Gideon.

גִּדְעֹנִי → גִּדְעֹנִי.

גִּדְעֹם *n. place* Gidom.

גִּדְעֹנִי *n. pers.* Gideoni.

גדף *pi* revile.

גְּדֻּפָה → גִּדּוּפָה.

גדר *q* erect a stone wall, wall up.

גָּדֵר stone wall, wall.

גֶּדֶר *n. place* Geder.

גְּדֹר *n. pers., n. place* Gedor.

גְּדֵרָה* I stone wall, fold.

גְּדֵרָה II *n. place* Gederah.

גְּדֵרוֹת *n. place* Gederoth.

גְּדֵרִי *gent.* Gederite.

גְּדֶרֶת wall.

גְּדֵרָתִי *gent.* Gederathite.

גְּדֵרֹתַיִם *n. place* Gederothaim.

גֵּה *rd.* זֶה *(Ezek. 47.13)*.

נהה *q* heal.

גֵּהָה healing.

נהר *q* bend down, crouch.

גַּו* back; *w.* הִשְׁלִיךְ אַחֲרֵי reject.

I גַּו back.

II גַּו community.

I גּוֹב swarm of locusts.

II גּוֹב *n. place* Gob.

גּוֹג *n. pers.* Gog.

גּוּר *q* make a raid, attack.

I גֵּוָה back.

II גֵּוָה pride, arrogance.

גּוז *q* drive in, sweep away.

גּוֹזָל young bird.

גּוֹזָן *n. terr.* Gozan.

גוח גיח → .

גּוֹי swarm, nation.

גְּוִיָּה body; corpse.

גּול גיל → .

גּוֹלָה deportation; those deported.

גּוֹלָן *n. place* Golan.

גּוּמָץ pit.

גּוּנִי *n. pers.* Guni; *gent.* Gunite.

גּוע *q* perish, die.

גּוף *hi* shut.

גּוּפָה* corpse.

I גּור *q* stay as client, alien.
        hitpol stay as client, alien.

II גּור *q* attack.

III גּור *q* be afraid, stand in awe.

גּוֹר* lion cub.

I גּוּר young *(still sucking)*.

II גּוּר *n. place* Gur.

גּוּר־בַּעַל *n. place* Gur-baal.

גּוֹרָל lot, allotment, destiny.

גֵּז shearing, mowing.

גִּזְבָּר treasurer.

גזה *q* cut off.

גִּזָּה fleece, wool.

גְּזוֹנִי *gent.* Gizonite.

גזז *q* clip, shear.

   ni be removed, destroyed.

גָּזֵז *n. pers.* Gazez.

גָּזִית squared stone.

גזל *q* tear away, seize possession of, plunder, rob; *Micah 3.2* flay.

   ni be stolen.

גֵּזֶל robbery.

גָּזֵל robbery, stolen goods.

גְּזֵלָה robbery, stolen goods.

גָּזָם locust?, caterpillar?

גַּזָּם *n. pers.* Gazzam.

גֶּזַע* tree-stump; shoot.

גזר I *q* cut, fell; *Job 22.28* decide.

   ni be cut off, separated; be lost; *Esther 2.1* be decreed.

גזר II *q* devour.

גֶּזֶר I* part cut off, portion.

גֶּזֶר II *n. place* Gezer.

גְּזֵרָה separated area; *Lam. 4.7* cutting?, form?

גְּזֵרָה unfruitful.

נחה *q Ps. 22.10* draw out?

גָּחוֹן belly.

גָּחוֹן → גִּיחוֹן.

גֶּחֲזִי → גֵּיחֲזִי.

גֶּחָל*, נַחַל*, coal, glow.

גַּחֶלֶת

גַּחַם *n. pers.* Gaham.

גַּחַר *n. pers.* Gahar.

גַּי, גַּיְ valley.

גַּיְא, גֵּיא, גֵּיא valley.

גֵּי(א) (בֶּן־)הִנֹּם *n. place* Valley of Hinnom.

גֵּיא(־)(ה)מֶלַח *n. place* Valley of Salt.

גֵּיא צְפַתָה *n. place* Valley of Zephathah.

גִּיד sinew.

גֵּי הַצְּבֹעִים *n. place* Valley of Zeboim.

נִיחַ   *q* burst out.

     hi burst out; *Ezek. 32.2* snort?

גִּיחַ   *n. place* Giah.

גִּיחוֹן   the spring Gihon; *n. river* Gihon.

גֵּיחֲזִי   *n. pers.* Gehazi.

גֵּי יִפְתַּח־אֵל   *n. place* Valley of Iphtah-el.

גִיל   *q* rejoice, shout for joy.

I°* גִּיל   age (-group).

II גִּיל   rejoicing.

גִּילָה   rejoicing.

גִּילֹנִי   *gent.* Gilonite.

גִּינַת   *n. pers.* Ginath.

גֵּירִים   *pl. of* גֵּר.

גִּישׁ   *rd. Q (Job 7.5)* crust.

גֵּישָׁן   *n. pers.* Geshan.

I גַּל   heap of stones.

II גַּל   wave.

גֹּל*   bowl.

גַּלָּב*   barber.

גִּלְבֹּעַ   *n. place* Gilboa.

גַּלְגַּל   wheel; *Isa. 17.13; Ps. 83.14* wheel-shaped thistle-ball.

I* גִּלְגָּל   wheel.

II גִּלְגָּל   *n. place* Gilgal.

גֻּלְגֹּלֶת   skull, head.

גֶּלֶד°*   skin.

גלה   *q* lay bare, uncover; (have to) go into exile.

     ni uncover oneself, disclose oneself, make oneself known; be
         uncovered, laid bare, revealed; be taken into exile.

     pi lay bare, uncover, open; disclose, reveal.

     pu be uncovered; *pt.* open.

     hi take into exile.

     ho be taken into exile.

     hitp uncover oneself, declare oneself.

גֹּלָה   → גּוֹלָה.

גִּלֹה   *n. place* Giloh.

גֻּלָּה   bowl; torus; spring; *Josh. 15.19b; Judg. 1.15b n. place.*

גִּלּוּל*   idol.

גְּלוֹם*   garment.

גִּלּוֹן   rd. Q (Josh. 20.8; 21.27).

גָּלוּת   deportation; those deported.

גלח   pi shave.

     pu be shaved.

     hitp shave oneself, have oneself shaved.

גִּלָּיוֹן   tablet; hand-mirror.

I גָּלִיל*   pivot, cylinder; ring.

II גָּלִיל   n. terr. Galilee.

גְּלִילָה   circuit, district.

גְּלִילוֹת   n. place Geliloth.

גַּלִּים   n. place Gallim.

גָּלְיָת   n. pers. Goliath.

גלל   q roll, roll away.

     ni be rolled together; roll, flow.

     poal pt. rolled.

     hitpo fall upon, roll.

     pilp roll away.

     hitpalp roll on.

     hi → q.

I גָּלָל   dung.

II גָּלָל°   n. pers. Galal.

III גָּלָל*   only w. בְּ on account of.

גָּלֲלוֹ, גְּלָלֵי   forms of I גָּלָל.

גְּלָלַי°   n. pers. Gilalai.

גלם   q roll up.

גֹּלֶם°*   formless thing, embryo.

גַּלְמוּד   barren.

גַּלְנִי   → גִּילֹנִי.

גלע   hitp break out.

גִּלְעָד   n. pers., n. place., n. terr. Gilead.

גַּלְעֵד   n. place Galed.

גִּלְעָדִי   gent. Gileadite.

גלש   q come down.

גַּם   together with, also, for one's part, even, yet; גַּם—גַּם not only—but also, negative neither—nor.

נמא *pi* swallow up.

hi give to sip.

גֹּמֶא papyrus.

גֹּמֶד *linear measure* gomed (⅔ *of a cubit?*).

גַּמָּדִים *n. peop.* Gammadites.

גָּמוּל *n. pers.* Gamul.

גְּמוּל deed, reward.

גְּמוּלָה deed, reward.

גִּמְזוֹ *n. place* Gimzo.

גמל *q* become ready, ripe; ripen; wean; deal with, show; reward.

ni be weaned.

גָּמָל camel.

גְּמַלִּי *n. pers.* Gemalli.

גַּמְלִיאֵל *n. pers.* Gamaliel.

גמר *q* be at an end, bring to an end.

גֹּמֶר *n. pers. f., n. peop.* Gomer.

גְּמַרְיָה(וּ) *n. pers.* Gemariah.

גַּן garden.

גנב *q* steal; deceive.

ni be stolen.

pi steal; deceive.

pu be stolen; *Job 4.12* come stealing.

hitp steal away.

גַּנָּב thief.

גְּנֵבָה thing stolen.

גְּנֻבַת *n. pers.* Genubath.

גַּנָּה* , גַּנָּה garden.

I גְּנָזִים* treasures.

II גְּנָזִים* carpets?

גַּנְזַךְ* treasury.

גנן *q* enclose, defend.

hi → *q*.

גִּנְּתוֹי *n. pers.* Ginnethoi.

גִּנְּתוֹן *n. pers.* Ginnethon.

נעה *q* low.

גֹּעָה* *n. place* Goah.

נעל   *q* abhor.

    ni be fouled.

    hi Job 21.10 fail (*in impregnation*).

גַּעַל   *n. pers.* Gaal.

גֹּעַל   abhorrence.

נער   *q* rebuke, threaten.

גְּעָרָה   rebuke, threat.

געשׁ   *q* shake.

    pu be shaken.

    hitp shake.

    hitpo shake.

גַּעַשׁ   *n. place* Gaash.

גַּעְתָּם   *n. pers.* Gatam.

I   *גַּף   back.

II   *גַּף   בְּנַפּוֹ he alone.

גֶּפֶן   *f.* tendril, vine; grape-vine.

גֹּפֶר   *kind of wood* gopher.

גָּפְרִית   sulphur.

גֵּר   client, alien.

גִּר   chalk.

גֵּרָא   *n. pers.* Gera.

גָּרָב   eruption.

גָּרֵב   *n. pers., n. place* Gareb.

*גַּרְגַּר   olive.

*גַּרְגְּרוֹת   throat, neck.

גִּרְגָּשִׁי   *gent.* Girgashite.

גרד   *hitp* scrape oneself.

גרה   *pi* excite.

    hitp excite oneself, engage oneself (*in conflict, war*); *Dan. 11.10a*
      prepare for war, *11.10b rd.* Q press on.

I   גֵּרָה   cud.

II   גֵּרָה   *unit of weight* gerah ($\frac{1}{20}$ *of a shekel, 0.572 g*).

*גֹּרָה   lion cub.

גָּרוֹן   throat, neck.

גֵּרוּת   lodging-place.

גרז   *ni* be removed.

גִּרְזִי   *rd.* Q (*I Sam. 27.8*) *gent.* Gizrite.

גְּרִזִים   *n. place* Gerizim.

גַּרְזֶן axe, chisel.

גּוֹרָל →　.גֹּרָל

נרם q *dub.*

　　pi gnaw.

גֶּרֶם bone; *II Kings 9.13* self.

גַּרְמִי *gent.* Garmite.

גֹּרֶן *f.* threshing-floor.

גֹּרֶן הָאָטָד *n. place* Goren-ha-atad.

גֹּרֶן כִּידֹן *n. place* Goren-kidon.

גֹּרֶן נָכוֹן *n. place* Goren-nacon.

נרם q be worn out.

　　hi make break.

נרע q shave, clip; reduce, deduct, withdraw.

　　ni be reduced, deducted, withdrawn.

　　pi extract.

נרף q sweep away.

נרר q carry away; *w.* גֵּרָה chew the cud.

　　poal pt. sawn.

גְּרָר *n. place* Gerar.

גֶּרֶשׂ *crushed grain* groats.

נרשׁ q drive out, divorce; *Isa. 57.20* throw up.

　　ni be cast away; be troubled.

　　pi drive out.

　　pu be driven out.

גֶּרֶשׁ produce?

גְּרֻשָׁה* expropriation.

גֵּרְשׁוֹם *n. pers.* Gershom.

גֵּרְשׁוֹן *n. pers.* Gershon.

גֵּרְשֹׁם →　.גֵּרְשׁוֹם

גֵּרְשֻׁנִּי *gent.* Gershonite.

גְּשׁוּר, גְּשׁוּרָה *n. terr., n. peop.* Geshur.

גְּשׁוּרִי *gent.* Geshurite.

נשׁם *hi* send rain.

I גֶּשֶׁם torrent of rain, rain; *pl. also* rainy season.

II גֶּשֶׁם *n. pers.* Geshem.

גֹּשֶׁם* rain.

גַּשְׁמוּ *n. pers.* Gashmu.

גֹּשֶׁן *n. place, n. terr.* Goshen.

גִּשְׁפָּא *n. pers.* Gishpa.

גשש *pi* grope.

גַּת I *f.* wine-press.

גַּת II *n. place* Gath.

גַּת הַחֵפֶר *n. place* Gath-hepher.

גִּתִּי *gent.* Gittite.

גִּתַּיִם* *n. place* Gittaim.

גִּתִּית *musical term.*

גֶּתֶר *n. pers.* Gether.

גַּת־רִמּוֹן *n. place* Gath-rimmon.

ר

דָּאַב *q* languish, faint.

דְּאָבָה despair.

דְּאָבוֹן* despair.

דָּאַג *q* fear; be anxious, care for, be afraid.

דָּאַג → דָּג.

דֹּאֵג *n. pers.* Doeg.

דְּאָגָה anxious care.

דָּאָה *q* fly, swoop down *(birds of prey)*; soar *(God)*.

דָּאָה kite, fork-tailed kite.

דֹּאר *n. place* Dor.

דֹּב bear, she-bear.

דֹּבֶא* *dub.*

דָבַב *q* moisten.

דִּבָּה report, calumny.

דְּבוֹרָה I bee.

דְּבוֹרָה II *n. pers. f.* Deborah.

דְּבִיר I hindermost room *(of the temple).*

דְּבִיר II *n. pers., n. place* Debir.

דְּבֵלָה cake of figs *(from pressed figs).*

דִּבְלָה* *rd.* רִבְלָה *(Ezek. 6.14).*

דִּבְלַיִם *n. pers.* Diblaim.

דבק *q* cling to, be attached to; hold fast to something, stick.

    pu be held together.

    hi catch up with, overtake; make to cling; pursue.

    ho pt. stuck.

דָּבֵק attached.

דֶּבֶק soldering; *I Kings 22.34; II Chron. 18.33* baldric?

I דבר *pi* turn away; drive away; exterminate.

    hi w. תַּחַת drive out, subdue.

II דבר *q* speak.

    ni speak with one another.

    pi speak, talk.

    pu be spoken.

    hitp speak with one another.

דָּבָר word; matter, event, affair; allotment, output; something, *negative* nothing.

דֶּבֶר plague.

דֹּבֶר* pasture.

דְּבִר *n. place* Debir.

דַּבֵּר word.

דִּבְרָה* *Job 5.8* cause; *Ps. 110.4* manner; *w.* עַל־ *also* because of, in order that.

דְּבֹרָה → דְּבוֹרָה.

דֹּבְרוֹת rafts.

דִּבְרִי *n. pers.* Dibri.

דָּבְרַת *n. place* Daberath.

דַּבֶּרֶת* word.

דְּבַשׁ honey.

I דַּבֶּשֶׁת hump.

II דַּבֶּשֶׁת *n. place* Dabbesheth.

דָּג fish; *Neh. 13.16 coll.*

דנה *q* become numerous.

דָּגָה *coll.* fish; *Jonah 2.2* a fish.

דָּגוֹן *n. deity* Dagon.

דגל *q* raise the standard; *pt. pass. Cant. 5.10* distinguished.

    ni pt. trooped round the standard.

דֶּגֶל standard > division.

דָּגָן grain, corn.

דגר q brood?

דַּד* du. breasts.

לֹד → דּוֹד.

דדה hitp go?

לְדוֹ → דּוֹדוֹ.

דְּדָוָהוּ n. pers. Dodavahu.

דֹּדִי rd. Q (II Sam. 23.9).

דְּדָן n. peop. Dedanites; n. pers., n. terr. Dedan.

דְּדָנִים n. peop. Dedanites.

דֹּדָנִים n. peop. Dodanim.

דהם ni pt. confounded.

דהר q dash.

דַּהֲרָה* dashing.

דּוֹאֵג → דִּאֵג.

דוב° hi waste.

דּוֹב → דֹּב.

דַּוָּג* fisherman.

דּוּגָה Amos 4.2 w. סִירוֹת fish-hooks, fishing tackle.

דּוֹד lover, beloved; (paternal) uncle; pl. also love, enjoyment of love.

דּוּד cooking-pot; basket.

דָּוִד n. pers. David.

I דּוּדָאִים* Jer. 24.1 baskets.

II דּוּדָאִים mandrakes.

דּוֹדָה* (paternal) aunt.

דּוֹדוֹ n. pers. Dodo.

דּוֹדַי n. pers. Dodai.

דוה q be unwell, menstruate.

דָּוֶה unwell, menstruating; sick, ill.

דוח hi rinse.

דְּוַי illness.

דַּוָּי sick, ill.

דּוֹאֵג n. pers. Doeg.

דָּוִיד → דָּוִד.

דוך q pound.

דּוּכִיפַת hoopoe.

I דּוּמָה silence (term for the underworld).

דּוּמָה II   *n. pers., n. peop., n. place, n. terr.* Dumah.

דּוּמָיָה   silence.

דּוּמָם   silently.

דּוּמֶּשֶׂק   *n. place* Damascus.

דּוֹן   *q* rule?

דּוֹנַג   wax.

דּוּץ°   *q* skip.

דּוּר   *q Ezek. 24.5* pile up in a circle; *Ps. 84.11* go about, dwell.

דּוּר   *Isa. 22.18* ball; *Isa. 29.3 w.* כְּ around.

דּוֹר I   camp.

דּוֹר II   age, generation, posterity; company, community.

דּוֹר III   *n. place* Dor.

דּוּשׁ   *q* trample down, thresh.
       ni be trampled down.
       ho be threshed.

דחה   *q* push, push in.
       ni be overthrown.
       pu be overthrown.

דחח   *ni* be pushed, driven away.

דְּחִי   tripping, stumbling.

דֹּחַן   millet.

דחף   *q pt. pass.* swift.
       ni hurry.

דחק   *q* push, oppress.

דַּי   sufficiency, need; enough; *w.* בְּ for, as often as; *w.* כְּ according to, as much as; *w.* מִן as often as; לְמַדַּי enough.

דִּיבוֹן, דִּיבֹן   *n. place* Dibon.

דִּיג   *q* fish.

דַּיָּג*   fisherman.

דַּיָּה   *unclean bird.*

דְּיוֹ   ink.

דִּי זָהָב   *n. place* Dizahab.

דִּימוֹן   *n. place* Dimon.

דִּימוֹנָה   *n. place* Dimonah.

דִּין   *q* administer justice, effect justice, pass judgment.
       ni dispute.

דִּין case, legal claim, lawsuit, judgment; *Esther 1.13* justice.

דַּיָּן judge.

דִּינָה *n. pers. f.* Dinah.

דִּיפַת *n. pers.* Diphath.

דָּיֵק siege-work.

דַּיִשׁ threshing-time.

I דִּישׁוֹן, דִּישֹׁן *n. pers., n. peop.* Dishon.

II דִּישֹׁן *animal permitted for food* bison?

דִּישָׁן *n. pers., n. peop.* Dishan.

דַּךְ oppressed.

דכא *ni pt.* oppressed.
pi shatter, crush.
pu be shattered.
hitp lie crushed.

דַּכָּא crushed, dejected; *Deut. 23.2* crushing; *Ps. 90.3* dust.

דכה *q rd. ni (Ps. 10.10).*
ni be crushed.
pi crush.

דֳּכִי* pounding.

I דַּל door.

II דַּל poor; mean, helpless, weak, destitute.

דלג *q* leap.
pi leap, climb.

I דלה *q* draw.
pi draw up.

II דלה *q Prov. 26.7* hang down?, dangle?

I דַּלָּה *Isa. 38.12* thrum.

II דַּלָּה* *Cant. 7.6* flowing hair.

III דַּלָּה* *coll. and pl.* the poor.

דלח *q* muddy.

דְּלִי bucket.

דְּלָיָה(וּ) *n. pers.* Delaiah.

דְּלִילָה *n. pers. f.* Delilah.

דָּלִית* tendrils, foliage.

I דלל *q* be/become small, low; *Isa. 38.14* languish?

II דלל *q Job 28.4* dangle.

דִּלְעָן‎ *n. place* Dilan.

I דלף‎ *q* leak.

II דלף‎ *q* be sleepless.

דֶּלֶף‎ leaking roof.

דַּלְפוֹן‎ *n. pers.* Dalphon.

דלק‎ *q* set on fire, burn; pursue hotly.
hi kindle, inflame.

דַּלֶּקֶת‎ fever-heat.

דֶּלֶת‎ door-leaf, door; *II Kings 12.10* lid; *Jer. 36.23* column.

דָּם‎ blood; bloodshed, guilt of bloodshed.

I דמה‎ *q* be like, equal to.
pi compare, ponder, devise.
hitp make oneself like.

II דמה‎ *q* be still, cease; *Jer. 6.2; Hos. 4.5 dub.*
ni be silenced, reduced to silence; be destroyed.

דֻּמָה‎ *Ezek. 27.32 text corr.*

דְּמוּת‎ copy, likeness, form.

דְּמִי‎ half.

דֳמִי‎ quiet.

דְּמִיָּה‎ → דּוּמִיָּה‎.

דִּמְיוֹן‎* resemblance.

דמם‎ *q* stand still, keep silent, be motionless, be dumb; perish.
ni be silenced; be devastated, perish.
poel quieten.
hi bring to a halt; cause to perish.

דְּמָמָה‎ calm.

דֹּמֶן‎ dung.

דִּמְנָה‎ *n. place* Dimnah.

דמע‎ *q* weep.

דֶּמַע‎* abundance?, juice?

דִּמְעָה‎ *coll.* tears.

דַּמֶּשֶׂק‎ *n. place* Damascus.

דְּמֶשֶׁק‎ damask?

דָּן‎ *n. pers., n. peop., n. place, n. terr.* Dan.

דָּנִיֵּאל → דָּנִיֵּאל.

דַּנָּה *n. place* Dannah.

דִּנְהָבָה *n. place* Dinhabah.

דָּנִי *gent.* Danite.

דָּנִיֵּאל *n. pers.* Daniel.

דַּע* knowledge.

דֵּעָה knowledge.

דְּעוּאֵל *n. pers.* Deuel.

דעך *q* be extinguished.

    ni dry up.

    pu be extinguished.

דַּעַת knowledge, skill, perception, discernment; intimacy, association.

דֳפִי blemish.

דפק *q* drive too hard; knock.

    hitp jostle each other.

דָּפְקָה *n. place* Dophkah.

דַּק thin, fine, low.

דֹּק veil?

דִּקְלָה *n. pers.* Diklah.

דקק *q* crush; be pulverized.

    hi crush; pulverize.

    ho be crushed.

דקר *q* pierce.

    ni be pierced.

    pu pt. pierced.

דֶּקֶר *n. pers.* Deker.

דַּר *costly paving.*

דֹּר → II דּוֹר.

דְּרָאוֹן aversion.

דָּרְבָן, דָּרְבֹן* goad.

דַּרְדַּע *n. pers.* Darda.

דַּרְדַּר thistles.

דָּרוֹם south; *Job 37.17* south wind.

I דְּרוֹר *f.* swallow?

II דְּרוֹר drops.

III דְּרוֹר release.

דָּרְיָוֶשׁ, *n. pers.* Darius.

דַּרְיָוֶשׁ *rd.* דָּרְיֹשׁ *(Ezra 10.16).*

דרך *q* tread; tread grapes; bend *(the bow)*.

hi cause to tread; make firm by treading; bend *(the bow)*; *Judg. 20.43 dub.*

דֶּרֶךְ *m. and f.* way, distance, journey; manner, custom, behaviour, course of life, condition.

דַּרְפְּמוֹנִים drachmae.

דַּרְמֶשֶׂק° *n. place* Damascus.

דָּרַע *n. pers.* Dara.

דַּרְקוֹן *n. pers.* Darkon.

דרשׁ *q* seek, inquire, require, care for.

ni be sought, let oneself be sought.

דשׁא *q* become green.

hi produce fresh growth.

דֶּשֶׁא fresh growth, grass.

דִּישׁוֹן, דִּשׁן → דִּישׁוֹן.

דשׁן *q* become fat.

pi make fat, smear with fat; clear of fat ashes; *Ps. 20.4* regard as fat.

pu be made fat.

hotpaal be satiated with fat > drip.

דֶּשֶׁן fatness, fat ashes.

דָּשֵׁן fat, full of sap.

דָּת *f.* decree, law.

דֹּתַיִן* *n. place* Dothain.

דֹּתָן *n. place* Dothan.

דָּתָן *n. pers.* Dathan.

ה

הֵא here!, see!

הֶאָח aha!, fine!

הָאֲרָרִי *gent.* Hararite.

הַב (הָבָה, הָבִי, הָבוּ) *imv. of* יהב give!, come on!

הַבְהָבִי *Hos. 8.13 dub.*

הָבוּ → הַב.

הֵבוּ *Hos. 4.18 dub.*

הָבִי → הַב.

הבל *q* be empty, vain.
hi make empty, vain.

I הֶבֶל breath > vanity, transitoriness; *also of idols.*

II הֶבֶל *n. pers.* Abel.

הבר *q* divide; *pt. w.* שָׁמַיִם astrologer.

הֵגֵא *n. pers.* Hege.

הַגִּדְגָּדָה → גֻּדְגֹּדָה.

I הגה *q* coo, growl, murmur; meditate, reflect; speak.
hi cause to murmur; mutter.
poel? Isa. 59.13 speak.

II הגה *q* separate, remove.

הֶגֶה murmuring, moaning; rumbling *(thunder).*

הָגוּת meditation.

הֵגַי *n. pers.* Hegai.

הָגִיג* sighing.

הִגָּיוֹן murmuring, plotting; sounding?; *Ps. 9.17 liturgical direction.*

הָנִין* *Ezek. 42.12* suitable?

הָגָר *n. pers. f.* Hagar.

הַגְרִי *n. peop.* Hagrite.

הֵד shouts of joy *(properly an interjection).*

הֲדַד *n. pers.* Hadad.

הֲדַדְעֶזֶר *n. pers.* Hadadezer.

הֲדַד־רִמּוֹן *Zech. 12.11* name of a god or *n. place*
Hadad-rimmon.

הדה *q* stretch out.

הֹדּוּ *n. terr.* Hoddu, India.

הֲדוּרִים *Isa. 45.2 dub.*

הֲדוֹרָם *n. pers.* Hadoram.

הִדַּי *n. pers.* Hiddai.

הוֹדַיְוָהוּ *rd. Q (I Chron. 3.24) n. pers.* Hodaiah.

הרך *q* trample down.

הֲדֹם footstool.

הֲדַס   myrtle.

הֲדַסָּה   *n. pers. f.* Hadassah.

הדף   *q* push, drive out.

הדר   *q* honour, favour.
     ni be honoured.
     hitp put on airs.

הֲדַר   *n. pers.* Hadar.

הָדָר   honour, ornament, splendour, majesty.

הֶדֶר   adornment.

הֲדָרָה*   adornment.

הֲדֹרָם   → הֲדֹורָם.

הָהּ   ah!, alas!

הוֹ   alas!

הוא   → הוה I.

הוּא   he; that.

הוֹבְנִים   *rd. Q (Ezek. 27.15)* ebony.

הוֹד   I   majesty, splendour.

הוֹד   II   *n. pers.* Hod.

הוֹדְוָה   *n. pers.* Hodvah.

הוֹדַוְיָה   *n. pers.* Hodaviah.

הוֹדִיָּה   *n. pers.* Hodiah.

הוה   I   *q* fall.

הוה°   II   *q* become; remain.

הַוָּה*   destruction; outrage; desire.

הֹוָה   disaster, destruction.

הוֹהָם   *n. pers.* Hoham.

הוֹי   alas! *(in lamentation for the dead, prophetic diatribe).*

הוֹלֵלוֹת, הוֹלֵלוּת   folly.

הוֹלֵם   *pt. q. of* הלם.

הום   *q* throw into confusion.
     ni be in a stir.
     hi throw into confusion; be in a stir.

הוֹמָם   *n. pers.* Homam.

הון   *hi* regard as easy.

הוֹן   goods, wealth; *adv.* enough.

הוֹשָׁמָע   *n. pers.* Hoshama.

הוֹשֵׁעַ   *n. pers.* Hosea.

הוֹשַׁעְיָה   *n. pers.* Hoshaiah.

הות → התת.

הוֹתִיר   *n. pers.* Hothir.

הֹזה   *q* pant.

הִי   cry of woe.

הִיא   *f. sg.* she; that.

הֵידָד   shouts of joy *(properly an interjection).*

הֻיְדֹת   songs of praise.

היה   *q* happen, become, be.

     ni happen, take place.

הַיָּה*   destruction, disaster.

הֵיךְ°   how?

הֵיכָל   palace; temple, *principal room of the temple.*

הֵילֵל   morning star.

הֵימָם   *n. pers.* Hemam.

הֵימָן   *n. pers.* Heman.

הִין   *liquid measure* hin *(between 3.66 and 7.5 l).*

הכר   *q* press?

הַכָּרָה*   *w.* פָּנִים partiality.

הלא   *ni pt.* far removed.

הָלְאָה   further, onwards.

הִלּוּלִים   festival.

הַלָּז   *m. and f.* this one; there.

הַלָּזֶה   this one.

הַלָּזוּ   this one.

הַלֵּחֹות   *rd. Q (Jer. 48.5).*

הֲלִיךְ*   step.

הֲלִיכָה*   way; *pl.* way, course, doings, caravan, procession.

הלך   *q* go, walk, act; go away, pass away.

     ni be made to pass away.

     pi go, walk, walk about; pass away; *Prov. 6.11 pt.* highwayman.

     hi cause to go, lead; bring.

     hitp go to and fro, traverse, walk, flow away *(water).*

הֵלֶךְ   *I Sam. 14.26* flowing; *II Sam. 12.4* visitor.

הלל I   *hi* cause to flash.

הלל II   *pi* shout with joy, glorify, praise, extol.

    pu be celebrated, praised.

    hitp boast; *Prov. 31.30* be praised.

הלל III   *q* be deluded.

    poel make a fool, a laughing-stock, of.

    poal pt. senseless.

    hitpo behave madly.

הִלֵּל   *n. pers.* Hillel.

הלם   *q* hammer, beat; stamp; overcome.

הֲלֹם   hither, here.

הֶלֶם   *n. pers.* Helem.

הַלְמוּת   hammer.

הָם   *n. place* Ham.

הָם*, הָמָה*   luxury?

הֵם   *m. pl.* they.

הַמְּדָתָא   *n. pers.* Hammedatha.

המה   *q* make an uproar, roar; growl, snarl, coo, bark; sound; groan; be agitated.

הֵמָּה   *m. pl.* they.

הֲמוּלָּה   → הֲמֻלָּה.

הָמוֹן   roar, tumult; crowd, wealth; commotion, agitation.

הֲמוֹנָה   *n. place?* Hamonah.

הֶמְיָה*   thrumming.

הֲמֻלָּה   roar?, throng?

המם   *q* confuse, exterminate; *Isa. 28.28* drive on; *Jer. 51.34 dub.*

הָמָן   *n. pers.* Haman.

הֲמָסִים   brushwood.

הֵן   see!; if *(Aram.)*.

הֵנָּה I   here, hither; until now.

הֵנָּה II   *f. pl.* they.

הִנֵּה   see!; if.

הֲנָחָה   remission, amnesty.

הִנֹּם   *n. pers.* Hinnom.

הֵנַע   *n. place* Hena.

הֲנָפָה   swinging.

הַס   hush!

הסה   *hi* still.

הָסוּרִים   *pt. pass. q of* אסר.

הֲפֻנָה*   cessation.

הָפַךְ   *q* turn *(trans.)*; overthrow, destroy; change; turn *(refl.)*, change into, become.

ni turn *(refl.)*; be overthrown, destroyed; be changed; change.

ho turn *(refl.)*.

hitp Gen. *3.24* whirl; *Judg. 7.13* roll; *Job 37.12* turn this way and that; *Job 38.14* be transformed.

הֶפֶךְ   opposite, perversity.

הֲפֵכָה   overthrow.

הֲפַכְפַּךְ   twisted.

הַצִּיץ   *n. place* Ziz.

הַצָּלָה   deliverance.

הַצְלֶלְפּוֹנִי   *n. pers. f.* Hazelelponi.

הֹצֶן   multitude?

הַקּוֹץ   *n. pers.* Hakkoz.

הַר   mountain, highlands.

הֹר   *n. place* Hor.

הָרָא   *n. terr.* Hara.

הַרְאֵל   *rd.* I אֲרִיאֵל *(Ezek. 43.15).*

הַרְבִּית   *rd. Q (II Sam. 14.11) inf. cstr. hi of* רבה.

הָרַג   *q* kill, slay; slaughter.

ni be killed.

pu be killed.

הֶרֶג   killing, murder.

הֲרֵגָה   killing, slaughter.

הָרָה   *q* conceive, be/become pregnant; *pt.* mother, parents.

pu be conceived.

poel? Isa. *59.13* conceive.

הָרָה   pregnant.

הָרֻם   *n. pers.* Harum.

הֲרוֹרִי   *gent.* Harorite.

הָרִיָּה*   pregnant.

הֵרָיוֹן   conception.

הָרָם   בֵּית הָרָם ←.

הֹרָם   *n. pers.* Horam.

הַרְמוֹן*   *unexplained.*

הָרָן   *n. pers.* Haran.

הֵרֹן*   pregnancy.

הרס   *q* tear down, pull down, destroy; break through, press forward;
Ps. 58.7 knock out.

ni be pulled down.

pi destroy.

הֶרֶס   destruction.

הֲרִסָה*   ruins.

הֲרִסֻת*   destruction.

הֲרָר*   *parallel form of* הַר.

הֲרָרִי, הֲרָרִי   *gent.* Hararite.

הָשֵׁם   *n. pers.* Hashem.

הַשְׁמָעוּת   information.

הָשַׁפּוֹת   אַשְׁפֹּת *with the article.*

הִתּוּךְ   melting.

הִתְחַבְּרוּת   *inf. hitp of* II חבר.

הֲתָךְ   *n. pers.* Hathach.

התל   *pi* mock.

הֲתֻלִים   mockery.

התת   *poel* overwhelm with reproofs.

ו

וְ, וּ   and; also, together with; that is; or; וְ—וְ not only—but also,
whether—or.

וְדָן   *n. place* Vedan.

וָהֵב   *n. place* Vaheb.

וָו*   peg.

וָזָר   guilty?

וַיְזָתָא   *n. pers.* Vaizatha.

וָלָד   child.

וַנְיָה   *n. pers.* Vaniah.

וָפְסִי   *n. pers.* Vophsi.

וַשְׁנִי   *n. pers.* Vashni.

וַשְׁתִּי   *n. pers. f.* Vashti.

ז

זְאֵב I wolf.

זְאֵב II *n. pers.* Zeeb.

זֹאת *f. sg.* this.

זבד° *q* present with.

זֶבֶד° gift.

זָבָד° *n. pers.* Zabad.

זַבְדִּי° *n. pers.* Zabdi.

זַבְדִּיאֵל° *n. pers.* Zabdiel.

זְבַדְיָה(וּ)° *n. pers.* Zebadiah.

זְבוּב *coll.* flies.

זָבוּד° *n. pers.* Zabud.

זְבוּלוּן, זְבֻלֻן *n. pers., n. peop.* Zebulun.

זְבוּלֹנִי *gent.* Zebulunite.

זבח *q* slaughter, sacrifice.

     pi sacrifice.

זֶבַח I sacrifice.

זֶבַח II *n. pers.* Zebah.

זַבַּי *n. pers.* Zabbai.

זְבִידָּה° *n. pers. f. rd. Q (II Kings 23.36)* Zebudah.

זְבִינָא° *n. pers.* Zebina.

זבל *q* honour?; live with?

זְבֻל I dwelling.

זְבֻל II *n. pers.* Zebul.

זְבֻלוּן → .זְבוּלוּן

זַג skin.

זֵד insolent, presumptuous.

זָדוֹן presumptuousness.

זֶה this; here; now; *also relative particle in poetry.*

זֹה *f. sg.* this.

זָהָב gold.

זהם *pi* fill with disgust.

זַהַם *n. pers.* Zaham.

זהר I *hi* shine.

זהר II *ni* let oneself be warned.

     hi warn.

זֹהַר brightness.

זִו Ziv *(name of a month, April/May)*.

זוֹ *f. sg.* this

זוּ *relative particle; Hab. 1.11 text corr.?; Ps. 62.12* this.

זוּב *q* flow; *Lam. 4.9* waste away?

זוֹב discharge.

זוּד → זיד.

זוּזִים *n. peop.* Zuzim.

זוֹחֵת *n. pers.* Zoheth.

זָוִית* corner.

זוּל *q* lavish.

זוּלָה* besides; *Josh. 11.13* except that.

זוּן *Prov. 17.4 hi of* I זון.

זוֹנָה prostitute.

זוּע *q* tremble.

     pilp shake.

זְוָעָה, זַוֲעָה, זוּעָ֑ה trembling, terror.

I זוּר *q* press out, crush.

II זוּר *q* turn away.

     ni turn away.

     ho pt. estranged.

III זוּר *q* be loathsome.

זָזָא *n. pers.* Zaza.

זחח *ni* be displaced, slip.

זחל *q* creep, crawl away.

זֹחֶלֶת serpent.

זיד *q* be presumptuous.

     hi act insolently, act presumptuously; be inflamed, instigate; *Gen. 25.29* boil.

זֵידוֹן* seething.

I זִיז swarm.

II זִיז udder, nipple.

זִיזָא *n. pers.* Ziza.

זִיזָה *n. pers.* Zizah.

זִינָא *n. pers.* Zina.

זִיעַ *n. pers.* Zia.

זִיף *n. pers., n. place* Ziph.

זִיפָה *n. pers.* Ziphah.

זִיפִי *gent.* Ziphite.

זִיקוֹת flaming arrows.

זַיִת olive-tree; *coll.* olives.

זֵיתָן *n. pers.* Zethan.

זַךְ pure, clear.

זכה *q* be pure.

　　pi keep pure.

　　hitp make oneself clean.

זְכוֹכִית glass.

זָכוּר* male.

זָכוּר mindful.

זַכּוּר *n. pers.* Zaccur.

זַכַּי *n. pers.* Zaccai.

זכך *q* be clear, pure; be bright.

　　hi cleanse.

זכר *q* recall, think of, remember.

　　ni be remembered, mentioned.

　　hi remind, mention; confess, praise.

זָכָר man; male.

זֵכֶר memory, mention, naming, invocation.

זֶכֶר *n. pers.* Zecher.

זִכָּרוֹן° memory, reminder, mention; memorial; event to be
　　remembered; maxim.

זִכְרִי *n. pers.* Zichri.

זְכַרְיָה(וּ) *n. pers.* Zechariah.

זֻלּוּת vileness.

זַלְזַלִּים tendrils.

זלל I *q* be profligate, vile.

　　hi despise.

זלל II *ni* quake, totter.

זַלְעָפָה*, זִלְעָפָה* intensity, fury.

זִלְפָּה *n. pers. f.* Zilpah.

זִמָּה I shameful deed, shame.

זִמָּה II *n. pers.* Zimmah.

זְמוֹרָה vine-branch, vine.

זַמְזֻמִּים *n. peop.* Zamzummim.

זָמִיר I pruning (*of vines*), trimming.

זָמִיר* II song.

זְמִירָה *n. pers.* Zemirah.

זמם‎ *q* consider, purpose.

זָמָם‎* plan.

זֹמָן‎ *pu pt.* appointed.

זְמָן‎ *(fixed)* time, date.

I זמר‎ *q* prune *(vines),* trim.
    ni be pruned *(vines),* be trimmed.

II זמר‎ *pi* sing, play a musical instrument; praise.

זֶמֶר‎ wild goat?, *species of gazelle?*

I זִמְרָה‎ song, sound.

II זִמְרָה‎* *Ex. 15.2; Isa. 12.2; Ps. 118.14* strength?

III זִמְרָה‎* fruit, produce.

זְמֹרָה‎ → זְמוֹרָה‎.

זִמְרִי‎ *n. pers., n. terr.* Zimri.

זִמְרָן‎ *n. pers.* Zimran.

זִמְרָת‎ → II זִמְרָה‎.

זַן‎ kind.

זנב‎ *pi* destroy the rearguard.

זָנָב‎ tail; stump.

זנה‎ *q* fornicate; be unfaithful; *Judg. 19.2* take a dislike to.
    pu have fornication committed.
    hi induce to commit fornication; fornicate.

זֹנָה‎ → זוֹנָה‎.

זָנוֹחַ‎ *n. pers., n. place* Zanoah.

זְנוּנִים‎ unchastity, fornication; unfaithfulness.

זְנוּת‎ unchastity, fornication; unfaithfulness.

I זנח‎ *hi* stink.

II זנח‎ *q* reject, cast off.
    hi declare rejected, reject.

זָנֹחַ‎ → זָנוֹחַ‎.

זנק‎ *pi* spring out.

זֵעָה‎* sweat.

זְוָעָה‎ trembling, terror.

זַעֲוָן‎ *n. pers.* Zaavan.

זעזע‎ *pilp of* זוע‎.

זְעֵיר‎° a little.

זעך‎ *ni* be extinguished.

זַעַם *q* curse, inveigh against, be angry with.

     ni pt. cursed.

זַעַם curse, anger.

זָעַף *q* be incensed; *Dan. 1.10* look wretched.

זַעַף rage, anger.

זָעֵף furious.

זָעַק *q* cry, call.

     ni be mustered; *I Sam. 14.20* assemble.

     hi cry; muster *(levies)*; *Jonah 3.7* have proclamation made;

       Zech. 6.8 call out to.

זְעָקָה outcry, lamentation.

זִפְרֹן* *n. place* Ziphron.

זֶפֶת *f.* pitch.

I זִקִּים fetters.

II זִקִּים flaming arrows.

זָקֵן *q* be/become old.

     hi become old.

זָקָן *m. and f.* beard.

זָקֵן old; old man; elder.

זֹקֶן old age.

זִקְנָה growing old.

זְקֻנִים time, condition of growing old, old age.

זָקַף *q* raise up.

זָקַק *q* filter, wash *(ore)*.

     pi refine.

     pu pt. strained, refined.

זָר foreign; foreigner; different, surprising, strange; unlawful.

זֵר moulding, band.

זָרָא diarrhoea with vomiting.

זרב *pu* become parched.

זְרֻבָּבֶל *n. pers.* Zerubbabel.

זֶרֶד *n. river* Zered.

I זרה *q* scatter, winnow.

     ni be dispersed.

     pi scatter, disperse, spread abroad; *Prov. 20.8,26* winnow.

     pu be spread, scattered.

II זרה *pi* measure off.

זְרוֹעַ arm, forearm; strength, force.

זֵרוּעַ sowing.

זַרְזִיף downpour.

זַרְזִיר *Prov. 30.31 text corr.*

זרח *q* rise, break out.

I ‎זֶרַח* rising *(sun)*.

II ‎זֶרַח *n. pers.* Zerah.

זַרְחִי *gent.* Zerahite.

זְרַחְיָה *n. pers.* Zerahiah.

זרם *q* wash away?

poel pour out.

זֶרֶם downpour.

‎זִרְמָה* penis.

זרע *q* sow.

ni be sown; be fertilized.

pu be sown.

hi produce seed; *Lev. 12.2* bear offspring.

זֶרַע sowing, seed; semen; offspring; family.

זֵרֹעִים, vegetables.

זֵרְעֹנִים°

זרק *q* scatter, sprinkle; *Hos. 7.9* be sprinkled.

pu be scattered.

זרר *q pass.?* be squeezed out.

poel sneeze.

זֶרֶשׁ *n. pers. f.* Zeresh.

זֶרֶת span *(c. 22 cm)*.

זַתּוּא *n. pers.* Zattu.

זֵתָם *n. pers.* Zetham.

זֵתַר *n. pers.* Zethar.

ח

‎חֹב* shirt-pocket.

חבא *ni* hide; be hidden, sheltered.

pu keep in hiding.

hi hide, keep hidden.

ho be kept hidden.

hitp keep in hiding; *Job 38.30* solidify.

חבב° *q* love.

חֹבָב *n. pers.* Hobab.

חבה *q* hide.

ni hide.

חָבוֹר *n. river* Habor.

חַבּוּרָה injury, bruise.

חבט *q* beat, beat out.

ni be beaten out.

חֲבַיָּה *n. pers.* Hobaiah.

חֶבְיוֹן veil.

I חבל *q* take in pledge.

ni be bound in pledge.

II חבל *q* act corruptly.

pi spoil, ruin.

pu be destroyed; be distraught.

III חבל *pi* conceive.

I חֶבֶל rope, line, cord; noose, snare; piece of ground; district, region; *I Sam. 10.5,10* band.

II חֶבֶל destruction.

חֵבֶל labour-pains, sufferings; foetus.

חֲבֹל pledge.

חֹבֵל mast?

חֹבֵל sailor.

חֲבֹלָה* pledge.

חֹבְלִים union.

חֲבַצֶּלֶת lily *(asphodel)*.

חֲבַצִּנְיָה *n. pers.* Habazziniah.

חבק *q* embrace; *Eccles. 4.5* fold *(the hands)*.

pi embrace; *Job 24.8; Lam. 4.5* take shelter.

חִבֻּק folding.

חֲבַקּוּק *n. pers.* Habakkuk.

I חבר *hi* be brilliant.

II חבר *q* be joined; cast *(spell)*.

pi join, ally.

pu be/become joined.

hitp ally oneself; be in trading partnership.

itpa be in trading partnership.

חֶבֶר I   league, association; binding, spell.

חֶבֶר II   *n. pers.* Heber.

חָבֵר   companion, associate; devotee.

חַבָּר*   partner.

חֲבַרְבֻּרֹת*   spots.

חֶבְרָה   association.

חַבּוּרָה*   injury, bruise.

חֶבְרוֹן   *n. pers., n. place* Hebron.

חֶבְרוֹנִי   *gent.* Hebronite.

חֶבְרִי   *gent.* Heberite.

חֶבְרֹנִי   → חֶבְרוֹנִי.

חֲבֶרֶת*   partner.

חֹבֶרֶת   set; hanging.

חבשׁ   *q* bind, bind round, bind up; saddle; *Ezek. 27.24* twist; *Job 34.17* hold the reins; *Job 40.13* confine.

pi bind up; dam up.

pu be bound up.

חֲבִתִּים   pans.

חַג   pilgrim-feast.

חָגָּא   confusion.

חָגָב I   locust.

חָגָב II   *n. pers.* Hagab.

חֲגָבָה   *n. pers.* Hagabah.

חגג   *q* keep a pilgrim-feast; *Ps. 107.27* reel.

חָגוּ*   refuge.

חָגוֹר*   girded.

חֲגוֹר   girdle.

חֲגוֹרָה   girdle; loincloth.

חַגַּי   *n. pers.* Haggai.

חַגִּי   *n. pers.* Haggi; *gent.* Haggite.

חַגִּיָּה   *n. pers.* Haggiah.

חַגִּית   *n. pers. f.* Haggith.

חָגְלָה   *n. pers. f.* Hoglah.

חגר   *q* gird; gird oneself.

חֲגוֹר, חֲגוֹרָה, חֲגֹרָה   → .

חַר I*   sharp.

II חַד° *Ezek. 33.30* one.

חדד *q* be aggressive.

ho be sharpened.

חֲדַד *n. pers.* Hadad.

חדה° *q* rejoice.

pi make glad.

חַדּוּדִים* points.

חֶדְוָה° joy.

חָדִיד *n. place* Hadid.

חדל *q* cease, desist from, neglect; fail to appear, be absent; rest.

חָדֵל *Ps. 39.5* ceasing, transient; *Ezek. 3.27* declining; *Isa. 53.3 dub.*

חֶדֶל abode of the dead?

חַדְלַי *n. pers.* Hadlai.

חֶרֶק nightshade.

חִדֶּקֶל *n. river* Tigris.

חדר *q* surround.

חֶדֶר inner room, chamber; innermost part.

חַדְרָךְ *n. place* Hadrach.

חדש *pi* renovate, renew.

hitp be revived, rejuvenated.

חָדָשׁ new, fresh.

I חֹדֶשׁ new moon, month; *Jer. 2.24* heat.

II חֹדֶשׁ *n. pers. f.* Hodesh.

חֲדָשָׁה *n. place* Hadashah.

חָדְשִׁי *n. place* Hodshi.

חֲדַתָּה° → חָצוֹר חֲדַתָּה.

חוב° *pi* bring into liability.

חוֹב° debt.

חוֹבָה *n. place* Hobah.

חוג *q* describe a circle.

חוּג circle, horizon.

חור° *q* pose a riddle.

חוה° *pi* proclaim, instruct.

I חַוָּה* camp, tent-village.

II חַוָּה *n. pers. f.* Eve.

חֹוֶה* → חֹזֶה.

חוֹזַי *n. pers.* Hozai.

חוֹחַ thorns; thorn, hook.

חֲבָתִים hiding-places.

חוּט thread.

חִוִּי *n. pers., gent.* Hivite.

חֲוִילָה *n. pers., n. terr.* Havilah.

I חוּל *q* dance a round dance, turn.
pol dance a round dance.
hitpol whirl.

II חוּל → I חיל.

חוּל *n. pers.* Hul.

I חוֹל sand.

II חוֹל *Job 29.18* phoenix.

חוּם dark-coloured.

חוֹמָה wall.

חוּם *q* be sad; have pity, spare.

חוֹף shore, coast.

חוּפָם *n. pers.* Hupham.

חוּפָמִי *gent.* Huphamite.

חוּץ alley; outside; *Eccles. 2.25* חוּץ מִן except.

חֻקֹק *n. place* Hukok.

חוּר *q* turn pale.

I חוּר linen.

II חוּר *n. pers.* Hur.

חוֹר → I חֹר.

חוֹרֵב → חֹרֵב.

חוֹרִי → II חֹרִי.

חוֹרִי linen.

חוּרִי *n. pers.* Huri.

חוּרַי *n. pers.* Hurai.

חוּרָם *n. pers.* Huram.

חַוְרָן *n. terr.* Hauran.

חוֹרֹנַיִם → חֹרֹנַיִם.

חוּשׁ *q* hasten; *Eccles. 2.25* be anxious?, enjoy?
hi hasten, speed; yield.

חוּשָׁה *n. pers.* Hushah.

חוּשַׁי *n. pers.* Hushai.

חוּשִׁים *n. pers. f.* Hushim.

חוּשָׁם → חֻשָׁם.

I חוֹתָם seal.

II חוֹתָם *n. pers.* Hotham.

חֲזָאֵל *n. pers.* Hazael.

חזה *q* see, behold; *Ex. 18.21* choose.

חָזֶה breast, brisket.

חֹזֶה seer.

חֲזָהאֵל → חֲזָאֵל.

חֲזוֹ *n. pers.* Hazo.

חָזוֹן vision, appearance.

חָזוֹת record of vision.

חָזוּת° vision; *Dan. 8.5,8* conspicuousness.

חֲזִיאֵל *n. pers.* Haziel.

חֲזָיָה *n. pers.* Hazaiah.

חֶזְיוֹן *n. pers.* Hezion.

חִזָּיוֹן vision, appearance.

חֲזִיז thundercloud.

חֲזִיר wild boar.

חֵזִיר *n. pers.* Hezir.

חזק *q* be/become firm, strong; *w.* עַל impel; *w.* בְּ be caught, hold fast; *w.* לְב be obdurate.

    pi make firm, strong; *w.* לֵב *and* פָּנִים harden, indurate; *Isa. 33.23* hold fast; *Isa. 22.21; Nahum 2.2* gird *(Aram.)*.

    hi make firm, strong; take hold of, hold fast; show oneself mighty.

    hitp strengthen oneself, show oneself strong.

חָזָק firm, hard, strong; severe.

חָזֵק strong, powerful.

חֵזֶק* strength.

חֹזֶק strength.

חֶזְקָה* gaining strength; *Isa. 8.11* impelling.

חָזְקָה power, strength; *II Kings 12.13* repair *(architectural)*.

חִזְקִי *n. pers.* Hizki.

חִזְקִיָּה(וּ) *n. pers.* Hezekiah.

חָח thorn, hook; *Ex. 35.22* clasp.

חטא *q* miss; be guilty, incur guilt, sin; *Hab. 2.10; Prov. 20.2* forfeit.

pi purify from sin, make sin-offering; *Gen. 31.39* be obliged to replace.

hi cause to sin, lead astray; *Judg. 20.16* miss; *Isa. 29.21* represent as guilty.

hitp purify oneself; *Job 41.17* draw back.

חֵטְא fault, guilt, sin.

חֵטָא* sinful; sinner.

חֲטָאָה offending.

חַטָּאָה fault, sin; sin-offering.

חֲטָאָה fault, sin.

חַטָּאת, חַטָּאת fault, sin; punishment for sin; sin-offering.

I חטב *q* hew.

pu pt. carved.

II חטב *q pt. pass.* variegated.

חִטָּה wheat.

חַטּוּשׁ *n. pers.* Hattush.

חֲטִיטָא *n. pers.* Hatita.

חַטִּיל *n. pers.* Hattil.

חֲטִיפָא *n. pers.* Hatiphah.

חטם *q* restrain oneself.

חטף° *q* seize.

חֹטֶר shoot, rod.

חַטָּאת → חַטָּת.

I חַי living; fresh; כָּעֵת חַיָּה in a year's time; → *also* חַיִּים.

II חַי* *I Sam. 18.18* kinsfolk?

חִיאֵל *n. pers.* Hiel.

חִידָה° riddle; *Hab. 2.6* veiled insinuation; *Dan. 8.23* intrigue.

חיה *q* live, remain alive, revive, recover.

pi let live, preserve alive; bring to life, call into being; revive; *Hos. 14.8* cultivate *(corn)*.

hi preserve alive; revive.

חָיֶה* *Ex. 1.19* having easy labour.

I חַיָּה animal *(usually not domesticated)*; being.

II חַיָּה* life; *Job 33.20; 38.39* appetite.

III חַיָּה band, host.

חַיּוּת life-span; *II Sam. 20.3* during the lifetime *(of the husband)*.

חַיִּים life, lifetime, life-span; happiness in life; sustenance.

I חיל *q* have labour-pains, be in labour; writhe, quake.

 pol make to have labour-pains; bring forth.

 polal be born; *Job 26.5* be made to quake.

 hi cause to quake.

 ho be born.

 hitpol writhe in anguish.

 hitpalp writhe in agitation.

II חיל *q* endure, be lasting.

III חיל *q* wait.

 pol wait.

 hitpol wait.

חַיִל strength, ability; wealth, property; military force, army; *Neh. 3.34* notables.

חֵיל outer fortification?, rampart?

חִיל labour-pains.

חִילָה labour-pains.

חִילֵז *n. place* Hilez.

חֶלֶךְ *n. terr.* Helech, Cilicia.

חֵילָם *n. place* Helam.

חִילֵן *n. place* Hilen.

חִין *Job 41.4 text corr.*

חַיִץ wall.

חִיצוֹן external, outer; secular; *w.* לְ on the outside.

חֵיק lap, bosom; fold of garment; region of the kidneys; *f.* cavity.

חִירָה *n. pers.* Hirah.

חִירוֹם *n. pers.* Hirom.

חִירָם *n. pers.* Hiram.

חִירֹת ← פִּי־הַחִירֹת.

חִישׁ quickly.

חֵךְ palate.

חכה *q* wait for.

 pi wait, await; delay.

חַכָּה fish-hook.

חֲכִילָה *n. place* Hachilah.

חֲכַלְיָה *n. pers.* Hacaliah.

חַכְלִילִי dark.

חַכְלִלוּת dimness.

חכם *q* be/become wise; act wisely.

pi make wise; instruct.

pu pt. instructed, experienced.

hi make wise.

hitp show oneself wise, shrewd.

חָכָם expert, skilled, skilful; experienced, shrewd, wise.

חָכְמָה accomplishment, skill; experience, shrewdness, wisdom.

חַכְמוֹנִי *n. pers.* Hachmoni.

חָכְמוֹת wisdom.

חֹל profane.

חֵל → חִיל.

חלא *q* fall ill.

hi make ill.

I *חֶלְאָה* rust.

II חֶלְאָה *n. pers. f.* Helah.

חֲלָאִים *pl. of* I חֲלִי.

חֶלְאָמָה → חֵילָם.

חָלָב milk.

I חֵלֶב fat; best, choicest part.

II חֵלֶב *n. pers.* Heleb.

חֶלְבָּה *n. place* Helbah.

חֶלְבּוֹן *n. place* Helbon.

חֶלְבְּנָה galbanum.

חֶלֶד life-span; world.

חֵלֶד *n. pers.* Heled.

חֹלֶד mole-rat.

חֻלְדָּה *n. pers. f.* Huldah.

חֶלְדַּי *n. pers.* Heldai.

חלה *q* be/become weak, sick.

ni become weak, sick; *pt.* severe, incurable.

pi make sick; *w.* פָּנִים appease.

pu be made weak.

hi make sick; *pt.* sickness.

ho be drained of strength.

hitp feel/feign to be sick.

חַלָּה   bread *(in the shape of a ring)*.

חֲלוֹם   dream.

חַלּוֹן   window aperture, window.

חֹלוֹן   *n. place* Holon.

חֲלוֹף   passing away?

חֲלוּשָׁה   defeat.

חֲלַח   *n. place* Halah.

חַלְחֻל   *n. place* Halhul.

חַלְחָלָה   shuddering.

חלט   *q* take to be favourable.

חֳלִי   sickness, suffering.

I חֲלִי   ornament.

II חֲלִי   *n. place* Hali.

חֶלְיָה*   ornament.

חָלִיל   flute.

חָלִילָה   far be it.

חֲלִיפָה*   turn, relief; *(change of)* clothing; *Ps. 55.20* mutual obligation.

חֲלִיצָה*   clothing, arms *(< that which may be stripped off)*.

חֶלְכָּאִים,   *unexplained.*
חֵלְכָה

I חלל   *ni* be profaned; defile oneself.

     pi defile; take into *(profane)* use; *Ezek. 28.16* cast out.

     pu pt. profaned.

     hi begin; *Ezek. 39.7* permit to be profaned; *Num. 30.3* break *(one's word)*.

     ho be begun.

II חלל   *q* be pierced.

     pi pierce.

     pu pt. pierced.

     poel pierce.

     poal pt. pierced.

III חלל   *pi* play the flute.

חָלָל   pierced; slain; deflowered.

חֲלָלָה   → חָלִילָה.

I חלם   *q* become robust.

     hi let recover.

II חלם   *q* dream.
     hi? cause to dream.
   חֲלֹם → חֲלוֹם.
   חֵלֶם   *n. pers.* Helem.
חַלָּמוּת   *species of plant* marsh-mallow *or* ox-tongue.
חַלָּמִישׁ   flint.
   חֵלֹן   *n. pers.* Helon.
   חֹלֹן → חֹלוֹן.
  I חלף   *q* pass by, pass away; *I Sam. 10.3* depart.
     pi change, alter.
     hi Gen. 31.7,41 alter; *Gen. 35.2; Ps. 102.27* change; *Lev. 27.10*
       replace; *Isa. 9.9* substitute; *Isa. 40.31; 41.1* renew; *Job 14.7*
       sprout again; *Job 29.20* send one after another.
II חלף   *q* pierce.
  I חֵלֶף°   in return for.
II חֵלֶף   *n. place* Heleph.
  I חלץ   *q* pull off; *Lam. 4.3 fig.* present *(the teats)*; *Hos. 5.6* withdraw.
     ni be delivered.
     pi tear out; deliver; *Ps. 7.5* despoil.
II חלץ   *q pt. pass.* armed.
     ni arm oneself.
     hi make sound.
  I חֲלֵץ*   loin.
II חֶלֶץ   *n. pers.* Helez.
  I חלק   *q* be smooth, false.
     hi make smooth; *w.* לָשׁוֹן *or* אֲמָרִים flatter.
II חלק   *q* divide, distribute, apportion; receive a share; give a share;
     II Chron. 28.21 plunder.
     ni be divided; divide.
     pi divide, distribute, apportion; scatter.
     pu be divided.
     hi share in an inheritance.
     hitp divide among themselves.
   חָלָק   smooth, insinuating; *Ezek. 12.24* deceitful; *pl. f. also* falseness,
     flattering thing; *Ps. 73.18* slippery place.
  I חֵלֶק   cajolery.

II חֵלֶק portion, share, possession, profit; lot.

III חֵלֶק n. pers. Helek.

חָלָק* smooth.

I חֶלְקָה* smoothness, cajolery.

II חֶלְקָה field.

חֲלֻקָּה* division.

חֲלַקּוֹת smoothness.

חֶלְקִי gent. Helekite.

חֶלְקַי n. pers. Helkai.

חִלְקִיָּה(וּ) n. pers. Hilkiah.

חֲלַקְלַקּוֹת slippery places; smoothness, falseness.

חֶלְקַת n. place Helkath.

חלשׁ q Ex. 17.13; Isa. 14.12 defeat; Job 14.10 be frail.

חַלָּשׁ weakling.

I חָם* father-in-law (husband's father).

II חָם hot.

III חָם n. pers. Ham > Egypt.

חֹם heat.

חֵמָא → I חֵמָה.

חֶמְאָה butter.

חמד q desire, long for; prize; pt. pass. Isa. 44.9 beloved; Ps. 39.12; Job 20.20 valuable object.

ni pt. desirable.

pi desire.

חֶמֶד grace, beauty.

חֶמְדָּה desirable thing, valuable, pleasantness.

חֲמֻדוֹת valuable objects; delicious; worthy of love.

חֶמְדָּן n. pers. Hemdan.

חֲמֻדֹת → חֲמֻדוֹת.

חֹמָה → חוֹמָה.

חַמָּה heat > sun.

I חֵמָה heat, arousal, rage; poison.

II חֵמָה → חֶמְאָה.

חַמּוּאֵל n. pers. Hammuel.

חֲמוּדוֹת, → חֲמֻדוֹת.
חֲמֻדֹת

חֲמוּטַל n. pers. f. Hamutal.

חָמוּל n. pers. Hamul.

חֲמוּלִי *gent.* Hamulite.

חַמּוֹן *n. place* Hammon.

*חָמוּץ vivid.

חָמוֹץ oppressor.

*חָמוּק curve.

I חֲמוֹר ass.

II חֲמוֹר *I Sam. 16.20* batch; *Judg. 15.16 w.* du. in heaps.

III חֲמוֹר *n. pers.* Hamor.

*חָמוֹת mother-in-law *(husband's mother)*.

חֹמֶט a reptile.

חָמְטָה *n. place* Humtah.

חֲמִיטַל *II Kings 24.18; Jer. 52.1* rd. Q.

חָמִיץ sorrel.

חֲמִישִׁי fifth; *f. also* fifth part; *I Kings 6.31* pentagonal.

חמל *q* have compassion; spare, save; *II Sam. 12.4* be unable to
　　　bring oneself; *w.* לֹא *also* without compassion.

*חֶמְלָה compassion.

חֶמְלָה compassion.

חמם *q* become warm, warm oneself; become heated, aroused.
　　　ni pt. inflamed, lustful.
　　　pi warm.
　　　hitp warm oneself.

*חַמָּן incense-altar.

חמם *q Jer. 22.3; Job 21.27* treat with violence, oppress; *Ezek. 22.26;*
　　　Zeph. 3.4 violate; *Job 15.33* shed; *Lam. 2.6* pull down.
　　　ni suffer violence.

חָמָם violence, wrong.

I חמץ *q* be/become leavened.
　　　hi taste leavened.
　　　hitp be embittered.

II חמץ *q* oppress.

חָמֵץ leavened material.

חֹמֶץ vinegar.

*חֲמָצָה *inf. q of* I חמץ.

חמק *q* turn aside, go away.
　　　hitp run hither and thither, vacillate.

I חמר   *q* foam; *Ex. 2.3* coat with pitch.
       poalal be in ferment.

II חמר   *poalal* be reddened.

חֶמֶר   wine.

I חֹמֶר   mud, clay; mire.

II חֹמֶר   *dry measure* homer *(between 200 and 450 l)*; *Ex. 8.10* heap.

III חֹמֶר   surge.

חֵמָר   asphalt, bitumen.

חֲמֹר   → I חֲמוֹר.

חַמְרָן   *n. pers.* Hamran.

חמשׁ   *q pt. pass.* in battle formation.
       pi take the fifth part.

חָמֵשׁ   five; *pl.* fifty.

I חֹמֶשׁ   *Gen. 47.26* fifth part.

II חֹמֶשׁ   abdomen, belly.

חֲמִישִׁי, חֲמִשִׁית   → חֲמִישִׁי.

חֵמֶת   skin.

חֲמָת   *n. place* Hamath.

חַמַּת   *n. pers., n. place* Hammath.

חֲמָתִי   *gent.* Hamathite.

חֵן   grace, beauty; favour, regard, approval; *Zech. 12.10* compassion.

חֵנָדָד   *n. pers.* Henadad.

חנה   *q* decline; encamp, set up a war camp.
       pi be gracious.

חַנָּה   *n. pers. f.* Hannah.

חֲנוֹךְ   *n. pers., n. place* Enoch.

חָנוּן   *n. pers.* Hanun.

חַנּוּן   kind, gracious.

°*חֲנוּת   vault.

I חנט   *q Gen. 50.2,26* embalm.

II חנט   *q Cant. 2.13* become ripe.

חֲנֻטִים   embalming.

חַנִּיאֵל   *n. pers.* Hanniel.

חֲנִיוֹת   *pl. of* חֲנוּת.

*חָנִיךְ   retainer?; trusty?

חֲנִינָה   kindness, favour.

חֲנִית spear.

חָנַךְ *q* train, dedicate.

חֲנֻכָּה dedication.

חֲנֹכִי *gent.* Enochite.

חִנָּם gratis, without payment; in vain; without cause, undeservedly.

חֲנַמְאֵל *n. pers.* Hanamel.

חֲנָמַל flood.

I חנן *q* be gracious, generous.
   ni Jer. 22.23 of אנח.
   pi make charming.
   poel have pity.
   ho find pity.
   hitp implore favour, pity.

II חנן *q* stink.

חָנָן *n. pers.* Hanan.

חֲנַנְאֵל *n. pers.* Hananel.

חֲנָנִי *n. pers.* Hanani.

חֲנַנְיָה(וּ) *n. pers.* Hananiah.

חָנֵס *n. place* Hanes.

חנף *q* be defiled, be godless; *Jer. 3.9* defile.
   hi defile; seduce.

חָנֵף godless.

חֹנֶף godlessness.

חֲנֻפָּה godlessness.

חנק *ni* strangle oneself.
   pi strangle.

חֲנָתוֹן *n. place* Hannathon.

I חסד *hitp* show oneself loyal.

II חסד° *pi* abuse.

I חֶסֶד joint obligation, loyalty, solidarity; *pl. also* demonstrations of favour, proofs of devotion.

II חֶסֶד disgrace.

III חֶסֶד *n. pers.* Hesed.

חֲסַדְיָה *n. pers.* Hasadiah.

חסה *q* shelter, seek refuge.

חֹסָה *n. pers., n. place* Hosah.

חָסוּת refuge.

חָסִיד loyal, pious.

חֲסִידָה stork?, heron?

חָסִיל locust?, cockroach?

חָסִין strong.

חסל q eat up.

חסם q muzzle, block.

חסן ni be stored up.

חֹסֶן store, treasure.

חָסֹן strong.

חספס pt. (pass.) flaky?

חסר q diminish; be empty; lack, want; suffer want.

    pi cause to lack, cause to want.

    hi cause to want, have want.

חָסֵר in want of, lacking.

חֶסֶר want.

חֹסֶר want.

חַסְרָה n. pers. Hasrah.

חֶסְרוֹן want.

חַף clean.

חפא pi II Kings 17.9 unexplained.

חפה q cover.

    ni be covered.

    pi overlay.

I חֻפָּה shelter; bridal chamber.

II חֻפָּה n. pers. Huppah.

חפז q hurry away.

    ni be driven away.

חִפָּזוֹן hurried flight, haste.

חֻפִּים, חֻפָּם n. pers. Huppim.

חֹפֶן hollow of the hand.

חָפְנִי n. pers. Hophni.

חפף q shelter.

I חפץ q be pleased, have pleasure; desire; be minded, feel inclined.

II חפץ q Job 40.17 hang?, stretch out?

חָפֵץ having pleasure in, willing.

חֵפֶץ delight, joy, pleasure; wish, desire; business, matter, affair (*Aram.*).

חֶפְצִי־בָה *n. pers. f.* Hephzibah.

חפר I *q* dig, paw; search out.

חפר II *q* be ashamed, be shamed.
    hi be abashed; act shamefully.

חֵפֶר *n. pers., n. place* Hepher.

חֶפְרִי *gent.* Hepherite.

חֲפָרַיִם *n. place* Hapharaim.

חָפְרַע *n. pers.* Hophra.

חֲפֹר פֵּרוֹת* *rd.* חֲפַרְפָּרוֹת shrews.

חפשׂ *q* search for, search thoroughly.
    ni be thoroughly searched.
    pi search for, search through, seek.
    pu hide?, be devised?
    hitp disguise oneself, be disfigured.

חֵפֶשׂ purpose?

חפשׁ *pu* be released.

חֹפֶשׁ material.

חָפְשָׁה release.

חָפְשׁוּת *rd. Q (II Chron. 26.21).*

חָפְשִׁי released, free.

חָפְשִׁית release; exempt from duties.

חֵץ arrow.

חצב *q* break, hew out, hew; split, dash to pieces.
    ni be hewed out.
    pu be hewed out.
    hi hew down.

חצה *q* divide, share, divide off; *Isa. 30.28 w.* עַד reach up to.
    ni be divided.

חֲצוֹצְרָה → חֲצֹצְרָה.

חָצוֹר *n. place* Hazor.

חָצוֹר חֲדַתָּה *n. place* Hazor-hadattah.

חֲצוֹת middle.

חֲצִי half; middle, half-way up.

חֵצִי arrow.

חָצִיר grass, reed; *Num. 11.15* leek.

חֵצֶן*, חֹצֶן bosom, fold of garment.

חָצַץ   *q* keep in file.

     pi distribute.

     pu be measured off for a limited span.

חָצָץ   gravel, pebbles.

חַצְצוֹן תָּמָר,   *n. place* Hazazon-tamar.
חַצְצֹן תָּמָר

חצצר   sound, blow the trumpet.

חֲצֹצְרָה   trumpet.

חָצֵר   settlement, court, enclosure.

חָצֹר   → חָצוֹר.

חֲצַר־אַדָּר   *n. place* Hazar-addar.

חֲצַר גַּדָּה   *n. place* Hazar-gaddah.

חֶצְרוֹ   *n. pers.* Hezro.

חֶצְרוֹן   *n. pers.*, *n. place* Hezron.

חֶצְרוֹנִי   *gent.* Hezronite.

חֲצֵרוֹת   *n. place* Hazeroth.

חֶצְרַי   *n. pers.* Hezrai.

חֲצַרְמָוֶת   *n. pers.* Hazarmaveth.

חֶצְרֹן   → חֶצְרוֹן.

חֶצְרֹנִי   → חֶצְרוֹנִי.

חֲצַר סוּסָה,   *n. place* Hazar-susah, Hazar-susim.
חֲצַר סוּסִים

חֲצַר עֵינוֹן,   *n. place* Hazar-enon, Hazar-enan.
חֲצַר עֵינָן

חֲצַר שׁוּעָל   *n. place* Hazar-shual.

חֲצֵרֹת   → חֲצֵרוֹת.

חֵק   → חֵיק.

חֹק   something fixed, laid down; measure, limit; fixed period; prescribed due, obligation, entitlement; ordinance, rule, precept, regulation, law; *Ps. 2.7* royal protocol.

חֻקָּה   *pu pt.* inscribed, drawn.

     hitp engrave.

חֻקָּה   something fixed, laid down; precept, statute, regulation, law; *Jer. 5.24* season.

חֲקוּפָא   *n. pers.* Hakupha.

חקק   *q* inscribe, engrave; lay down, fix, command; *Isa. 22.16* hew out.

pu pt. prescribed.

ho be inscribed.

poel regulate, lay down; *pt. also* commander's staff; leader.

חִקְקֵי *pl. cs. of* חֹק.

חקר *q* search, explore, examine.

ni be searched out; be calculated; be penetrable.

pi seek.

חֵקֶר investigation; exploration; something to be searched out.

I חֹר *freeman, noble.

II חֹר hole, cave.

חֹר hole, hiding-place.

חֲרָאִים* excrement, dung.

I חרב *q* dry up, be dried up; lie waste, desolate.

ni be laid waste.

pu be dried up.

hi dry up; lay waste, make desolate.

ho be laid waste.

II חרב *q* slay, cut down.

ni cut one another down.

ho II Kings 3.23 inf. abs. in conjunction with ni.

חָרֵב dry; laid waste, desolate.

חֶרֶב knife, dagger, sword; chisel; *Ezek. 26.9* iron instruments?

חֹרֶב dryness, heat; devastation, desolation.

חֹרֵב *n. place* Horeb.

חָרְבָּה desolate land, ruined habitation; *Job 3.14* pyramids.

חֲרָבָה that which is dry.

חֲרָבוֹן* dry heat.

חַרְבוֹנָא, *n. pers.* Harbona.

חַרְבוֹנָה

חרן *q* come out.

חַרְגֹּל *species of locust.*

חרד *q* tremble, quake.

hi terrify, strike with terror.

חָרֵד trembling, anxious, afraid.

חָרֹד *n. place* Harod.

I חֲרָדָה trembling, anxiety, terror.

II חֲרָדָה *n. place* Haradah.

חֲרֹדִי   *gent.* Harodite.

חרה   *q* burn, be kindled; become angry; *Isa. 24.6 dub.*
  ni pt. angry.
  hi become heated; be zealously engaged.
  hitp show oneself angered.
  tiphal compete.

חֹר הַגִּדְגָּד   *n. place* Hor-haggidgad.

חַרְהֲיָה   *n. pers.* Harhaiah.

חֲרוֹדִי   → חֲרֹדִי.

חֲרוּזִים   necklace.

חָרוּל   weed, thistle.

חֲרוּמַף   *n. pers.* Harumaph.

חָרוֹן   heat.

חֹרוֹן   → בֵּית חֹרוֹן.

חֹרוֹנַיִם   *n. place* Horonaim.

I חָרוּץ   gold.

II חָרוּץ   moat; cut; mutilated; threshing-sledge; *Joel 4.14* decision.

III חָרוּץ   diligent.

IV חָרוּץ   *n. pers.* Haruz.

חַרְחוּר   *n. pers.* Harhur.

חַרְחַס   *n. pers.* Harhas.

חַרְחֻר   feverishness, inflammation.

חֶרֶט   stylus.

חַרְטֹם*   learned person, soothsayer-priest.

חֲרִי   heat.

I חֹרִי   baking.

II חֹרִי   *n. pers.* Hori; *gent.* Horite.

חֲרֵי   *cstr. of* * חֲרָאִים.

חָרִיט*   container, money-bag.

חֲרִייוֹנִים   *rd.* חֲרֵי יוֹנִים (*II Kings 6.25*).

חָרִיף   *n. pers.* Hariph.

חֲרִיפִי   *rd. K* (*I Chron. 12.6*) *gent.* Hariphite.

I חָרִיץ*   slice, piece.

II חָרִיץ*   pickaxe, hoe.

חָרִישׁ   ploughing-time; that which is to be ploughed > cultivated ground.

חֲרִישִׁי*   *unexplained.*

חָרֻךְ *q* unexplained.

חֲרַכִּים lattice window.

I חרם *hi* lay under ban, devote by ban; exterminate.
ho be laid under ban.

II חרם *q pt. pass.* with slit nose.
hi Isa. *11.15* split.

I חֵרֶם ban; that which is laid under ban, goods under ban.

II חֵרֶם net.

חָרִם *n. pers.* Harim.

חָרֵם *n. place* Horem.

חָרְמָה *n. place* Hormah.

חֶרְמוֹן *n. place* Hermon.

חֶרְמוֹנִים summits of Hermon.

חֶרְמֹן → חֶרְמוֹן.

חֶרְמֵשׁ sickle.

חָרָן *n. pers., n. place* Haran.

חֹרֹנִי *gent.* Horonite.

חֹרֹנַיִם → חֹרוֹנַיִם.

חַרְנֶפֶר *n. pers.* Harnepher.

I חֶרֶס *f.* scab, itch.

II חֶרֶס sun.

III חֶרֶס *n. place* Heres.

חַרְסוּת *rd. Q (Jer. 19.2)* potsherd.

I חרף *q* winter.

II חרף *q* abuse, taunt.
pi abuse, taunt; provoke; despise.

III חרף *ni pt. Lev. 19.20* designated.

חָרֵף *n. pers.* Hareph.

חֹרֶף prime, youth; autumn; winter.

חֶרְפָּה abuse; disgrace, shame.

I חרץ *q* fix, determine; *w.* לָשׁוֹן threaten.
ni pt. that which is determined, decision.

II חרץ *q* hasten.

חַרְצֹב* fetter; pang.

חַרְצָן* stone.

חרק *q* grind.

חרר *q* glow, burn.

    ni be set on fire, scorched, inflamed.

    pilp cause to glow.

חֲרָרִים stony waste, lava-fields.

חֶרֶשׂ clay; potsherd.

חֲרֹשֶׁת → קִיר חֲרֹשֶׁת.

I חרשׁ *q* engrave; work, cut; plough; devise.

    ni be ploughed.

    hi devise.

II חרשׁ *q* be deaf, be silent.

    hi be silent, keep silence, pass over in silence; leave off, be inactive; reduce to silence.

    hitp keep quiet.

I *חֶרֶשׁ magic art.

II חֶרֶשׁ secretly.

III חֶרֶשׁ *n. pers.* Heresh.

חֹרֶשׁ wood.

חָרָשׁ worker.

חֵרֵשׁ deaf.

חַרְשָׁא *n. pers.* Harsha.

חֹרְשָׁה *n. place* Horesh.

חֲרֹשֶׁת working.

חֲרֹשֶׁת → קִיר חֲרֹשֶׁת.

חֲרֹשֶׁת הַגּוֹיִם *n. place* Harosheth-haggoiim.

°חרת *q* engrave.

חָרֵת *n. place* Hereth.

חֲשׂוּפָא *n. pers.* Hasupha.

חשׂךְ *q* keep back, spare, save; fail.

    ni be kept back, spared.

חשׂף *q* strip, bare; draw.

*חָשׂף small group, little flock.

חֲשֻׂפָא → חֲשׂוּפָא.

חשׁב *q* reckon, consider/regard as valuable; consider to be something; mean, devise, plan; *Ps. 40.18* care for; *pt. also* weaver, engineer.

    ni be reckoned, be regarded, be considered as.

    pi reckon; consider; devise, plan.

    hitp count oneself among.

חֵשֶׁב girdle.
חַשְׁבַּדָּנָה *n. pers.* Hashbaddanah.
חֲשֻׁבָה *n. pers.* Hashubah.
I חֶשְׁבּוֹן reckoning, perception.
II חֶשְׁבּוֹן *n. place* Heshbon.
חִשָּׁבוֹן* *pl.* devices; defensive devices.
חֲשַׁבְיָה(וּ) *n. pers.* Hashabiah.
חֲשַׁבְנָה *n. pers.* Hashabnah.
חֲשַׁבְנְיָה *n. pers.* Hashabneiah.
חשה *q* be inactive; keep silence.
　hi bid keep silence; be inactive; keep silence; hesitate.
חַשּׁוּב *n. pers.* Hasshub.
חָשׁוּק* tie-bar.
חֲשֵׁיכָה → חֲשֵׁכָה.
חֲשִׁים → חוּשִׁים.
חשׁךְ *q* be/become dark.
　hi darken, obscure; be dark.
חֹשֶׁךְ darkness, obscurity, darkening.
חָשֹׁךְ* dark > obscure.
חֲשֵׁכָה darkness.
חשׁל *ni pt.* straggler.
חָשֻׁם *n. pers.* Hashum.
חֻשָׁם *n. pers.* Husham.
חֻשִׁם *n. peop.* Hushim.
חֶשְׁמוֹן *n. place* Heshmon.
חַשְׁמַל electrum.
חַשְׁמֹנָה *n. place* Hashmonah.
חַשְׁמַנִּים articles in bronze.
חֹשֶׁן breast-piece.
חשׁק *q* be attached *to someone*, love.
　pi link.
　pu pt. linking *or* linked.
חֵשֶׁק desire.
חִשֻּׁק* spoke.
חִשֻּׁר* hub.
חֲשָׂרָה* gathering?
חָשָׁשׁ dry grass; foliage.
חֻשָׁתִי *gent.* Hushathite.

חַת   terror; filled with terror.

חֵת   *n. pers.* Heth.

I חתה   *q Ps. 52.7* strike down.

II חתה   *q* rake together.

חִתָּה*   terror.

חִתּוּל   bandage.

חִתְחַתִּים   terror.

חִתִּי   *gent.* Hittite.

חִתִּית   terror.

חתת   *ni* be fixed.

חתל   *pu* be swaddled.

     ho Ezek. 16.4 inf. abs. in conjunction with pu.

חֲתֻלָּה*   swaddling-band.

חֶתְלֹן   *n. place* Hethlon.

חתם   *q* seal, affix seal; *Job 33.16; Dan. 9.24* confirm.

     ni be sealed.

     pi lock oneself up.

     hi be stopped.

חֹתָם   → I חוֹתָם.

חֹתֶמֶת   sealing-apparatus.

חתן   *q pt.* father-in-law; *Deut. 27.23* mother-in-law *(wife's parents)*.

     hitp become related by marriage.

חָתָן   son-in-law; bridegroom; *II Kings 8.27* connected.

חֲתֻנָּה*   marriage.

חתף   *q* snatch away.

חֶתֶף   robber.

חתר   *q* break through; *Jonah 1.13* row.

חתת   *q* be dismayed, terrified.

     ni be shattered; be cast-down, terrified.

     pi Jer. 51.56 be broken in pieces; *Job 7.14* terrify.

     hi shatter; terrify, dismay.

I חֲתַת   terror.

II חֲתַת   *n. pers.* Hathath.

ט

טָאטָא sweep away.

טֹב → I טוֹב.

טָבְאַל n. pers. Tabeal.

טָבְאֵל n. pers. Tabeel.

טְבוּל* turban.

טַבּוּר navel.

טבח q slaughter, butcher.

טֶבַח I slaughter.

טֶבַח II n. pers. Tebah.

טַבָּח sg. butcher, cook; pl. bodyguard.

טַבָּחָה* cook.

טִבְחָה slaughter; slaughtered meat.

טִבְחַת n. place Tibhath.

טֹבִיָּה → טוֹבִיָּה.

טבל q dip, immerse.

     ni be dipped.

טְבַלְיָהוּ n. pers. Tebaliah.

טבע q penetrate, sink in.

     pu be submerged.

     ho be settled; Jer. 38.22 be sunk.

טַבָּעוֹת n. pers. Tabbaoth.

טַבַּעַת signet-ring, ring.

טַבְרִמֹּן n. pers. Tabrimmon.

טֵבֵת Tebeth (name of a month, December/January).

טַבָּת n. place Tabbath.

טָהוֹר clean, pure.

טהר q be clean, pure.

     pi purify, pronounce clean.

     pu pt. cleansed.

     hitp purify oneself.

טֹהַר purity; purification.

טֹהַר* lustre.

טָהֹר → טָהוֹר.

טָהֳרָה becoming clean; purification; rite of purification.

טוב q be good, fine, glad, preferable.

     hi act right.

טוב I good; pleasant, useful, proper, fair, benevolent; kind.

טוב II fragrance.

טוב III *n. terr.* Tob.

טוב good thing, wealth, prosperity, goodness, beauty.

טוב אֲדֹנִיָּה *n. pers.* Tob-adonijah.

טוֹבִיָּה(וּ) *n. pers.* Tobiah.

טוה *q* spin.

טוח *q* over-lay, coat.

ni be coated.

טוֹטָפֹת mark.

טול *pilp* fling down.

hi hurl, fling.

ho be flung down.

טוּר course, row.

טוּשׂ° *q* fly about.

טחה *pil pt.* range.

טְחוֹן hand-mill.

טֻחוֹת *Ps. 51.8 text corr.*; *Job 38.36* ibis.

טחח *q* be smeared.

טחן *q* grind, grind down, crush; *Eccles. 12.3 pt. f.* molar.

טַחֲנָה mill.

טְחֹרִים haemorrhoids.

טֹטָפֹת → טוֹטָפֹת.

טִיחַ mud-plaster.

טִיט mire, mud.

טִירָה* encampment, course of stones; *Cant. 8.9* battlement.

טַל dew; fine rain.

טלא *q pt. pass.* flecked.

pu pt. patched.

טְלָאִים I *n. place* Telaim.

טְלָאִים II *pl. of* טָלֶה.

טָלֶה lamb.

טַלְטֵלָה long throw.

טלל° *pi* roof.

טֶלֶם *n. pers. (Aram.), n. place* Telem.

טַלְמוֹן°, *n. pers.* Talmon.
טַלְמֹן°

טמא   *q* become unclean.
    ni defile oneself.
    pi defile, pronounce unclean.
    pu pt. defiled.
    hitp defile oneself.
    hotpaal be defiled.

טָמֵא   unclean.
טֻמְאָה   uncleanness.
טמה   *ni* be unclean?
טמן   *q* hide, fix secretly; bury secretly.
    ni hide.
    hi keep in hiding.

טֶנֶא   basket.
טנף°   *pi* soil.
טעה°   *hi* mislead.
טעם   *q* taste, take food; perceive.
טַעַם   taste, perception; sense; *Jonah 3.7* order, decree *(Aram.)*.
I טען   *pu pt.* pierced.
II טען°   *q* load.
טַף   *coll.* children; those not fit for marching; family.
I טפח   *pi* spread out.
II טפח   *pi* nurse.
טֶפַח   hand-breadth; *I Kings 7.9* corbel?
טֹפַח   hand-breadth.
טִפֻּחִים   nursing.
טפל   *q* smear, sully, plaster up.
טַפְסָר*, טִפְסָר   *designation of an official* tablet-writer?
טפף   *q* trip along.
טפש   *q* be insensitive.
טָפַת°   *n. pers. f.* Taphath.
טרד   *q* drip.
טֶרוֹם   before.
טרח   *hi* load.
טֹרַח   burden.
טָרִי*   fresh, moist.

טֶרֶם   beginning; not yet; before, ere.

I טרף   *q* tear, rend.

       ni be torn in pieces.

       pu be torn in pieces.

II טרף   *hi* give to eat.

I טֶרֶף   prey.

II טֶרֶף   food.

טָרָף   freshly plucked.

טְרֵפָה   that which has been torn in pieces.

י

יאב°   *q* long.

יֹאָב   → יוֹאָב.

יאה   *q* belong.

יְאוֹר   → יְאֹר.

יַאֲזַנְיָה(וּ)   *n. pers.* Jaazaniah.

יָאִיר   *n. peop.* Jair.

I יאל   *ni* act foolishly, show oneself to be a fool.

II יאל   *hi* be intent on something; resolve; set about.

יְאֹר   river, stream; *usu.* the Nile; *pl. usu.* arms of the Nile; *Job 28.10*

       galleries?

יָאֲרִי   *gent.* Jairite.

יאש   *ni* despair; *pt. also* futile.

       pi make despair.

יֹאָשׁ   → יוֹאָשׁ.

יֹאשִׁיָּה(וּ)   *n. pers.* Josiah.

יִאתוֹן   *rd. Q (Ezek. 40.15)* entrance?

יְאָתְרַי   *n. pers.* Jeatherai.

יבב   *pi* lament.

יְבוּל   produce.

יְבוּס   *n. place* Jebus.

יְבוּסִי   *gent.* Jebusite.

יִבְחָר   *n. pers.* Ibhar.

יָבִין   *n. pers.* Jabin.

יָבֵישׁ   → II יָבֵשׁ.

יָבֵל *hi* bring.

ho be brought.

I יָבָל* *channel.*

II יָבָל *n. pers.* Jabal.

יְבֵל → יְבוּל.

אֹבֵל → יוֹבֵל.

יִבְלְעָם *n. place* Ibleam.

יַבֶּלֶת *wart?*

יבם *pi* consummate a levirate marriage.

יָבָם* *brother-in-law (husband's brother).*

יְבָמָה* *sister-in-law.*

יַבְנְאֵל *n. place* Jabneel.

יַבְנֶה *n. place* Jabneh.

יִבְנְיָה *n. pers.* Ibneiah.

יִבְנִיָּה *n. pers.* Ibnijah.

יְבֻסִי → יְבוּסִי.

יַבֹּק *n. river* Jabbok.

יְבֶרֶכְיָהוּ *n. pers.* Jeberechiah.

יִבְשָׂם *n. pers.* Ibsam.

יבשׁ *q* dry up, be dry, wither.

pi dry up.

hi make dry, wither; dry up.

I יָבֵשׁ *dried, withered.*

II יָבֵשׁ *n. pers., n. place* Jabesh.

יַבָּשָׁה *the dry, dry ground, dry land.*

יַבֶּשֶׁת *dry land.*

יִגְאָל *n. pers.* Igal.

יגב *q pt.* labourer on the land?

יֶגֶב* *field?*

יָגְבְּהָה *n. place* Jogbehah.

יִגְדַּלְיָהוּ *n. pers.* Igdaliah.

I יגה *ni pt.* grieved.

pi grieve.

hi torment, grieve.

II יגה *hi II Sam. 20.13* clear away.

יָגוֹן *grief, torment.*

יָגוּר *n. place* Jagur.

יָגוֹר *fearing.*

יָנִיעַ* exhausted.

יְנִיעַ toil, labour; produce, acquisition, property.

יָגְלִי n. pers. Jogli.

יגע q be weary, labour for, toil.

    pi make weary, trouble.

    hi weary.

יְגַע proceeds of labour.

יָגֵעַ weary, wearisome.

יְגֵעָה* wearying.

יגר q fear.

יְגַר Aram. heap of stones.

יָד hand; side, bank; area, place; strength, might, power; monument, token; pl. handles, arm-rests, tenons; with numeral parts, times as much; Isa. 57.8 phallus; Ezek. 21.24 signpost.

יִדְאֲלָה n. place Idalah.

יִדְבָּשׁ n. pers. Idbash.

ידד q cast.

יְדִדוּת beloved.

I ידה q shoot.

    pi throw, throw down.

II ידה hi praise, confess.

    hitp confess.

יִדּוֹ n. pers. Iddo.

יַדּוּ n. pers. rd. Q (Ezra 10.43) Jaddai.

יָדוֹן n. pers. Jadon.

יַדּוּעַ n. pers. Jaddua.

יְדוּתוּן n. pers. Jeduthun.

יָדִיד* beloved; lovely.

יְדִידָה n. pers. f. Jedidah.

יְדִידְיָה n. pers. Jedidiah.

יְדִידֹת love.

יְדָיָה n. pers. Jedaiah.

יְדִיעֲאֵל n. pers. Jediael.

יְדִיתוּן n. pers. Jedithun.

יִדְלָף n. pers. Jidlaph.

יָדַע *q* notice, observe; learn, perceive, understand, know; care for, get to know, be acquainted with, be intimate with; lie with.

ni show oneself, make oneself known, be made known; be evident; be/become known, become recognized; *Jer. 31.19* attain insight.

pi cause to know.

pu pt. known, intimate.

poel direct?

hi cause to know, declare, make known.

ho be made known.

hitp make oneself known.

יָדָע *n. pers.* Jada.

יְדַעְיָה *n. pers.* Jedaiah.

יִדְּעֹנִי soothsaying spirit, soothsayer.

יְדֻתוּן → יְדוּתוּן.

יָהּ *contraction of Yahweh.*

יהב → הַב.

יְהָב °* load?, care?

יהר *hitp* profess oneself a Jew.

יְהֻד *n. place* Jehud.

יָהְדַּי *n. pers.* Jahdai.

יֵהוּא *n. pers.* Jehu.

יְהוֹאָחָז *n. pers.* Jehoahaz.

יְהוֹאָשׁ *n. pers.* Joash.

יְהוּד → יָהֻד.

יְהוּדָה *n. pers., n. peop., n. terr.* Judah.

יְהוּדִי *n. pers.* Jehudi; *gent.* Judaean; *n. peop.* Jew.

I יְהוּדִית *adv.* in Judaean.

II יְהוּדִית *n. pers. f.* Judith.

יהוה Yahweh.

יְהוֹזָבָד ° *n. pers.* Jehozabad.

יְהוֹחָנָן *n. pers.* Jehohanan.

יְהוֹיָדָע *n. pers.* Jehoiada.

יְהוֹיָכִין, יְהוֹיָכִן *n. pers.* Jehoiachin.

יְהוֹיָקִים, יְהוֹיָקֻם *n. pers.* Jehoiakim.

יְהוֹיָרִיב *n. pers.* Jehoiarib.

יְהוֹכַל *n. pers.* Jehucal.

יְהוֹנָדָב‎ *n. pers.* Jonadab.

יְהוֹנָתָן‎ *n. pers.* Jonathan.

יְהוֹסֵף‎ *n. pers.* Joseph.

יְהוֹעַדָּה‎ *n. pers.* Jehoaddah.

יְהוֹעַדִּ(י)ן‎ *n. pers. f.* Jehoaddan.

יְהוֹצָדָק‎ *n. pers.* Jehozadak.

יְהוֹרָם‎ *n. pers.* Joram.

יְהוֹשֶׁבַע‎ *n. pers. f.* Jehosheba.

יְהוֹשַׁבְעַת‎ *n. pers. f.* Jehoshabeath.

יְהוֹשׁוּעַ,‎ *n. pers.* Joshua.

יְהוֹשֻׁעַ‎

יְהוֹשָׁפָט‎ *n. pers.* Jehoshaphat.

יָהִיר‎ presumptuous, proud.

יַהֵל‎ *pi of* אהל‎.

יְהַלֶּלְאֵל‎ *n. pers.* Jehallelel.

יַהֲלֹם, יָהֲלֹם‎ jasper?

יַהַץ, יַהְצָה‎ *n. place* Jahaz.

יוֹאָב‎ *n. pers.* Joab.

יוֹאָח‎ *n. pers.* Joah.

יוֹאָחָז‎ *n. pers.* Joahaz.

יוֹאֵל‎ *n. pers.* Joel.

יוֹאָשׁ‎ *n. pers.* Joash.

יוֹב‎ *n. pers.* Job.

יוֹבָב‎ *n. pers., n. peop.* Jobab.

יוֹבֵל‎ ram; *w.* שָׁנָה‎ jubilee.

יוּבַל I‎ canal.

יוּבַל II‎ *n. pers.* Jubal.

יוֹזָבָד‎ *n. pers.* Jozabad.

יוֹחָא‎ *n. pers.* Joha.

יוֹחָנָן‎ *n. pers.* Johanan.

יוּטָּה‎ → יַטָּה‎.

יוֹיָדָע‎ *n. pers.* Joiada.

יוֹיָכִין‎ *n. pers.* Jehoiachin.

יוֹיָקִים‎ *n. pers.* Joiakim.

יוֹיָרִיב‎ *n. pers.* Joiarib.

יוֹכֶבֶד‎ *n. pers. f.* Jochebed.

יוּכַל‎ *n. pers.* Jucal.

יוֹם   day; *pl.* days; time, period; year; הַיּוֹם *also* today; כַּיּוֹם,

כְּהַיּוֹם now, first, *w.* הַזֶּה as it now is, as is now evident.

יוֹמָם   *adv.* during the day, by day.

יָוָן   *n. pers., n. terr.* Javan; *n. peop.* Greeks.

יָוָן   sludge, mire.

יוֹנָדָב   *n. pers.* Jonadab.

יוֹנָה I   dove.

יוֹנָה II   *n. pers.* Jonah.

יוֹנָה III   *pt. q of* ינה.

יְוָנִי*   *gent.* Greek.

יוֹנֵק, יוֹנֶקֶת*   suckling; shoot, sucker.

יוֹנָתָן   *n. pers.* Jonathan.

יוֹסֵף   *n. pers., n. peop.* Joseph.

יוֹסִפְיָה   *n. pers.* Josiphiah.

יוֹעֵאלָה   *n. pers.* Joelah.

יוֹעֵד   *n. pers.* Joed.

יוֹעֶזֶר   *n. pers.* Joezer.

יוֹעָשׁ   *n. pers.* Joash.

יוֹצֵאת   *Ps. 144.14* abortion.

יוֹצָדָק   *n. pers.* Jozadak.

יוֹצֵר   potter.

יוֹקִים   *n. pers.* Jokim.

יוֹרֶה   early rain.

יוֹרָה   *n. pers.* Jorah.

יוֹרַי   *n. pers.* Jorai.

יוֹרָם   *n. pers.* Joram.

יוּשַׁב חֶסֶד   *n. pers.* Jushab-hesed.

יוֹשִׁבְיָה   *n. pers.* Joshibiah.

יוֹשָׁה   *n. pers.* Joshah.

יוֹשַׁוְיָה   *n. pers.* Joshaviah.

יוֹשָׁפָט   *n. pers.* Joshaphat.

יוֹתָם   *n. pers.* Jotham.

יוֹתֵר   what is left; what is in excess, superfluous, too much; *w.* לְ

advantage; *adv.* excessively, more; *w.* שֶׁ it is unnecessary that.

יְזַוְאֵל   *n. pers. rd. Q (I Chron. 12.3)* Jeziel.

יִזִּיָּה   *n. pers.* Izziah.

יָזִיז   *n. pers.* Jaziz.

יְזְלִיאָה   *n. pers.* Izliah.

יֹזֶן   *pu pt.* rutting.

יְזַנְיָה(וּ)   *n. pers.* Jezaniah.

יֵזַע   sweat.

יִזְרָח   *rd.* זַרְחִי *(I Chron. 27.8)*.

יִזְרַחְיָה   *n. pers.* Izrahiah.

יִזְרְעֶאל   *n. pers., n. place* Jezreel.

יִזְרְעֵאלִי   *gent.* Jezreelite.

יֹחָא   → יוֹחָא.

יְחֻבָּה   *n. pers.* Jehubbah.

יחד   *q* come together, join.

     pi concentrate.

יַחַד   unitedness, totality; *adv.* together, all together, in the same place, at the same time, completely, likewise; *Ezra 4.3* alone.

יַחְדָּו   together, all together, at the same time, likewise.

יַחְדּוֹ°   *n. pers.* Jahdo.

יַחְדִּיאֵל°   *n. pers.* Jahdiel.

יֶחְדְּיָהוּ°   *n. pers.* Jehdeiah.

יַחְדָּיו   → יַחְדָּו.

יְחוּאֵל   *rd. Q (II Chron. 29.14)*.

יַחֲזִיאֵל°   *n. pers.* Jahaziel.

יַחְזְיָה°   *n. pers.* Jahzeiah.

יְחֶזְקֵאל   *n. pers.* Ezekiel.

יְחִזְקִיָּה(וּ)   *n. pers.* Hezekiah.

יַחְזְרָה   *n. pers.* Jahzerah.

יְחִיאֵל   *n. pers.* Jehiel.

יְחִיאֵלִי   *n. peop.* Jehieli.

יָחִיד   only, alone, solitary.

יְחִיָּה   *n. pers.* Jehiah.

יָחִיל   awaiting.

יחל   *ni* wait.

     pi wait.

     hi wait.

יַחְלְאֵל   *n. pers.* Jahleel.

יַחְלְאֵלִי   *gent.* Jahleelite.

יחם   *q* be in heat.

     pi be/make to be in heat; conceive.

יַחְמוּר   roebuck.

יַחְמַי   n. pers. Jahmai.

יָחֵף   barefoot.

יַחְצְאֵל   n. pers. Jahzeel.

יַחְצְאֵלִי   gent. Jahzeelite.

יַחְצִיאֵל   n. pers. Jahziel.

יחר   יִיחַר hi of אחר.

יחשׂ   hitp be entered in the genealogical table.

יַחַשׂ   w. סֵפֶר. genealogical table.

יַחַת   n. pers. Jahath.

יטב   q be good, go well; w. בְּעֵינֵי be pleasing; w. לֵב be glad.
     hi treat well, aright; do good; cheer; make ready.

יָטְבָה   n. place Jotbah.

יָטְבָתָה   n. place Jotbathah.

יֻטָּה   n. place Juttah.

יְטוּר   n. pers., n. peop. Jetur.

יַיִן   wine; drunkenness.

יַךְ   rd. Q (I Sam. 4.13).

יְכׇנְיָה   n. pers. Jeconiah.

יְכׇונְיָה   rd. Q (Jer. 27.20).

יכח   ni enter into legal argument; prove to be in the right.
     hi decide, judge; justify oneself, vindicate oneself; call to
         account; rebuke, chastise, punish.
     ho be chastised.
     hitp argue.

יְכׇילְיָה   rd. Q (II Chron. 26.3).

יָכִין   n. pers. Jachin (also the name of the right-hand pillar in front of
     the temple in Jerusalem).

יָכִינִי   gent. Jachinite.

יכל   q hold, bear, be able to; have power to, be capable of; prevail,
     defeat; Job 31.23 hold one's own against.

יְכׇלְיָהוּ   n. pers. f. Jecoliah.

יְכׇנְיָה(ו)   n. pers. Jeconiah.

יָלַד   *q* bear; beget.

     ni be born.

     pi assist at childbirth; *pt. f.* midwife.

     pu be born.

     hi cause to bear; beget.

     ho be born.

     hitp be entered in the genealogical table.

יֶלֶד   boy, child; youth, young; *Ex. 21.22 pl.* foetus.

יַלְדָּה   girl, child.

יַלְדוּת   childhood, youth.

יִלּוֹד   born.

יָלוֹן   *n. pers.* Jalon.

יָלִיד*   son; יְלִיד בַּיִת house-born slave.

יָלַל   *hi* howl, lament.

יְלֵל   howling.

יְלָלָה*   howling, wailing.

יָלַע   *impf. q of* I לָעַע.

יַלֶּפֶת   herpes.

יֶלֶק   locust *(crawling, wingless)*.

יַלְקוּט   shepherd's pouch.

יָם   sea, lake; the west; river; *Ezek. 32.2* arm of the Nile.

יְמוּאֵל   *n. pers.* Jemuel.

יְמִימָה   *n. pers. f.* Jemimah.

I יָמִין   right side, right; the south, south.

II יָמִין   *n. pers.* Jamin.

יָמִינִי   *gent.* Jaminite.

יְמִינִי   *rd. Q (Ezek. 4.6; II Chron. 3.17).*

יְמִינִי   *gent.* Benjamite.

יִמְלָא, יִמְלָה   *n. pers.* Imla.

יַמְלֵךְ   *n. pers.* Jamlech.

יֵמִם   vipers.

יָמַן   *hi* go, keep to the right; *pt. also* right-handed.

יִמְנָה   *n. pers.* Imnah.

יְמָנִי   right; south.

יִמְנָע   *n. pers.* Imna.

יָמַר   *hi of* מוּר.

     hitp boast?

יִמְרָה   *n. pers.* Imrah.

יָמֵשׁ   *hi* let touch.

יָנָה   *q* be cruel.

     hi oppress.

יָנוֹחַ   *n. place* Janoah.

יָנוֹחָה   *n. place* Janohah.

יָנוּם   *n. place* Janum.

יְנִיקָה*   sucker.

יָנַק   *q* suck.

     hi suckle, nurse; *Deut. 32.13* make to suck.

יַנְשׁוּף, יַנְשׁוֹף   long-eared owl?; bee-eater?

I יסד   *q* found, erect; lay down, determine.

     ni be founded.

     pi found; determine; appoint.

     pu be founded.

     ho be founded.

II יסד   *ni* combine.

יְסָד   beginning?

יְסֹד, יְסוֹד   foundation-wall, base.

יְסוּדָה*   foundation.

יִסּוֹר   fault-finder.

יִסּוּרַי   *rd. Q (Jer. 17.13)*.

יִסְכָּה   *n. pers. f.* Iscah.

יִסְמַכְיָהוּ   *n. pers.* Ismachiah.

יָסַף   *q* add; continue.

     ni be added.

     hi add; increase, multiply, surpass; continue.

יסר   *q* instruct.

     ni let oneself be instructed.

     pi correct, chastise.

     hi chastise.

     nitp let oneself be warned.

יַעְבֵּץ   *n. pers., n. place* Jabez.

יָעַד   *q* fix, assign.

     ni let oneself be met, appear; assemble; make an appointment.

     hi summon.

     ho pt. ordered, directed.

יַעְדַּי *n. pers. rd.* Q *(II Chron. 9.29)* Iddo.

יעה *q* sweep away.

יְעוּאֵל *n. pers.* Jeuel.

יְעוּץ *n. pers.* Jeuz.

יָעוּר *n. pers. rd.* Q *(I Chron. 20.5)* Jair.

יְעוּשׁ *n. pers.* Jeush.

יעז *ni pt.* insolent.

יַעֲזִיאֵל *n. pers.* Jaaziel.

יַעֲזִיָּהוּ *n. pers.* Jaaziah.

יַעְזֵיר, יַעְזֵר *n. place* Jazer.

יעט *hi of* I עטה.

יְעִיאֵל *n. pers.* Jeiel.

יָעִים shovels.

יָעִיר *n. pers.* Jair.

יָעִישׁ *n. pers.* Jeish.

יַעְכָּן *n. pers.* Jacan.

יעל *hi* profit, be of use.

I *יָעֵל mountain-goat.

II יָעֵל *n. pers. f.* Jael.

יַעֲלָא, יַעֲלָה *n. pers.* Jaalah.

*יַעֲלָה female mountain-goat.

יַעְלָם *n. pers.* Jalam.

יַעַן cause for; on account of, because.

*יָעֵן ostrich.

יַעֲנָה *w.* בַּת ostrich.

יַעֲנַי *n. pers.* Jaanai.

יעף *q* become weary.
ho pt. wearied?

יָעֵף weary.

*יָעֵף weariness?; swift course?

יעץ *q* advise, counsel, intend, resolve.
ni take counsel together, give advice, consult, resolve.
hitp take counsel together.

יַעֲקֹב *n. pers.* Jacob; *fig. for Israel.*

יַעֲקֹבָה *n. pers.* Jaakobah.

יַעֲקוֹב → יַעֲקֹב.

יַעֲקָן *n. pers.* Jaakan.

I יַעַר thicket, wood; forest; *Eccles. 2.6* park.

יַעַר II honeycomb.

יַעַר III n. *place* Jaar.

יַעְרָה* honeycomb.

יַעְרָה n. *pers.* Jarah.

יַעֲרֵי אֹרְגִים n. *pers.* Jaare-oregim.

יַעֲרֶשְׁיָה n. *pers.* Jaareshiah.

יַעֲשׂוֹ n. *pers.* Jaasau.

יַעֲשִׂיאֵל n. *pers.* Jaasiel.

יִפְדְיָה n. *pers.* Iphdeiah.

יפה q be beautiful.

pi adorn.

hitp beautify oneself.

יָפֶה beautiful; well-ordered, excellent.

יְפֵה־פִיָה beautiful.

יָפוֹ(א) n. *place* Joppa.

יפח hitp groan.

יָפֵחַ* panting.

יְפִי* beauty.

יָפִיעַ n. *pers.*, n. *place* Japhia.

יַפְלֵט n. *pers.* Japhlet.

יַפְלֵטִי gent. Japhletite.

יְפֻנֶּה n. *pers.* Jephunneh.

יפע hi shine out brightly.

יִפְעָה* brightness.

יֶפֶת n. *pers.* Jepheth.

יִפְתָּח n. *pers.* Jephthah; n. *place* Iphtah.

יִפְתַּח־אֵל n. *place* Jiphtah-el.

יצא q go out, come out, sally out; issue, be descended; escape, elude; extend *(boundary)*; be spent *(money)*; be sold *(commodity)*; end *(time)*.

hi lead out, bring forth, march out; produce, bring out; remove, dismiss.

ho be led out.

יצב hitp take one's stand, hold one's own against.

יָצַנ *hi* set down, place, put; *Gen. 33.15* leave behind; *Amos 5.15* bring to effect.

     ho be left behind.

I יִצְהָר   oil.

II יִצְהָר   *n. pers.* Izhar.

יִצְהָרִי   *gent.* Izharite.

יָצוּעַ*   couch.

יָצוּעַ   *rd. Q* extension.

יִצְחָק   *n. pers.* Isaac; *fig. for Israel.*

יִצְחָר   *n. pers. rd. Q* Zohar *or rd. K* Izhar.

יצע   *hi* spread out a couch.

     ho be spread out as couch.

יצק   *q* pour out, empty out; flow; cast.

     hi pour out; *II Kings 4.5 rd.* מוֹצֶקֶת pour in.

     ho be poured out, cast; *Job 11.15* unshakeable.

יְצֻקָה*   casting.

יצר   *q* form, fashion; *pt. also* potter.

     ni be fashioned.

     pu be predetermined.

     ho be formed.

I יֵצֶר   form.

II יֵצֶר   *n. pers.* Jezer.

יֹצֵר   → יוֹצֵר.

יִצְרִי   *n. pers.* Izri; *gent.* Jezerite.

יְצֻרִים*   members.

יצת   *q* kindle, burn.

     ni be kindled, be burned.

     hi kindle.

יֶקֶב   vat; winepress.

יֶקֶב־זְאֵב   *n. place* Winepress of Zeeb.

יִקְבֵי הַמֶּלֶךְ   *n. place* King's Winepresses.

יַקַבְצְאֵל   *n. place* Jekabzeel.

יקד   *q* burn.

     ho be kindled, set on fire.

יְקֹד   burning.

יָקְדְעָם   *n. place* Jokdeam.

יָקֶה   *n. pers.* Jakeh.

יְקָהָה* obedience.

יְקוֹד → יְקֹד.

יָקוּד hearth.

יָקוֹט rd. קַיִט (קִשְׁרֵי) (*Job 8.14*) gossamer.

יְקוּם existence, living being.

יָקוֹשׁ, יָקֹשׁ fowler.

יְקוּתִיאֵל n. pers. Jekuthiel.

יָקְטָן n. pers. Joktan.

יָקִים n. pers. Jakim.

יַקִּיר dear, precious.

יְקַמְיָה n. pers. Jekamiah.

יְקַמְעָם n. pers. Jekameam.

יָקְמְעָם n. place Jokmeam.

יָקְמְעָם n. place Jokmoam.

יָקְנְעָם n. place Jokneam.

יָקְנְעָם n. place Joknoam.

יקע q be dislocated; turn away from, be alienated.

    hi expose.

    ho be exposed.

יְקִפָּאוֹן rd. Q (*Zech. 14.6*) frost.

יקץ q awake.

יקר q be precious, costly; *I Sam. 18.30* be respected; *Ps. 139.17* be
    weighty.

    hi make costly, rare.

יָקָר costly, precious; *I Sam. 3.1* rare; *Jer. 15.19* noble.

יְקָר° precious things; worth, price; lustre, respect.

יִקְרָה* meeting.

יקשׁ q set a trap; *pt.* fowler.

    ni be caught; become entangled.

    pu be caught.

יָקְשָׁן n. pers. Jokshan.

יָקְתְאֵל n. place Joktheel.

ירא q fear, be afraid.

    ni be feared; *pt. also* fearful.

    pi fill with fear.

יָרֵא in awe, fearful.

יִרְאָה fear, reverence.

יִרְאוֹן n. place Iron.

יְרָאִיָּה   *n. pers.* Irijah.

רָב (מַלְכִּי)   *rd.* (*Hos. 5.13; 10.6*) great (king).

יְרֻבַּעַל   *n. pers.* Jerubbaal.

יָרָבְעָם   *n. pers.* Jeroboam.

יְרֻבֶּשֶׁת   *n. pers. derogatory form of* יְרֻבַּעַל Jerubbesheth.

ירד   *q* go down, come down, descend; *also fig.*

     hi send down, bring down, lead down, take down; lower.

     ho be led down, be thrown down; *Num. 10.17* be taken down.

יֶרֶד   *n. pers.* Jared.

יַרְדֵּן   *n. river* Jordan.

I ירה   *q* throw, shoot; *Gen. 31.51* erect; *Job 38.6* lay.

     ni be shot through.

     hi shoot.

II ירה   *hi Hos. 6.3* water?

     ho Prov. 11.25 be watered, refreshed?

III ירה   *hi* direct, teach.

יְרוּאֵל   *n. place* Jeruel.

יָרוֹחַ   *n. pers.* Jaroah.

יָרוֹק   green thing.

יְרוּשָׁא, יְרוּשָׁה   *n. pers. f.* Jerushah.

יְרוּשָׁלַיִם   *n. place* Jerusalem.

I יֶרַח   month.

II יֶרַח   *n. pers.* Jerah.

יָרֵחַ   moon.

יְרֵחוֹ, יְרִחוֹ   *n. place* Jericho.

יְרֹחָם   *n. pers.* Jeroham.

יְרַחְמְאֵל   *n. pers.* Jerahmeel.

יְרַחְמְאֵלִי   *gent.* Jerahmeelite.

יַרְחָע   *n. pers.* Jarha.

ירט   *q Job 16.11* throw; *Num. 22.32* be precipitate?

יְרִיאֵל   *n. pers.* Jeriel.

I *יָרִיב   opponent.

II יָרִיב   *n. pers.* Jarib.

יְרִיבַי   *n. pers.* Jeribai.

יְרִיָּה(וּ)   *n. pers.* Jeriah.

יְרִיחֹה, יְרִיחוֹ   *n. place* Jericho.

יְרִימוֹת   *n. pers.* Jerimoth.

יְרֵימוֹת   *n. pers.* Jeremoth.

יְרִיעָה   tent-curtain.

יְרִיעוֹת   *n. pers. f.* Jerioth.

יָרֵךְ   thigh, loin, side; *Ex. 25.31; 37.17; Num. 8.4* shaft.

יַרְכָּה*   rear, remotest part.

יֹרָם   → יוֹרָם.

יַרְמוּת   *n. place* Jarmuth.

יְרֵמוֹת   *n. pers.* Jeramoth.

יְרֵמוֹת   *n. pers.* Jeremoth.

יְרֵמַי   *n. pers.* Jeremai.

יִרְמְיָה(וּ)   *n. pers.* Jeremiah.

ירע   *q* quiver, be afraid.

יִרְפְּאֵל   *n. place* Irpeel.

ירק   *q* spit.

יָרָק   vegetables.

יֶרֶק   green thing.

יַרְקוֹן   *n. river* Jarkon.

יֵרָקוֹן   mildew; *Jer. 30.6* pallor.

יָרְקְעָם   *n. pers.* Jorkoam.

יְרַקְרַק   yellowish green, pale green.

ירשׁ   *q* take possession of, subdue, dispossess; inherit; *pt. also* conqueror.

     ni be impoverished.

     pi take possession of.

     hi drive away; take possession of; impoverish; make to suffer for.

יְרֵשָׁה   possession.

יְרֻשָּׁה   possession.

יִשְׂחָק   *n. pers.* Isaac.

יְשִׂימָאֵל   *n. pers.* Jesimiel.

יִשְׂרָאֵל   *n. pers., n. peop.* Israel.

יִשַׂרְאֵלָה   *n. pers.* Jesarelah.

יִשְׂרְאֵלִי   *gent.* Israelite.

יִשָּׂשכָר   *n. pers., n. peop.* Issachar.

יֵשׁ   there exists, there is.

יָשַׁב   *q* sit down, sit, stay, dwell; be inhabited.

     ni be inhabited.

     pi set up.

     hi set; make to stay; make to dwell; settle; *Ezra 10; Neh. 13* marry.

     ho be inhabited; be settled.

יֹשֵׁב בַּשֶּׁבֶת   *n. pers.* Josheb-basshebeth.

יָשָׁבְאָב   *n. pers.* Jeshebeab.

יִשְׁבָּח°   *n. pers.* Ishbah.

יָשֻׁבִי לֶחֶם   *n. pers.* Jashubi-lehem.

יָשָׁבְעָם   *n. pers.* Jashobeam.

יִשְׁבָּק   *n. pers.* Ishbak.

יָשְׁבְּקָשָׁה   *n. pers.* Joshbekashah.

יָשׁוּב   *n. pers.* Jashub.

יָשׁוּבִי   *gent.* Jashubite.

יִשְׁוָה   *n. pers.* Ishvah.

יְשׁוֹחָיָה   *n. pers.* Jeshohaiah.

יִשְׁוִי   *n. pers.* Ishvi; *gent.* Ishvite.

יֵשׁוּעַ   *n. pers.*, *n. place* Jeshua.

יְשׁוּעָה   help, salvation.

יֶשַׁח*   *unexplained.*

יִשְׁטֹ°   *hi* stretch out.

יִשַׁי   *n. pers.* Jesse.

יָשִׁיב   *n. pers.* Jashib.

יִשִּׁיָּה(וּ)   *n. pers.* Isshiah.

יְשִׁימוֹן   wilderness.

יְשִׁימָוֶת   destruction?

יִשִׁימֹן   → יְשִׁימוֹן.

יָשִׁישׁ   aged.

יְשִׁישַׁי   *n. pers.* Jeshishai.

יִשְׁמָא   *n. pers.* Ishma.

יְשִׁמ(וֹ)ן   → יְשִׁימוֹן.

יִשְׁמָעֵאל   *n. pers.* Ishmael.

יִשְׁמְעֵא(א)לִי   *gent.* Ishmaelite.

יִשְׁמַעְיָה(וּ)   *n. pers.* Ishmaiah.

יִשְׁמְרַי   *n. pers.* Ishmerai.

I יָשֵׁן   *q* fall asleep, sleep.

      pi make to sleep.

II יָשֵׁן   *ni* be long established; be old, belong to the preceding year.

   יָשָׁן   old, of the preceding year.

I יָשֵׁן   sleeping.

II יָשֵׁן   *n. pers.* Jashen.

  יְשָׁנָה   *n. place* Jeshanah.

   יֹשַׁע   *ni* accept help, receive help, be saved; be victorious.

      hi help, save, come to the aid.

   יֵשַׁע   help, deliverance, salvation, prosperity.

  יִשְׁעִי   *n. pers.* Ishi.

יְשַׁעְיָה(וּ)   *n. pers.* Isaiah.

  יִשְׁפָּה   *n. pers.* Ishpah.

  יָשְׁפֵה   jade.

  יִשְׁפָּן   *n. pers.* Ishpan.

   יָשַׁר   *q* be straight, level, right.

      pi make straight, level; go straight ahead, lead.

      pu pt. beaten flat; foil.

      hi level; make look straight ahead.

   יָשָׁר   straight, level, right, reliable, upright.

   יֵשֶׁר   *n. pers.* Jesher.

   יֹשֶׁר   straightness, uprightness; what is right; *Job 33.23* duty.

*יִשְׁרָה   uprightness.

  יְשֻׁרוּן   Jeshurun *(honorific name for Israel)*.

   יָשֵׁשׁ   decrepit.

   יָתֵד   tent-peg; *Zech. 10.4* support.

   יָתוֹם   fatherless boy, orphan *(bereaved of one parent)*.

   יָתוּר   that which is espied.

   יַתִּיר   *n. place* Jattir.

  יִתְלָה   *n. place* Ithlah.

  יִתְמָה   *n. pers.* Ithmah.

יַתְנִיאֵל   *n. pers.* Jathniel.

  יִתְנָן   *n. place* Ithnan.

   יתר   *q pt.* → יוֹתֵר.

      ni be left over, remain over.

      hi leave over, have over > *inf. abs.* more than enough; have abundance; have pre-eminence.

I יֶתֶר bowstring, cord.
II יֶתֶר remainder, abundance.
III יֶתֶר *n. pers.* Jether.
יַתִּיר → ‏יַתִּיר.
יֹתֵר → ‏יוֹתֵר.
יִתְרָא *n. pers.* Ithra.
יִתְרָה savings.
יִתְרוֹ *n. pers.* Jethro.
°יִתְרוֹן profit; advantage.
יִתְרִי *gent.* Ithrite.
יִתְרָן *n. pers.* Ithran.
יִתְרְעָם *n. pers.* Ithream.
יֹתֶרֶת lobe (of the liver).
יֵתֶת *n. peop.?* Jetheth.

כ

כְּ as, exactly as, corresponding to, according to; when, as soon
as, supposing that; כַּאֲשֶׁר as, because, as though, when; *w.* כֵּן
as — so, the more — the more.

כאב *q* suffer pain.
   hi cause pain; *II Kings 3.19* ruin.

כְּאֵב pain.

כאה *ni* be disheartened.
   hi dishearten.

כָּאֹר *rd.* כִּיאֹר *(Amos 8.8)*.

כַּאֲשֶׁר → ‏כְּ.

כבד *q* be heavy, obtuse, important, honoured; *II Sam. 13.25* be
   troublesome.
   ni be honoured, enjoy reputation; behave creditably, get oneself glory.
   pi honour; reward; *I Sam. 6.6* make obtuse.
   pu be honoured; *pt.* respected.

hi make heavy, make weigh heavily; make dull, obdurate; make important, numerous; make respected.

hitp make oneself numerous, give oneself airs.

I כָּבֵד heavy, burdensome, oppressive; numerous; arduous; obtuse, obdurate; slow.

II כָּבֵד liver.

כָּבוֹד → כָּבוֹד.

כֹּבֶד heaviness, force, mass.

כְּבֵדֻת difficulty.

כבה *q* be extinguished.

pi extinguish.

כָּבוֹד heaviness, burden; importance, possessions, reputation; person, self; dignity, splendour; distinction, honour, glory; *Ps. 149.5* song of praise.

כְּבוּדָּה valuables, splendour.

כָּבוּל *n. place* Cabul.

כַּבּוֹן *n. place* Cabbon.

כַּבִּיר strong, mighty, much.

כָּבִיר* skin?

כֶּבֶל° fetter.

כבס *q* full.

pi cleanse, wash away.

pu be washed.

hotpaal be washed out.

כבר *hi* make many; *pt.* in abundance.

I כְּבָר° long since.

II כְּבָר *n. river* Chebar.

I כְּבָרָה sieve.

II כִּבְרָה* space; a distance away.

כֶּבֶשׂ lamb.

כִּבְשָׂה ewe-lamb.

כבשׁ *q* subdue, tread down; rape.

ni be subdued, be brought into bondage.

pi subdue.

hi rd. Q (*Jer. 34.11*).

כֶּבֶשׁ footstool.

כִּבְשָׁן furnace.

כַּד jar.

כַּדּוּר hank, ball.

כְּדִי → דַי.

כַּדְכֹּד ruby?

כְּדָרְלָעֹמֶר, n. pers. Chedorlaomer.
כְּדָר־לָעֹמֶר

כֹּה thus; here, hither; now.

כהה q become expressionless, weak.

pi fade, lose heart; I Sam. 3.13 reprimand.

כֵּהֶה* expressionless, pale; disheartened; dim, smouldering.

כֵּהָה alleviation.

כהן pi officiate as priest.

כֹּהֵן priest.

כְּהֻנָּה priesthood, office of priest, clergy.

כּוּב n. terr.? Cub.

כּוֹבַע helmet.

כוה ni be scorched, be burned.

כְּוִיָּה branding.

כּוֹחַ → I כֹּחַ.

כּוֹכָב star.

כּוּל q comprehend.

hi hold, contain; endure.

pilp contain, hold in; supply; endure; Ps. 112.5 manage.

polp be supplied.

כּוּל → כֹּל.

כּוּמָז woman's adornment.

כון q rd. pol (Job 31.15).

ni stand firm, be well-rounded; be firm, secured; endure;
be ready, prepared; be established; pt. f. also that which is
trustworthy, right.

pol set up, prepare, establish; set up firmly, enduringly; aim
(arrow).

polal be prepared.

hi provide, make ready; fix, determine, direct, appoint; make
firm; prepare; do something without being distracted,
steadfastly.

ho be set up.

hitpol be established, take up position.

כּוּן   *n. place* Cun.

כַּוָּן*   sacrificial cake.

כָּנַנְיָהוּ   *n. pers. rd. K* Conaniah.

כּוֹס I   *f.* cup.

כּוֹס II   *species of owl* screech-owl?

כּוּר   furnace.

כּוֹרֶשׁ   *n. pers.* Cyrus.

כּוּשׁ   *n. pers., n. terr.* Cush, Ethiopia.

כּוּשִׁי   *n. pers.* Cushi; *gent.* Cushite, Ethiopian.

כּוּשָׁן   *n. peop.* Cushan.

כּוּשַׁן רִשְׁעָתַיִם   *n. pers.* Cushan-rishathaim.

כּוֹשָׂרָה*   prosperity.

כּוּת, כּוּתָה   *n. terr.* Cuth.

כּוֹתֶרֶת   → כֹּתֶרֶת.

כזב   *q* lie.

ni prove lying, false.

pi lie, deceive, fail.

hi accuse of lying.

כָּזָב   lie, deception, fraud.

כֹּזְבָא   *n. place* Cozeba.

כָּזְבִּי   *n. pers. f.* Cozbi.

כְּזִיב   *n. place* Chezib.

כֹּחַ I   strength, power; ability, fitness; produce, wealth, property.

כֹּחַ II   *species of lizard.*

כחד   *ni* be hidden; go astray, perish.

pi keep hidden, hide.

hi destroy; *Job 20.12* dissolve.

כחל   *q* paint.

כחשׁ   *q* grow lean.

ni feign submission.

pi lie, deceive; deny, disown.

hitp act deceitfully.

כַּחַשׁ   decline; lying.

כֶּחָשׁ*   untruthful.

כִּי I thus; then, just so; rather, but, nevertheless; because, for; that; as, while, when, if; even if, though; see!, there!

כִּי II *Isa. 3.24* branding.

כִּי אִם except, unless; but, rather, however, yet; only; surely.

כִּיד* downfall.

כִּידוֹד* spark.

כִּידוֹן javelin.

כִּידוֹר attack.

כִּידֹן *n. pers.* Chidon.

כִּיּוּן *rd.* כֵּיוָן *(Amos 5.26) n. pers.* Kewan *(Saturn)*.

כִּיּוֹר basin, cauldron; *II Chron. 6.13* stand?

כִּילַי deceiver?

כֵּילַפּת wedge?

כִּימָה Pleiades.

כִּיס bag.

כִּיר* small stove.

כִּיֹר → כִּיּוֹר.

כִּישׁוֹר spindle-whorl.

כָּכָה thus.

כִּכָּר *f.* round disc; *unit of weight* talent *(c. 34 kg)*; encircling area.

כֹּל totality, whole; entire, all, each; anyone, anything; all kinds; whenever, as often as.

כלא *q* hold back, withhold; restrain; shut up, imprison.
    ni be restrained, held back.

כֶּלֶא prison.

כֶּלֶא *rd.* כֵּלֶה *(Ezek. 36.5)*.

כִּלְאָב *n. pers.* Chileab.

כִּלְאַיִם of two kinds.

כֶּלֶב dog.

כָּלֵב *n. pers.* Caleb.

כָּלִבִּי *gent.* Calebite.

כלה *q* cease, come to/be at an end; be/become finished; pass away; be determined, resolved; languish, become weak.

pi complete, finish with, cease; annihilate, destroy; make to waste away; do something completely.

pu be completed, at an end.

כָּלֶה*   languishing.

כָּלָה   annihilation, end.

כַּלָּה   daughter-in-law, bride.

כְּלֻהִי   *n. pers. text corr.*

כְּלוּב I   basket, cage.

כְּלוּב II   *n. pers.* Chelub.

כְּלוּבַי   *n. pers.* Chelubai.

כְּלוּלֹת*   bridal time.

כֶּלַח I   vigour.

כֶּלַח II   *n. place* Calah.

כָּל־חֹזֶה   *n. pers.* Col-hozeh.

כְּלִי   container, vessel; instrument, tool, article, weapon; *Isa. 18.2* boat.

כֵּלַי   → כִּילַי.

כְּלִיא   *rd. K* prison.

כִּלְיָה*   kidney.

כִּלָּיוֹן   annihilation; languishing.

כִּלְיוֹן   *n. pers.* Chilion.

כָּלִיל   entire, perfect; whole; whole-offering.

כַּלְכֹּל   *n. pers.* Calcol.

כלל   *q* perfect.

כְּלָל   *n. pers.* Chelal.

כלם   *ni* be humiliated, insulted; be ashamed; be confounded.

hi abuse, shame, bring disgrace upon.

ho be shamed, insulted.

כִּלְמַד   *n. terr.* Chilmad? *text corr.*

כְּלִמָּה   insult.

כְּלִמּוּת   insult.

כַּלְנֶה, כַּלְנוֹ   *n. place* Calneh.

כמה   *q* languish.

כִּמְהָם   *n. pers.* Chimham.

כִּמְהָן   *n. pers.* Chimhan.

כְּמוֹ   as, when.

כְּמוֹהֶם   *rd. Q (Jer. 41.17).*

כְּמוֹשׁ   *n. deity* Chemosh.

כְּמִישׁ   → כְּמוֹשׁ.

כַּמֹּן   cummin.

כמס   *q pt. pass.* stored up.

כמר   *ni* become hot, be aroused.

כֹּמֶר*   priest *(of alien gods)*.

I כֵּן   thus, even so; so much, so greatly, so long; for, therefore; כְּכֵן then; עַד־כֵּן as yet; עַל־כֵּן therefore.

II כֵּן   steadfast, erect, straight; correct, true, right.

III כֵּן   stand, place; office.

IV כֵּן   gnat.

כנה   *pi* give someone an honorific name > flatter.

כַּנֶּה   *n. place* Canneh.

כַּנָּה   *imv. q of* כנן.

כִּנּוֹר   zither.

כָּנוֹת   *rd. Q pl. of* כְּנָת*.

כָּנְיָהוּ   *n. pers.* Coniah, Jehoiachin.

כִּנָּם   *coll.* gnats.

כנן   *q* cover?, protect?

כְּנָנִי   *n. pers.* Chenani.

כְּנַנְיָה(וּ)   *n. pers.* Chenaniah.

כנס   *q* gather.

pi gather together.

hitp wrap oneself.

כנע   *ni* be defeated, bowed, humbled; humble oneself.

hi subjugate, humble.

כְּנְעָה*   load, bundle.

כְּנַעַן   *n. pers., n. peop., n. terr.* Canaan; *fig. coll.* merchants.

כְּנַעֲנָה   *n. pers.* Chenaanah.

כְּנַעֲנִי   *gent.* Canaanite; *fig.* merchant.

כְּנַעֲנִי*   merchant.

כנף   *ni* hide.

כָּנָף   *f.* wing; corner; extremity, limit.

כִּנֶּרֶת,   *n. place* Chinnereth, Gennesaret.
כִּנְרוֹת, כִּנֲרוֹת

כְּנָת*   colleague.

כֶּסֶא   full moon.

כִּסֵּא chair, seat, throne.

כסה *q* cover, conceal.

    ni be covered.

    pi cover, cover up; hide, keep secret; conceal in itself.

    pu be covered, concealed.

    hitp cover oneself; *Prov. 26.26* be wrapped up.

כֵּסֶה → כִּסֵּא.

כִּסֶּה → כִּסֵּא.

כָּסוּי* covering.

כְּסֻלּוֹת *n. place* Chesuloth.

כְּסוּת covering, cover, clothing.

כסח *q pt. pass.* cut away.

כִּסְיָה throne of Yahweh.

I כְּסִיל foolish; fool.

II כְּסִיל Orion; *pl.* large constellations?

III כְּסִיל *n. place* Chesil.

כְּסִילוּת foolishness.

כסל *q* be foolish.

I כֶּסֶל loin.

II כֶּסֶל imperturbability, confidence; *Eccles. 7.25* foolishness.

כִּסְלָה *Ps. 85.9* foolishness; *Job 4.6* confidence.

כִּסְלֵו Chislev *(name of a month, November/December)*.

כִּסְלוֹן *n. pers.* Chislon.

כְּסָלוֹן *n. place* Chesalon.

כִּסְלוֹת תָּבֹר *n. place* Chisloth-tabor.

כַּסְלֻחִים *n. peop.* Casluhim.

כִּסְלָיו → כִּסְלֵו.

כסם *q* clip.

כֻּסְּמִים spelt.

כֻּסֶּמֶת spelt.

כסס *q* count.

כסף *q* long, desire.

    ni long; *Zeph. 2.1* be ashamed.

כֶּסֶף silver, money.

כָּסִפְיָא *n. place* Casiphia.

כֶּסֶת* band.

כעס   *q* be angry.

     pi provoke to anger.

     hi make angry, vex, insult.

כַּעַשׂ, פַּעַשׂ   anger, vexation.

כַּף   *f.* hollow of the hand, palm, hand; *Lev. 11.27* paw; *w.* רֶגֶל sole; *Lev. 23.40* branch; *m.* pan, vessel.

כַּף°*   rock.

כפה   *q* avert, pacify.

כִּפָּה   reed-shoot, frond.

כְּפוֹר I   cup.

כְּפוֹר II   hoar-frost.

כָּפִיס   stucco?, rafter?

כְּפִיר   young lion.

כְּפִירָה,   *n. place* Chephirah.

כְּפִירִים

כפל   *q* put doubled.

     ni be doubled.

כֶּפֶל   doubling; *du.* double; *Isa. 40.2* exchange value, equivalent.

כפן°   *q* stretch out.

כָּפָן°   hunger.

כפף   *q* bend.

     ni bow down.

כפר   *q* smear, coat with pitch.

     pi cover, atone for, make expiation for, purify; avert.

     pu be atoned for; *Isa. 28.18* be annulled.

     hitp be atoned for.

     nitp be atoned for.

כָּפָר°*   village.

כֹּפֶר° I   village.

כֹּפֶר II   asphalt.

כֹּפֶר III   henna.

כֹּפֶר IV   hush-money, ransom.

כְּפֹר   → כְּפוֹר II.

כִּפֻּרִים   atonement; *w.* יוֹם day of atonement.

כַּפֹּרֶת   cover.

כפשׁ   *hi* press down.

כַּפְתּוֹר,I   knob, capital; nodule.
כַּפְתֹּר

II כַּפְתּוֹר   *n. terr.* Caphtor.
כַּפְתֹּרִי*   *gent.* Caphtorite.
I כַּר   ram; battering-ram.
II כַּר   pasture.
III כַּר   saddle-bag.
כֹּר   *dry measure* cor *(between 220 and 450 l)*.
כרבל   *pu pt.* wrapped.
I כרה   *q* dig.
     ni be dug.
II כרה   *q* bargain (for).
III כרה   *q w.* כֵּרָה give a feast.
כָּרָה*   *unexplained.*
כֵּרָה   feast.
I כְּרוּב   cherub.
II כְּרוּב   *n. place* Cherub.
כָּרִי   *gent.* Carite.
כְּרִית   *n. river* Cherith.
כְּרִיתוּת,   dismissal, divorce.
כְּרִיתֻת
כַּרֹּב   edge.
כַּרְכֹּם   saffron.
כַּרְכְּמִישׁ,   *n. place* Carchemish.
כַּרְכְּמִשׁ
כַּרְכַּס   *n. pers.* Carcas.
כִּרְכָּרָה*   female camel.
כֶּרֶם   *m. and f.* vineyard.
כֹּרֵם*   vine-dresser.
כַּרְמִי   *n. pers.* Carmi; *gent.* Carmite.
כַּרְמִיל   crimson.
I כַּרְמֶל   orchard.
II כַּרְמֶל   fresh corn.
III כַּרְמֶל   *n. place* Carmel.
כַּרְמְלִי   *gent.* Carmelite.
כְּרָן   *n. pers.* Cheran.
כרסם   *pi* chew away.

כרע *q* kneel down, recline *(of animals)*; bow down; buckle at the knees, collapse.

hi force to the knees; *Judg. 11.35* bow someone down.

כְּרָעַיִם *f.* shanks; *Lev. 11.21* legs for jumping.

כַּרְפַּס fine fabric.

כרר *pilp* dance.

כָּרֵשׂ* belly.

כֹּרֵשׁ → כּוֹרֶשׁ.

כַּרְשְׁנָא *n. pers.* Carshena.

כרת *q* cut off, hew down, fell; exterminate; *w.* בְּרִית enter into/impose an obligation.

ni be felled, exterminated, destroyed; *Josh. 3f.* be divided.

pu be cut down, cut off.

hi exterminate, destroy.

ho be cut off.

כְּרֻתוֹת beams.

כְּרֵתִי *gent.* Cherethite, Cretan.

כְּרֵתֹת → כְּרֻתוֹת.

כֶּשֶׂב lamb.

כִּשְׂבָּה ewe-lamb.

כֶּשֶׂד *n. pers.* Chesed.

כַּשְׂדִּים *n. peop.* Chaldeans; *n. terr.* Chaldea; *Dan. 2.2,4* wise men, astrologers.

כשׂה *q* gorge oneself.

כְּשִׂי → כּוּשִׁי.

כַּשִּׁיל axe.

כשׁל *q* stumble, stagger; be exhausted.

ni stumble, stagger; be exhausted.

pi rd. Q (Ezek. 36.14).

hi cause to stumble, stagger.

ho pt. brought to downfall.

כִּשָּׁלוֹן stumbling, fall.

כשׁף *pi* practise sorcery.

כֶּשֶׁף* sorcery.

כַּשָּׁף* sorcerer.

כשׁר° *q* succeed, please.

hi succeed?

כִּשָׁרוֹן° success, gain.

כתב *q* write, record, write upon.
   ni be written, recorded.
   pi write zealously.

כְּתָב° piece of writing, roll; script.

כְּתֹבֶת writing.

כִּתִּיִּים, כִּתִּים *n. peop.* Kittim.

כָּתִית pounded; pure.

כֹּתֶל* wall.

כִּתְלִישׁ *n. place* Chithlish.

כתם° *ni* be stained.

כֶּתֶם gold.

כֻּתֹּנֶת, כְּתֹנֶת tunic.

כָּתֵף, כָּתֵף *f.* shoulder, shoulder-blade, shoulder-piece; side-piece, side-
   wall; slope.

כתר *pi* encircle; have patience *(Aram.)*.
   hi encircle; crown *(Aram.)*.

כֶּתֶר° crown; head-adornment.

כֹּתֶרֶת capital.

כתשׁ *q* pound.

כתת *q* crush, pound; hammer.
   pi crush; hammer.
   pu be crushed.
   hi disperse.
   ho be crushed, dispersed.

ל

לְ towards, up to; at, even to, until, till nearly, after; within; with
   regard to; to; for; namely; according to; on account of; *sign of
   the dative;* לְ *of authorship.*

לֹא not, un-.

לֻא → לוּ.

לֹא דְבַר *n. place* Lo-debar.

לָאָה   *q* be/become weary; give up.

     ni be exhausted, exert oneself; be unable.

     hi weary.

לֵאָה   *n. pers. f.* Leah.

לְאוֹם   → לְאֹם.

לָאט   *pf. q of* לוט.

לְאַט   gently, softly.

לָאט   → לָט.

לָאֵל   *n. pers.* Lael.

לְאֹם   nation; *Prov. 11.26* people.

לְאֻמִּים   *n. peop.* Leummim.

לֵב   heart, interior; *fig.* disposition, will, mind, conscience.

לְבֹא*   *n. place?* Labo.

לָבָא*   lion.

לְבָאָה*   lioness.

לְבָאוֹת   *n. place* Lebaoth.

לבב I   *ni* become intelligent.

     pi cause beating of the heart.

לבב II   *pi* prepare.

לֵבָב   → לֵב.

לְבִבָה*   heart-shaped cake?

לְבַד   → בַּד I.

לַבָּה*   flame.

לִבָּה*   heart.

לָבוֹא*   → לְבֹא.

לְבוֹנָה I   → לְבֹנָה.

לְבוֹנָה II   *n. place* Lebonah.

לְבוּשׁ   clothing, garment.

לָבוּשׁ   clothed.

לבט   *ni* be trampled down.

לָבִיא   lion.

לְבִיָּא   lioness.

לֵבִים   → לוּבִים.

לבן I   *hi* make white, purify; become white.

     hitp be purified.

לבן II   *q* make bricks.

I לָבָן   white.

II לָבָן   *n. pers., n. place* Laban.

I לְבָנָה   full moon.

II לְבָנָה   *n. pers.* Lebanah.

לְבֹנָה   frankincense.

לְבֵנָה   brick; *Ex. 24.10* platform.

לִבְנֶה   storax tree.

לִבְנָה   *n. place* Libnah.

לְבָנוֹן   *n. place* Lebanon.

לִבְנִי   *n. pers.* Libni; *gent.* Libnite.

לִבְנָת   *n. river* Libnath.

לֵב קָמַי   *code-name for* Chaldeans.

לבשׁ   *q* dress, clothe; put on; cover oneself.

　　　　pu pt. clothed; *Ezra 3.10* in vestments.

　　　　hi clothe; put on.

לָבֵשׁ, לְבֻשׁ   → לָבוּשׁ, לְבוּשׁ, לְבֻשׁ.

לֹג   *liquid measure* log *(between 0.3 and 0.625 l)*.

לֹד   *n. place* Lod.

לִדְבִר   *n. place* Lidebir.

לֵדָה   childbirth.

לֹה   *rd.* לֹא *(Deut. 3.11)*.

לַהַב   flame; blade.

לֶהָבָה   flame; blade.

לְהָבִים   *n. peop.* Lehabim.

לַהַג   studying.

לַהַד   *n. pers.* Lahad.

להה   *q* be exhausted.

　　　　hitpalp behave senselessly.

להט   *q* consume.

　　　　pi consume; scorch.

לַהַט   blade.

לְהָטִים*   sorceries.

להם   *hitp pt.* titbit.

לָהֵן   *Ruth 1.13* therefore.

לַהֲקָה*   band.

לֹא, לוּא   if; if only, O that.

לוּבִים   *n. people* Libyans.

לוּד   *n. people* Lud, Lydians.

לֹא דְבָר ← לוֹ דְבָר.

I לוה ‎ *q* accompany.

‎ *ni* attach oneself to someone, be bound.

II לוה ‎ *q* borrow.

‎ *hi* lend.

לוז ‎ *q* leave.

‎ *ni pt.* perverted, perversion.

‎ *hi* leave.

I לוז ‎ almond tree.

II לוז ‎ *n. place* Luz.

לוּחַ ‎ tablet; plank, board.

לוּחִית ‎ *n. place* Luhith.

לוֹחֵשׁ ‎ *n. pers.* Lohesh.

לוט ‎ *q* cover, wrap up.

‎ *hi* cover.

I לוֹט ‎ covering.

II לוֹט ‎ *n. pers.* Lot.

לוֹטָן ‎ *n. pers.* Lotan.

לֵוִי ‎ Levite; *n. pers., n. people* Levi.

לוְיָה* ‎ garland.

לִוְיָתָן ‎ Leviathan, serpent; *Job 40.25* crocodile.

לֻל* ‎ staircase?, trap-door?

לוּלֵא, לוּלֵי ‎ if not; unless; *Ps. 27.13* surely.

לון ‎ *ni* murmur.

‎ *hi* murmur.

לוין ← לִין.

לושׁ ‎ *q* knead.

לָושׁ ‎ *rd. Q (II Sam. 3.15).*

לָז, לָזֶה, הַלֵּזוּ ← הַלָּז, הַלָּזֶה, הַלֵּזוּ.

לָזוּת* ‎ perversity.

לַח ‎ moist, fresh, new.

לֵחַ* ‎ freshness.

לְחוּם ‎ *unexplained.*

לְחוֹת ← לוּחִית.

I לְחִי ‎ jaw, cheek.

II לְחִי ‎ *n. place* Lehi.

בְּאֵר לַחַי רֹאִי ← לַחַי רֹאִי.

לחַךְ *q* crop.

  pi lick, lick up; consume.

I לחם *q* fight.

  ni fight, wage war, besiege, be victorious.

II לחם *q* eat.

לֶחֶם battle?

לֶחֶם bread, food; corn.

לֶחֶם → לְחוּם.

לַחְמִי *n. pers.* Lahmi.

לַחְמָס *n. place* Lahmas.

לחץ *q* push, press, oppress, afflict, persecute.

  ni press oneself.

לַחַץ oppression, affliction.

לחשׁ *pi* charm.

  hitp whisper with one another.

לַחַשׁ whispering, charming; *Isa. 3.20* humming shell.

לָט occult art; *w.* בְּ secretly.

לֹט mastic bark.

לְטָאָה gecko.

לְטוּשִׁים *n. peop.* Letushim.

לטשׁ *q* hammer, sharpen; *pt.* smith.

  pu pt. sharpened.

לֹיָה* garland.

לַיִל, לַיְלָה night, by night.

לִילִית *n. pers. f.* Lilith.

לין *q* stay the night, remain all night.

  hitpol stay the night, lodge.

ליץ *q* boast.

  pol pt. arrogant?

  hi be spokesman, interpret; mock.

  hitpol mock.

I לַיִשׁ lion.

II לַיִשׁ *n. pers., n. place* Laish.

לַיְשָׁה *n. place* Laishah.

לכד *q* catch, capture; occupy, cut off; *Josh. 7.14* designate; *I Sam. 14.47* assume.

  ni be caught, captured; be chosen.

  hitp be compacted together.

לָכַד capture.

לֵכָה n. *place* Lecah.

לָכִישׁ n. *place* Lachish.

לָכֵן therefore, for that reason.

לֻלָאֹת loops, nooses.

למד q learn.

    pi teach; train.

    pu be taught, trained.

לִמֻּד accustomed; pupil, disciple.

לָמָּה, why? *usually of inquiry.*

לָמָה, לָמֶה

לְמוֹ for, with respect to.

לְמוּאֵל, לְמוֹאֵל n. *pers.* Lemuel.

לִמֻּד → לִמֻּד.

לֶמֶךְ n. *pers.* Lamech.

לְמִן from then/there on.

לְמַעַן → מַעַן.

לָן* *pt. q of* לִין.

לֹעַ* throat.

לעב° *hi* scoff.

לענ q scoff.

    ni speak in a foreign language.

    hi mock, deride.

לַעַג stammering; scoffing, mockery.

לָעֵג* speaking in a foreign language.

לַעְדָּה n. *pers.* Laadah.

לַעְדָּן n. *pers.* Laadan.

לעז° q speak incomprehensibly.

לעט *hi* let gulp down.

לַעֲנָה wormwood.

I לעע q speak rashly.

II לעע q swallow up.

לַפִּיד torch.

לַפִּידוֹת n. *pers.* Lappidoth.

לפת q clasp.

    ni be diverted; bend forward.

לֵץ mocker.

לָצוֹן mockery.

לַקּוּם *n. place* Lakkum.

לקח *q* take, grasp, seize; take away; take with one, for oneself; receive; take up; fetch, bring; carry off; *Prov. 31.16* acquire.

ni be taken away, carried off; be fetched.

pu be taken, taken away, carried off; be brought.

hitp flare up, flash.

לֶקַח teaching, persuasion, insight.

לִקְחִי *n. pers.* Likhi.

לקט *q* gather, glean.

pi glean, collect.

pu be gleaned.

hitp gather.

לֶקֶט gleanings.

לקק *q* lap.

pi lap.

לקש *pi* plunder.

לֶקֶשׁ late crop.

לָשָׁד* cake; marrow.

לָשׁוֹן tongue, language.

לִשְׁכָּה room, hall, chamber.

לֶשֶׁם I *precious stone.*

לֶשֶׁם II *n. place* Leshem.

לשן *poel* slander.

hi slander.

לָשֹׁן → לָשׁוֹן.

לֶשַׁע *n. place* Lasha.

לַשָּׁרוֹן → שָׁרוֹן.

לַת *inf. q of* ילד.

לֶתֶךְ grain-measure lethech *(between 110 and 225 l).*

מ

מַאֲבוּס* granary.

מוֹאָבִי → מֹאָבִי.

מְאֹד strength, power; very.

מֵאָה I hundred; *du.* two hundred; *pl.* hundreds.

מֵאָה II *n. place* Meah.

מַאֲוַי* eager desire.

מְאוּם, מְאֹם stain, blemish.

מְאוּמָה anything at all.

מָאוֹר lamp, luminary; lampstand; *Ps. 90.8; Prov. 15.30* light.

מְאוּרָה* young?

מֹאזְנַיִם scales.

מֵאיֹות *pl. of* I מֵאָה.

מַאֲכָל food, food-stuff.

מַאֲכֶלֶת knife.

מַאֲכֹלֶת feed.

מַאֲמָץ* exertion.

מַאֲמָר°* word, command.

מאן *pi* refuse.

מאס I *q* despise, abhor; refuse, reject; *Job 42.6* retract.
ni be rejected.

מאס II *ni* run, vanish.

מַאֲפֶה* something baked.

מַאֲפֵל darkness.

מַאְפֵּלְיָה darkness.

מאר *hi pt.* painful, malignant.

מַאֲרָב ambush.

מְאֵרָה curse.

מִבְדָּלוֹת enclaves.

מָבוֹא entrance; entering; setting *(of the sun)* > west.

מְבוּכָה confusion.

מַבּוּל heavenly ocean; deluge.

מְבוֹנִים *rd. Q (II Chron. 35.3).*

מְבוּסָה trampling down.

מַבּוּעַ spring.

מְבוּקָה waste.

מִבְחוֹר choice, the best.

מִבְחָר I* choice, the best.

מִבְחָר II *n. peop.?* Mibhar.

מַבָּט* hope.

מִבְטָא rash undertaking.

מִבְטָח trust; security.

מַבְלִיגִית* cheering.

מִבְנֶה* structure.

מְבֻנַּי n. pers. Mebunnai.

מִבְצָר I fortified place, fortification, fortress.

מִבְצָר II n. peop.? Mibzar.

מִבְרָח* fugitive.

מִבְשָׂם n. pers. Mibsam.

מְבֻשִׁים* private parts.

מְבַשְׁלוֹת cooking-places.

מַג part of a Bab. official title.

מַגְבִּישׁ n. pers. Magbish.

מִגְבָּלֹת cords.

מִגְבָּעָה* head-band.

מֶגֶד gift; the best.

מְגִדּוֹ(ן) n. place Megiddo.

מִגְדּוֹל → מִגְדָּל.

מַגְדִּיאֵל n. peop.? Magdiel.

מִגְדִּיל rd. K (II Sam. 22.51).

מִגְדָּל I tower; Neh. 8.4 podium; Cant. 5.13 cabinet?

מִגְדָּל* II part of n. place Migdal.

מִגְדֹּל n. place Migdol.

מִגְדָּנוֹת costly gifts, valuables.

מָגוֹג n. pers., n. terr. Magog.

מָגוֹר terror.

מָגוּר* Ps. 55.16 unexplained.

מְגוֹרָה* terror.

מְגוּרָה grain-pit.

מְגוּרִים* status of client, residence.

מַגְזֵרָה* axe.

מַגָּל sickle.

מְגִלָּה scroll.

מְגַמָּה* striving?

מגן pi give up, hand over; Prov. 4.9 bestow upon.

מָגֵן I shield; Job 41.7 scale.

מָגֵן II shameless.

מָגִנָּה* insolence.

מִגְעֶרֶת threat.

מַגֵּפָה plague.

מַגְפִּיעָשׁ *n. pers.* Magpiash.

סגר *q pt. pass.* given up.

    pi throw down *(Aram.).*

מְגֵרָה stone-saw.

מִגְרוֹן *n. place* Migron.

מִגְרָעוֹת ledges, recesses.

מֶגְרָפָה* shovel?, clod?

מִגְרָשׁ pasture; uncultivated land.

מִגְרָשׁוֹת waves?

מַד* garment.

מִדְבָּר I steppe, desert.

מִדְבָּר* II speech.

מדד *q* measure.

    ni be measured.

    pi measure off, measure out.

    hitpo stretch out.

מִדָּה I measurement, size; *following* tall, spacious.

מִדָּה* II tax.

מַדְהֵבָה *l.* מַרְהֵבָה *(Isa. 14.4)* assault.

מַדּוּ* garment.

מַדְוֶה* I garment.

מַדְוֶה* II illness, disease.

מַדּוּחִים misleading.

מָדוֹן I, מִדְיָן* dispute, quarrel.

מָדוֹן II *n. place* Madon.

מַדּוּעַ why? *usually reproachful.*

מְדוּרָה pile of wood.

מִדְחֶה downfall.

מַדְחֵפָה* blow.

מָדַי *n. pers.* Madai; *n. peop.* Medes; *n. terr.* Media.

מָדִי *gent.* Median.

מַדִּי מַה־דַּי >.

מִדְיָן* I dispute, quarrel.

מִדְיָן II *n. pers., n. terr.* Midian; *n. peop.* Midianites.

מִדִּין I garments.

מִדִּין II *n. place* Middin.

מָדִין rd. מִדָּה (II Sam. 21.20).

מְדִינָה° circuit, area of jurisdiction, satrapy, province.

מְדִינִי gent. Midianite.

מְדֹכָה mortar.

מַדְמֵן n. place Madmen.

I מַדְמֵנָה dunghill.

II מַדְמֵנָה n. place Madmenah.

מַדְמַנָּה n. pers., n. place Madmannah.

מְדָן n. pers. Medan.

מְדָנִים gent. Medanites.

מַדָּע°, מַדָּע° understanding; Eccles. 10.20 bedroom.

מֹדַע relative.

מַדּוּעַ → מַדּוּעַ.

מֹדַעַת* relative.

מַדְקָרָה* thrust.

מַדְרֵגָה rocky terrace.

מִדְרָךְ* foot's-breadth.

מִדְרָשׁ* interpretation, exposition.

מְדֻשָׁה* that which is threshed.

מָה what?, how?, why?; what; how!, עַד־מָה how long?

מהה hitpalp linger.

מְהוּמָה uproar, tumult; confusion, alarm.

מְהוּמָן n. pers. Mehuman.

מְהֵיטַבְאֵל n. pers. m. (Aram.) and f. Mehetabel.

מָהִיר skilled, diligent.

מהל q pt. pass. adulterated.

מַהֲלָךְ* way, journey, passage; pl. access.

מַהֲלָל* recognition.

מַהֲלַלְאֵל n. pers. Mahalalel.

מַהֲלֻמוֹת blows, thrashing.

מהמה → מהה.

מַהֲמֹרוֹת pits filled with rain-water.

מַהְפֵּכָה* overthrow.

מַהְפֶּכֶת stocks.

I מהר ni act hastily; pt. rash, impetuous, dismayed.
pi hurry; hasten; imv. also quickly.

II מהר q acquire (by payment of the bride-price).

מֹהַר bride-price.

מְהֵרָה haste; in haste.

מַהְרַי *n. pers.* Maharai.

מַהֲתַלּוֹת deceptions.

מוֹאָב *n. pers., n. terr.* Moab; *n. peop.* Moabites.

מוֹאָבִי *gent.* Moabite.

מוֹאָל → מוּל.

מוֹבָא entrance.

מוּג *q* reel.

    ni heave, surge to and fro.

    pol soften, dissolve.

    hitpol melt, be in commotion.

מוּד *pol* shake.

מוּט *q* totter.

    ni totter, shake.

    hi bring down upon.

    hitpol reel to and fro.

מוֹט stand, pole.

מוֹטָה yoke, bearer.

מוּךְ *q* come down, be reduced to poverty.

מוּל I *q* circumcise.

    ni be circumcised.

מוּל II *hi* ward off.

מוּל, מוֹל before, facing; פָּנִים מוּל front; מִמּוּל before, in front of, towards.

מוֹלָדָה *n. place* Moladah.

מוֹלֶדֶת offspring, relatives; *pl. also* descent.

מוּלָה* circumcision.

מוֹלִיד *n. pers.* Molid.

מוּם → מְאוּם.

מוּמָה → מְאוּמָה.

מוֹמְכָן *rd. Q (Esther 1.16).*

מוּסָב* circuit?

מוּסָד* foundation-wall, foundation.

מוּסָד foundation.

מוּסָדָה foundation.

מוֹסָדָה* *m.* foundation-wall, foundation.

מוֹסֵר* fetter.

מוּסָר   chastisement, discipline; reminder, warning.

I *מוֹסֵרָה   fetter.

II מוֹסֵרָה   *n. place* Moserah.

מוֹעֵד   meeting-place, place of assembly; assembly, meeting; fixed date; appointed time, time of festival.

*מוֹעָד   assembly point?

מוּעָדָה   appointment.

מוֹעַדְיָה   *n. pr.* Moadiah.

מוּעָף   darkness.

*מוֹעֵצָה   counsel, plan.

מוּעָקָה   *Ps. 66.11 unexplained.*

מוּפָז   *pt. ho of* I פזז.

מֵיפַעַת → מוּפַעַת.

מוֹפֵת   sign.

I מוֹצָא   exit, going out; utterance; departure; rising *(sun)* > east.

II מוֹצָא   *n. pers.* Moza.

*מוֹצָאָה   origin; latrine.

I מוּצָק   (metal) casting.

II מוּצָק   affliction.

*מוּצָקָה   casting; pipe.

מוּק°   *hi* deride.

מוֹקֵד   hearth.

מוֹקְדָה   hearth.

מוֹקֵשׁ   trap, snare.

מוּר → מֹר.

מוּר   *ni* alter.

       hi exchange, alter.

מוֹרָא   fear, terror; reverence.

מוֹרַג   threshing-sledge.

מוֹרָד   slope; *I Kings 7.29* pendants.

מוֹרֶה   early rain.

I מוֹרָה   *m.* razor.

II מוֹרָה → מוֹרָא.

מוֹרָט   *pt. pu of* מרט.

מוֹרִיָּה → מוֹרִיָּה.

I *מוֹרָשׁ   possession.

II *מוֹרָשׁ   desire.

מוֹרָשָׁה	acquisition, possession.
מוֹרֶשֶׁת גַּת	n. place Moresheth-gath.
מוֹרַשְׁתִּי	gent. Morashtite.
מוּשׁ I	q feel.
	hi let feel; be able to feel, grasp.
מוּשׁ II	q withdraw, cease; remove.
מוֹשָׁב	chair, seat; home, place of residence; location, site; company; dwelling; inhabitants.
מוּשִׁי	n. pers. Mushi; gent. Mushite.
מוֹשָׁעָה*	help.
מוּת	q die.
	pol kill, give the death-blow.
	hi put to death, kill, have killed.
	ho be killed, suffer death.
מָוֶת	death, dying; pestilence; abode of the dead.
מוֹתָר°	advantage, superiority.
מִזְבֵּחַ	altar.
מֶזֶג	mixed wine.
מָזֶה*	weakened.
מִזָּה	n. pers. Mizzah.
מָזוּ*	granary.
מְזוּזָה	door-post.
מָזוֹן	food.
מָזוֹר I	festering wound, sore.
מָזוֹר II	trap?, ambush?
מֵזַח I	dockyard.
מֵזַח II	girdle.
מְזִיחַ	girdle.
מַזְכִּיר	spokesman (official title).
מִזְלֵג*	meat-fork.
מַזְלֵג	meat-fork.
מַזָּלוֹת	signs of the zodiac.
מְזִמָּה	thinking, plan; calculation, machination; prudence.
מִזְמוֹר	psalm.
מַזְמֵרָה*	vine-dresser's knife.
מְזַמֶּרֶת*	snuffers.
מִזְעָר	few.
מִזְרֶה	winnowing-fork.

מַזָרוֹת southern signs of the zodiac?

מִזְרָח rising *(sun)* > east.

מְזָרִים north winds.

*מִזְרָע sown land.

מִזְרָק basin.

*מֵחַ fatling *(sheep)*.

מֹחַ marrow.

°מחא *q* strike, clap.

מַחֲבֵא hiding-place.

מַחֲבֹאִים hiding-places.

מְחַבְּרוֹת binders, clamps.

מַחְבֶּרֶת seam, set.

מַחֲבַת griddle.

מַחְגֹרֶת girding.

I מחה *q* wipe off, wipe away; destroy.

     ni be wiped out, destroyed.

     hi blot out.

II °מחה *q* strike, meet.

III מחה *pu pt.* full of marrow.

מְחוּגָה compasses.

*מָחוֹז harbour.

מְחוּיָאֵל *n. pers.* Mehujael.

מַחֲוִים *gent.* Mahavite.

I מָחוֹל round dance.

II מָחוֹל *n. pers.* Mahol.

מַחֲזֶה appearance, vision.

מֶחֱזָה window.

מַחֲזִיאוֹת *n. pers.* Mahazioth.

°מְחִי blow.

מְחִידָא *n. pers.* Mehida.

מִחְיָה preservation of life; renewal, new tissue; supplies, sustenance; reviving.

מְחִיָאֵל *n. pers.* Mehijael.

I מְחִיר equivalent value, purchase-price, payment.

II מְחִיר *n. pers.* Mehir.

*מַחֲלֶה sickness.

מַחְלָה *n. pers. m. and f.* Mahalah.

מַחֲלָה sickness.

מְחֹלָה* round dance.

מְחִלָּה* hole.

מַחְלוֹן n. pers. Mahlon.

מַחְלִי n. pers. Mahli; gent. Mahlite.

מַחֲלָיִים injuries.

מַחְלָף* dub.

מַחְלְפוֹת* plaits.

מַחֲלָצוֹת fine garments.

מַחְלְקוֹת n. pers. Mahlekoth.

מַחֲלֹקֶת share, division.

מָחֲלַת I liturgical direction.

מָחֲלַת II, n. pers. Mahalath.

מָחֲלַת

מְחֹלָתִי gent. Meholathite.

מַחֲמָאֹת milk-foods.

מַחְמָד* desirable thing, valuable; desire; Hos. 9.16 darling.

מַחְמֹד* valuable.

מַחְמָל unexplained.

מַחְמֶצֶת anything leavened.

מַחֲנֶה camping-place, war-camp, travellers' camp; host, army.

מַחֲנֵה־דָן n. place Mahaneh-dan.

מַחֲנַיִם n. place Mahanaim.

מַחֲנָק suffocation.

מַחְסֶה, מַחֲסֶה refuge.

מַחְסוֹם rein?, muzzle?

מַחְסוֹר want, loss.

מַחְסֵיָה n. pers. Mahseiah.

מחץ q shatter.

מַחַץ wound.

מֻחְצָב w. אֶבֶן dressed.

מֶחֱצָה half.

מַחֲצִית half, middle.

מחק° q shatter.

מֶחְקָר* depth.

מָחָר tomorrow.

מֹחֲרָאוֹת rd. K (II Kings 10.27) latrine.

מַחֲרֵשָׁה*, ploughshare.

מַחֲרֶשֶׁת*

מָחֳרָת following day.

מַחְשֹׂף peeling off the bark.

מַחֲשָׁבָה, thought, intention, plan; invention.
מַחֲשֶׁבֶת,
מַחֲשֶׁבֶת

מַחְשָׁךְ dark place, hiding-place.

מַחַת n. pers. Mahath.

מְחִתָּה terror; destruction.

מַחְתָּה fire-pan, brazier.

מַחְתֶּרֶת housebreaking.

מַטְאֲטֵא besom.

מַטְבֵּחַ slaughtering-place.

מַטֶּה stick, staff; tribe; *Ezek. 19 also* branch.

מַטָּה below.

מִטָּה bed.

מֻטֶּה perversion.

מַטֶּה* spread.

מַטְוֶה yarn.

מָטִיל* bar.

מַטְמוֹן (hidden) treasure.

מַטָּע planting.

מַטְעַמּוֹת*, titbits.
מַטְעַמִּים

מִטְפַּחַת wrap.

מטר *ni* have rain.
hi send rain.

מָטָר rain.

מַטָּרָא° target.

מַטְרֵד n. pers. f. Matred.

מַטָּרָה° target; guard.

מַטְרִי gent. Matrite.

מִי* water, waters; *Isa. 52.5 rd. Q.*

מִי who?, who; whoever; מִי יִתֵּן who gives? > O that!

מֵידְבָא n. place Medeba.

מֵידָד n. pers. Medad.

מוֹדַע rd. Q (Ruth 2.1) relative.

מֵי הַיַּרְקוֹן n. place Me-jarkon.

מֵי זָהָב   *n. pers.* Me-zahab.

מֵיטָב*   the best.

מִיכָא   *n. pers.* Mica.

מִיכָאֵל   *n. pers.* Michael.

מִיכָה   *n. pers.* Micah.

מִיכָהוּ   *rd. Q (II Chron. 18.8).*

מִיכָיָה(וּ)   *n. pers.* Micaiah.

מִיכָיְהוּ   *n. pers.* Micaiah.

מִיכַל   *n. pers. f.* Michal; *II Sam. 17.20 unexplained.*

מַיִם   → מַי.

מִיָּמִ(י)ן   *n. pers.* Mijamin.

מִין*   kind, species.

מֵינֶקֶת   wet-nurse.

מיסָך   *rd. Q (II Kings 16.18)* covered-way?

מֵיפַעַת   *n. place* Mephaath.

מִיץ   pressing.

מִיצִיאוּ   *rd. Q (II Chron. 32.21)* issuing.

מִישׁ   → מוּשׁ.

מֵישָׁא   *n. pers.* Mesha.

מִישָׁאֵל   *n. pers.* Mishael.

מִישׁוֹר   plain, level; uprightness; *Ps. 67.5* justly.

מֵישַׁךְ   *n. pers.* Meshach.

מֵישַׁע   *n. pers.* Mesha.

מֵישָׁע   *n. pers.* Mesha.

מִישֹׁר   → מִישׁוֹר.

מֵישָׁרִים   rectitude, uprightness; uprightly, justly; *Dan. 11.6* settlement.

מֵיתָר*   bow-string; tent-cord.

מַכְאוֹב   pain, suffering.

מַכְבֵּנָה   *n. pers.* Machbenah.

מַכְבַּנַּי   *n. pers.* Machbannai.

מַכְבֵּר   blanket?

מִכְבָּר   grating.

מַכָּה   stroke, wound; plague; defeat.

מִכְוָה   burn.

מָכוֹן   abode, foundation.

מְכוֹנָה   place, abode; stand.

מְכוֹרָה*   descent (also pl.).

מָכִי *n. pers.* Machi.

מָכִיר *n. pers., n. peop.* Machir.

מָכִירִי *gent.* Machirite.

מכך *q* sink down.

ni become sunken.

ho be brought low.

מִכְלָא*, מִכְלָה fold.

מִכְלוֹל perfection.

מִכְלוֹת perfection, purity.

מִכְלָל* perfection.

מַכְלֻלִים gorgeous garments.

מַפֹּלֶת food.

מִכְמַנִּים*° treasures.

מִכְמָס *n. place* Michmas.

מִכְמָר, מַכְמֹר* net.

מִכְמֶרֶת*, fishing-net.

מִכְמֹרֶת

מִכְמָשׁ → מִכְמָס.

מִכְמְתָת *n. place* Michmethath.

מַכְנַדְבַי *n. pers.* Machnadebai.

I מְכֹנָה → מְכוֹנָה.

II מְכֹנָה *n. place* Meconah.

מִכְנָס* drawers.

מֶכֶס tax.

מִכְסָה* number, amount.

מִכְסֶה covering.

מִכְבֶּה covering; clothing; deck.

מַכְפֵּלָה *n. place* Machpelah.

מכר *q* sell, give up.

ni sell oneself, be sold.

hitp sell oneself, give oneself over.

מֶכֶר purchase-price; ware.

מַכָּר* acquaintance?

מִכְרֶה* pit.

מְכֵרָה* sword?

מִכְרִי *n. pers.* Michri.

מְכֵרָתִי *gent.* Mecherathite.

מִכְשׁוֹל, מִכְשֹׁל offence, obstacle.

מַכְשֵׁלָה ruin.

מִכְתָּב writing, document.

מְכִתָּה* that which is shattered.

מִכְתָּם *designation of a song.*

מַכְתֵּשׁ I mortar; molar.

מַכְתֵּשׁ II *n. place* Machtesh.

מלא *q* be full, be complete, be at an end; fill.

    ni be filled, fulfilled; *Eccles. 6.7* be satisfied.

    pi fulfil, fill; *w.* יָד *also* install, consecrate; *w.* אַחֲרֵי hold constantly to.

    pu pt. set.

    hitp band together.

מָלֵא full.

מְלֹא fullness.

מְלֵאָה full produce.

מִלֵּאָה* setting.

מִלֻּאִים installation; setting.

מַלְאָךְ messenger.

מְלָאכָה mission, duty, business, work, service; article.

מַלְאָכוּת* message.

מַלְאָכִי *n. pers.?* Malachi.

מִלֵּאת fullness?

מַלְבּוּשׁ garment.

מַלְבֵּן brick-mould?, brick-kiln?, brick-terrace?

מלה *pi* fill.

מִלָּה° word; byword.

מְלֹא, מְלוֹא, מְלוֹא → מָלֵא.

מִלּוֹא mound, acropolis; Millo.

מִלּוּאִים → מִלֻּאִים.

מַלּוּחַ salt-wort.

מַלּוּךְ *n. pers.* Malluch.

מְלוּכָה kingship, royal-house, royal-.

מְלוּכִי *rd.* מַלּוּךְ *(Neh. 12.14).*

מָלוֹן camp for the night.

מְלוּנָה watchman's hut.

מַלּוֹתִי *n. pers.* Mallothi.

מלח I *ni* be dispersed.

מלח II *q* salt.

pu pt. salted.

ho be rubbed down with salt water.

I *מֶלַח   rags.

II מֶלַח   salt.

*מַלָּח   sailor.

מְלֵחָה   salt land.

מִלְחָמָה   fight, battle, war; *Ps. 76.4* weapon?

I מלט   *ni* make for safety, escape.

     pi save; *II Kings 23.18* leave undisturbed; *Isa. 34.15* lay
       (eggs)?

     hi save; *Isa. 66.7* bear.

     hitp fly out *(sparks).*

II מלט   *hitp* become hairless.

°מֶלֶט   mortar.

מְלַטְיָה   *n. pers.* Melatiah.

*מְלִילָה   (rubbed) ears *(of corn).*

מְלִיצָה   cryptic remark.

I מלך   *q* be king, rule; *Prov. 30.22* come to power.

     hi appoint as king.

     ho be appointed as king.

II °מלך   *ni* take counsel with oneself.

I מֶלֶךְ   king.

II מֶלֶךְ   *n. pers.* Melech.

מֹלֶךְ   *derogatory form of* I מֶלֶךְ *(title of a god)* Molech.

*מַלְכֹּדֶת   trap.

מַלְכָּה   queen *(also wife of the king).*

מְלֻכָה   → מְלוּכָה.

מִלְכָּה   *n. pers. f.* Milcah.

מַלְכוּת   royal power; royal dignity; reign; kingdom; royal.

מַלְכִּיאֵל   *n. pers.* Malchiel.

מַלְכִּיאֵלִי   *gent.* Malchielite.

מַלְכִּיָּה(וּ)   *n. pers.* Malchijah.

מַלְכִּי־צֶדֶק   *n. pers.* Melchizedek.

מַלְכִּירָם   *n. pers.* Malchiram.

מַלְכִּי־שׁוּעַ   *n. pers.* Malchishua.

מַלְכָּם   *n. pers.* Malcam.

מִלְכֹּם Milcom (*name of a god*).

מַלְפֵּן rd. Q (*II Sam. 12.31*).

מַלְכֶּת queen.

מֹלֶכֶת *n. pers. f.* (Ham)molecheth.

I מלל *q* wither.

poel wilt.

hitpo be limp?

II מלל *q* circumcise.

ni be circumcised; be cut off.

III°מלל *q* give a signal.

pi speak, announce.

מְלָלַי *n. pers.* Milalai.

מַלְמָד* goad.

מלץ *ni* be smooth.

מֶלְצַר overseer (*Bab. official title*).

מלק *q* nip off.

מַלְקוֹחַ booty; *du.* palate.

מַלְקוֹשׁ late rain.

מֶלְקָחַיִם snuffers.

מֶלְתָּחָה wardrobe.

מַלְתָּעוֹת* jaw-bones.

מַמְּגֻרָה* grain-pit.

מֵמַד* measurement.

מְמוּכָן *n. pers.* Memucan.

מְמוֹתִים* death.

מַמְזֵר bastard.

מִמְכָּר sale, ware, that which is sold.

מִמְכֶּרֶת sale.

מַמְלָכָה sovereignty; royal dignity; reign; kingdom; royal; kingship; king.

מַמְלָכוּת reign, sovereignty, kingdom.

מַמְלֶכֶת reign.

מִמְסָךְ spiced wine.

מֶמֶר bitterness, vexation.

מַמְרֵא *n. pers.*, *n. place* Mamre.

מַמְרֹרִים bitterness.

מַמְשַׁח *dub.*

מִמְשָׁל dominion; *pl.* leaders.

מֶמְשָׁלָה dominion, domain; might.

מִמְשָׁק* possession?

מַמְתַקִּים sweet things.

I מָן manna.

II מָן what?

I מֵן* string.

II מֵן* Ps. 68.24 portion? text corr.

מִן portion of > of, from; out of, away from, on, -wards; on from, immediately after, since, after; because of, before, since; without, far from; so that; used in comparisons.

מְנָאוֹת pl. of מְנָת.

מַנְגִּינָה* mocking song.

מנה q count, destine.

ni be counted, able to be counted.

pi allot, assign, appoint (Aram.).

pu pt. appointed.

מָנֶה unit of weight mina (50 shekels, 571.2 g).

מָנָה portion, share.

מֹנָה* pl. times.

מִנְהָג way of driving.

מִנְהָרָה* cleft.

מָנוֹד* shaking.

I מָנוֹחַ resting-place.

II מָנוֹחַ n. pers. Manoah.

מְנוּחָה rest, resting-place; II Sam. 14.17 reassurance.

מָנוֹן scorner?

מָנוֹס place of refuge, refuge.

מְנוּסָה flight.

מָנוֹר weaver's beam.

מְנוֹרָה lampstand.

מִנְּזָרִים* watchmen.

מִנְחָה gift; offering, grain-offering.

מָנַחַה מְנֻחָה → מְנֻחָה.

מְנָחוֹת n. peop. Menuhoth.

מְנַחֵם n. pers. Menahem.

מָנַחַת n. pers., n. place Manahath.

מָנַחְתִּי gent. Manahathite.

מְנִי (god of) destiny.

מְנִי I	*n. terr.* Minni.
מְנִי, II מְנִי	*poetic form of* מֶן.
מְנָיוֹת	*pl. of* מָנָת.
מִנְיָמִ(י)ן	*n. pers.* Miniamin.
מִנִּית	*n. place* Minnith.
מִנְלָם	*dub.*
מנע	*q* hold back, withhold, refuse.
	ni allow oneself to be held back, be withheld.
מַנְעוּל	lock, bolt.
מִנְעָל*	bolt, lock.
מַנְעַמִּים	titbits.
מְנַעַנְעִים	sistrum, rattle.
מְנַצֵּחַ	→ נצח.
מְנַקִּית*	offering-bowl.
מֵינֶקֶת	→ מֵינֶקֶת.
מְנוֹרָה	→ מְנוֹרָה.
מְנַשֶּׁה	*n. pers., n. peop.* Manasseh.
מְנַשִּׁי	*gent.* Manassite.
מְנָת	share.
מֶס	*dub.*
מַס	forced labour; *coll.* forced labourers.
מֵסַב	party at table, surroundings, round about.
מְסִבָּה*	*pl.* round about.
מַסְגֵּר	locksmith?, master-builder?; prison.
מִסְגֶּרֶת	bulwark; moulding.
מַסָּד	foundation.
מִסְדְּרוֹן*	porch?, privy?
מסה	*hi* make to melt, wash, dissolve, consume.
מַסָּה I	proving, trying.
מַסָּה* II	despair.
מַסָּה III	*n. place* Massah.
מִסָּה*	according to the measure of, according to the circumstances of.
מַסְוֶה	covering.
מְסוּכָה	thorn-hedge.
מַסָּח	alternately.
מִסְחָר*	trade.
מסך	*q* mix.
מֶסֶך	admixture of spices.

מָסָךְ covering, curtain; *fig.* protection.

מְסֻכָּה* covering.

I מַסֵּכָה cast image; *Isa. 30.1* drink-offering?

II מַסֵּכָה covering.

מִסְכֵּן poor, needy.

מִסְכְּנוֹת stores, storehouses.

מִסְכֵּנֻת poverty.

מַסֶּכֶת warp.

מְסִלָּה highway, course.

מַסְלוּל highway.

מַסְמֵר*, nail.

מַסְמֵר*

מַשְׂמְרָה* nail.

מסס *q* despair?

ni melt, dissolve; become weak, despair.

hi make to melt.

מַסַּע breaking up, setting out; stage of a journey, station.

מַסָּע quarrying; *Job 41.18* missile?

מִסְעָד prop?

מִסְפֵּד mourning custom, mourning rites, lamentation.

מִסְפּוֹא fodder.

מִסְפָּחוֹת veils.

מִסְפַּחַת scab.

I מִסְפָּר number, counting; narration.

II מִסְפָּר *n. pers.* Mispar.

מִסְפֶּרֶת *n. pers. m.* Mispereth.

מסר *q* unexplained.

ni be enlisted?

מֹסֵרוֹת *n. place* Moseroth.

מֹסְרָם *rd.* מוּסָר *(Job 33.16).*

מָסֹרֶת bond?

מִסְתּוֹר hiding-place.

מַסְתֵּר covering.

מִסְתָּר hiding-place.

מַעֲבָּד* deed.

מַעֲבֶה* foundry?

מַעֲבָר* ford, passage, pass; *Isa. 30.32* stroke.

מַעֲבָרָה ford, passage; pass.

מַעְגָּל I   wagon-track, track, course.

מַעְגָּל II   camp-circle.

מעד   *q* totter.
> *pu pt. rd. q.*
> *hi* cause to totter.

מֹעַד → מוֹעֵד.

מַעֲדַי   *n. pers.* Maadai.

מַעֲדְיָה   *n. pers.* Maadiah.

מַעֲדַנִּים   titbits, refreshment.

מַעֲדַנֹּת   fetters.

מַעְדֵּר   hoe.

מֶעָה*   grain.

מֵעָה → מֵעִים.

מָעוֹג   anything baked?

מָעוֹז   place of refuge, mountain stronghold; protection.

מָעוֹךְ   *n. pers.* Maoch.

מָעוֹן I   lurking-place, (place of) residence, dwelling.

מָעוֹן II   *n. pers., n. peop., n. place* Maon.

מְעוּנִים   *n. peop.* Meunites.

מְעוֹנֹתַי   *n. pers.* Meonothai.

מָעוּף*   darkness.

מָעוֹר*   private part.

מָעֹז → מָעוֹז.

מַעַזְיָה(וּ)   *n. pers.* Maaziah.

מָעֹזֵן*   *rd.* מָעוֹז *(Isa. 23.11).*

מעט   *q* be/become few; decrease.
> *pi* become few.
> *hi* make small; *Jer. 10.24; Ezek. 29.15* destroy.

מְעַט   fewness, little; few, a few; moment.

מְעֻטָּה   *rd.* מְרוּטָה *(Ezek. 21.20).*

מַעֲטֶה*   mantle.

מַעֲטָפֶת*   outer garment.

מְעִי   heap.

מֵעִי   *n. pers.* Maai.

מְעִיל   robe.

מֵעִים*   intestines, inward part; belly.

מַעְיָן   site of a spring, spring.

מָעְיָנִים   *rd. Q (I Chron. 4.41).*

מָעַד ‎ *q pt. pass.* crushed, thrust.
pu be handled.

מַעֲכָה ‎ *n. pers. m. and f., n. terr.* Maacah.

מַעֲכַת ‎ *n. terr.* Maacath.

מַעֲכָתִי ‎ *gent.* Maacathite.

מָעַל ‎ *q* be faithless, misappropriate.

I מַעַל ‎ misappropriation, unfaithfulness, apostasy.

II מַעַל ‎ above.

מֹעַל ‎ lifting up.

מַעֲלֶה ‎ ascent, rise; pass; *Neh. 9.4* rostrum.

מַעֲלָה ‎ step; *Pss. 120–134* pilgrimage; *Ezra 7.9* ascent; *Ezek. 11.5* that which arises.

מַעְלָה ‎ upwards; onwards.

מַעֲלֵה עַקְרַבִּים ‎ *n. place* Ascent of the Scorpions.

מַעֲלִיל* ‎ *rd. Q (Zech. 1.4).*

מַעֲלָל* ‎ deed.

מַעֲמָד* ‎ service; position; duty.

מָעֳמָד ‎ footing.

מַעֲמָסָה ‎ *w.* אֶבֶן ‎ heavy stone.

מַעֲמַקִּים ‎ depths.

מַעַן ‎ *always w.* לְ ‎ with regard to; for the sake of, because of; in order that.

I מַעֲנֶה ‎ answer.

II מַעֲנֶה* ‎ purpose.

מַעֲנָה ‎ furrow.

מְעֹנָה ‎ residence, lurking-place.

מַעֲנוֹת* ‎ *rd. Q (Ps. 129.3)* furrow.

מַעַץ ‎ *n. pers.* Maaz.

מַעֲצֵבָה ‎ torment.

מַעֲצָד ‎ bill-hook.

מַעְצוֹר ‎ impediment.

מַעְצָר ‎ mastery.

מַעֲקֶה ‎ parapet.

מַעֲקַשִּׁים ‎ rough country.

מַעַר ‎ nakedness.

I מַעֲרָב* ‎ merchandise.

II מַעֲרָב ‎ setting *(sun)* > west.

מְעָרָה* ‎ surroundings, vicinity.

מְעָרָה I   cave.

מְעָרָה* II   bare ground.

מַעֲרִיץ*   terror.

מַעֲרָךְ*   consideration.

מַעֲרָכָה   row, course; battle-line.

מַעֲרֶכֶת   row, layer, line.

מַעֲרֻמִּים*   naked ones.

מַעֲרָצָה   fright.

מְעָרָת   n. place Maarath.

מַעֲשֶׂה   deed, conduct, work, labour; Isa. 32.17 produce.

מַעֲשַׂי   n. pers. Maasai.

מַעֲשֵׂיָה(וּ)   n. pers. Maaseiah.

מַעֲשֵׂר   a tenth, the tithe.

מַעֲשַׁקּוֹת   extortions.

מֹף   n. place Memphis.

מְפִי(־)בֹשֶׁת   → בֹשֶׁת.

מִפְגָּע   target.

מַפָּח*   expiring.

מַפֻּחַ   bellows.

מְפִי(־)בֹשֶׁת   n. pers. derogatory form of מְרִי־בַעַל Mephibosheth.

מֻפִּים   n. pers. Muppim.

מֵפִיץ   club.

מַפָּל   Amos 8.6 waste; Job 41.15 pendulous underparts.

מִפְלָאָה*   wonderful work.

מִפְלַגָּה*   division.

מַפֵּלָה, מַפָּלָה   ruins, ruin.

מִפְלָט   place of refuge.

מִפְלֶצֶת   abhorrent cult image.

מִפְלָשׂ*   suspension.

מַפֶּלֶת   fall, ruin; Ezek. 31.13 felled trunk; Judg. 14.8 carcass.

מִפְעָל*   deed.

מֵפַעַת   → מֵיפַעַת.

מַפָּץ*   destruction.

מַפֵּץ   hammer.

מִפְקָד   appointment, muster.

מִפְרָץ*   landing-place.

מַפְרֶקֶת*   neck.

מִפְרָשׂ*   sail, layer.

מִפְשָׂעָה buttocks.

מִפְתָּח* opening.

מַפְתֵּחַ key.

מִפְתָּן pedestal, threshold.

מֵץ oppressor.

מֹץ chaff.

מצא *q* attain, meet(with), find; obtain.

ni be found, let oneself be found; be sufficient.

hi bring up to, cause to find; deliver up; *Job 37.13* bring to pass.

מֹצָא → I מוֹצָא.

מַצָּב place of standing, outpost, office.

מֻצָּב *Judg. 9.6* monumental stone; *Isa. 29.3* outpost?

מַצָּבָה outpost, guard.

מַצֵּבָה massebah, monumental stone; *Jer. 43.13* obelisk.

מְצֹבָיָה *gent.?* Mezobaite.

מַצֶּבֶת I *Isa. 6.13* tree-stump.

מַצֶּבֶת II → מַצֵּבָה.

מְצָד place difficult of access; mountain fastness, stronghold.

מְצָדָה, מְצָדָה → מְצוֹדָה II, מְצֻדָה.

מצה *q* squeeze out, drain.

ni be squeezed out, drained.

מַצָּה I unleavened bread, matzah.

מַצָּה II dispute, quarrel.

מֹצָה *n. place* Mozah.

מִצְהָלָה* neighing.

מָצוֹד* noose; *Eccles. 9.14* bulwark.

מְצוּדָה I net; prey.

מְצוּדָה II inaccessible place, mountain stronghold.

מְצוֹדָה net; *Isa. 29.7 dub.*

מִצְוָה order, command, commandment; right.

מְצוּלָה, depth.

מְצוֹלָה*

מָצוֹק affliction.

מָצוּק pillar.

מְצוּקָה affliction.

מָצוֹר I affliction.

מָצוֹר II siege; siege-works.

מָצוֹר III *n. terr.* Egypt.

מְצוּרָה fortress, fortification.

מֵצַח brow.

מִצְחָה* greave.

מְצִלָּה* bell.

מְצָלָה → מְצוֹלָה.

מְצִלְתַּיִם cymbals.

מִצְנֶפֶת turban, head-band.

מַצָּע bed.

מִצְעָד* step; *pl. also* train.

מִצְעָר small, insignificant thing.

מִצְפֶּה I watch-tower.

מִצְפֶּה II *n. place* Mizpeh.

מִצְפָּה *n. place* Mizpah.

מַצְפֻּנִים* hiding-places.

מצץ *q* drink deeply.

מֵצַר affliction.

מְצָרָה → מְצוּרָה.

מִצְרִי *gent.* Egyptian.

מִצְרַיִם *n. terr.* Egypt; *n. peop.* Egyptians.

מַצְרֵף crucible.

מַצֻּת* strife.

מָק, מַק decay, smell of decay.

מַקֶּבֶת I hammer.

מַקֶּבֶת II excavation.

מַקֵּדָה *n. place* Makkedah.

מִקְדָּשׁ holy place, sanctuary; holy thing.

מַקְהֵל* assembly.

מַקְהֵלֹת *n. place* Makheloth.

מִקְוֵא → מִקְוֶה II.

מִקְוֶה I hope.

מִקְוֶה* II collection.

מִקְוָה basin, ditch.

מָקוֹם place, position, abode; region; space; *Eccles. 10.4* post.

מָקוֹר spring.

מִקָּח* taking.

מַקָּחוֹת wares.

מִקְטָר* place of burning.

מְקַטְּרוֹת incense-altars.

מְקְטֶרֶת censer.

מַקֵּל branch, rod; staff, stick.

מִקְלוֹת *n. pers.* Mikloth.

מִקְלָט refuge, asylum.

מִקְלַעַת wood-carving.

מִקְנֶה acquisition, possession; cattle (possessed by one).

מִקְנָה acquisition, purchase.

מִקְנֵיָהוּ *n. pers.* Mikneiah.

מִקְסָם* soothsaying.

מָקַץ *n. place* Makaz.

מִקְצוֹעַ, מִקְצֹעַ corner.

מַקְצֻעָה* rasp.

מִקְצָת → קְצָת.

מקק *ni* rot, fester; rot away, decay; dissolve.

hi make to rot away.

מָקוֹר → מָקוֹר.

מִקְרָא proclamation, convoking festival; *Isa. 4.5 pl.* place of assembly; *Neh. 8.8* reading aloud.

מִקְרֶה chance, happening; fate, condition.

מְקָרֶה beams.

מְקֵרָה cooling.

מִקְשֶׁה hair-curling.

מִקְשָׁה I turned, chased work.

מִקְשָׁה II field of cucumbers.

מִקְשׁוֹת → מוֹקֵשׁ.

מַר I drop.

מַר II bitter, bitterly, embittered.

מֹר myrrh.

מרא I *q* be obstinate.

מרא II *hi* spring up.

מוֹרָא → מוֹרָא.

מָרָא *f. of* II מַר.

מַרְאֶה seeing; look, appearance; apparition, sight, vision; brilliance.

מַרְאָה sight, vision; *Ex. 38.8* mirror.

מֻרְאָה* crop.

מַרְאוֹן *text corr.*

מָרֵאשָׁה   *n. place* Mareshah.

מֵרַאֲשׁוֹת*   head.

מֵרַב   *n. pers. f.* Merab.

מַרְבַדִּים   coverlets.

מִרְבֶּה   capacity.

מַרְבֶּה   increase, abundance.

מַרְבִּית   large number, majority; *Lev. 25.37* usury.

מִרְבָּץ*   resting-place.

מַרְבֵּץ   resting-place.

מַרְבֵּק   fattening, feeding-stuff.

מַרְגּוֹעַ   resting-place.

מַרְגְּלֹת*   foot.

מַרְגֵּמָה   heap of stones.

מַרְגֵּעָה   resting-place.

מרד   *q* revolt, rebel.

מֶרֶד I   revolt.

מֶרֶד II   *n. pers.* Mered.

מַרְדּוּת°   revolt.

מְרֹדָךְ   *n. deity derogatory form of* Marduk.

מְרֹדַךְ בַּלְאֲדָן   *n. pers. derogatory form of* Marduk-baladan.

מָרְדְּכַי, מָרְדֳּכַי   *n. pers.* Mordecai.

מִרְדָּף   persecution?

מרה   *q* be obstinate.

  hi be obstinate.

מֹרָה*   grief, sorrow.

מָרָה   *n. place* Marah.

מָרוּד*   homelessness; homeless.

מֵרוֹז   *n. place* Meroz.

מָרוֹחַ*   crushing.

מָרוֹם   height; high, *also adv.* on high; exalted.

מֵרוֹם   *n. place* Merom.

מֵרוֹץ   running.

מְרוּצָה* I   course, running.

מְרוּצָה II   oppression, extortion.

מְרוּקִים*   beauty treatment.

מָרוֹת   *n. place* Maroth.

מַרְזֵחַ, מִרְזַח*   revelry, cultic feast; noise.

מרח   *q* apply.

מֶרְחָב spacious place, expanse.

מֶרְחָק distance, expanse; *II Sam. 15.17* last.

מַרְחֶשֶׁת cooking-pot.

מרט *q* pull out; whet; wear away.

    ni become bald.

    pu be burnished, be smooth; be whetted.

מְרִי obstinacy.

מְרִיא fatling.

מְרִיב בַּעַל *n. pers.* Meribbaal.

I מְרִיבָה strife.

II מְרִיבָה *n. place* Meribah.

מְרִי־בַעַל *n. pers.* Meribaal.

מְרָיָה *n. pers.* Meraiah.

מֹרִיָּה *n. place* Moriah.

מְרָיוֹת *n. pers.* Meraioth.

מִרְיָם *n. pers. f. (m.? I Chron. 4.17)* Miriam.

מְרִירוּת bitterness, affliction.

מְרִירִי bitter.

מֹרֶךְ faint-heartedness.

מֶרְכָּב *coll.* chariots; saddle, seat.

מֶרְכָּבָה chariot.

מַרְכֹּלֶת market.

I מִרְמָה fraud, treachery.

II מִרְמָה *n. pers.* Mirmah.

מְרֵמוֹת *n. pers.* Meremoth.

מִרְמָס that which is trampled, trampled ground.

מֵרֹנֹתִי *gent.* Meronothite.

מֶרֶס *n. pers.* Meres.

מַרְסְנָא *n. pers.* Marsena.

מֵרַע evil.

מֵרֵעַ* friend.

מִרְעֶה pasture; fodder.

מַרְעִית pasturage; flock.

מַרְעֲלָה *n. place* Maralah.

I מַרְפֵּא healing.

II מַרְפֵּא calmness.

מַרְפֵּה → I מַרְפֵּא.

מַרְפֵּשׂ* that which is turbid.

מרץ   *ni* be crippling, devastating.

     hi provoke.

מְרֻצָּה   → I מְרוּצָה.

מַרְצֵעַ   awl.

מַרְצֶפֶת   pavement.

מרק   *q* polish, burnish.

     pu be scoured.

     hi cleanse, purify.

מָרָק   broth.

מֶרְקָח*   spice.

מִרְקָחָה   ointment; ointment-pot.

מִרְקַחַת   ointment-mixture.

מרר   *q* be/become bitter; be incensed; be embittered; be in
       despair.

     pi make bitter, provoke; *w.* בְּכִי weep bitterly.

     hi afflict, embitter; lament bitterly.

     hitpalp be enraged.

מַר*   bitter.

מְרֵרָה*   gall.

מְרֹרָה*   gall; poison.

מְרָרִי   *n. pers.* Merari; *gent.* Merarite.

מָרֵשָׁה   *n. pers.*, *n. place* Mareshah.

מִרְשַׁעַת   infamy; *fig.* infamous woman.

מוֹרַשְׁתִּי   → מוֹרַשְׁתִּי.

מְרָתַיִם   double obstinacy; *derogatory form of* Babylon.

I מַשָּׂא   bearing; burden; tribute; *Ezek. 24.25* longing.

II מַשָּׂא   utterance.

III מַשָּׂא   *n. pers.* Massa.

מַשֹּׂא   partiality.

מַשְׂאָה   lifting up.

מַשְׂאוֹת   *Aram. inf. of* נשׂא *(q)*.

מַשְׂאֵת   lifting up, ascending; signal; burden; tax; gift, present.

מִשְׂגָּב   high ground, refuge.

מַשְׂגֶּנֶת   *pt. hi of* נשׂג

מְשׂוּכָה*   thorn-hedge.

מַשּׂוֹר   saw.

מְשׂוּרָה   measure *(for liquids)*.

מָשׂושׂ joy.

מִשְׂחָק laughter.

מַשְׂטֵמָה enmity.

מְשׂוּכָה* thorn-hedge.

מַשְׂכִּיל *designation of a song.*

מַשְׂכִּית figure, image, imagination.

מַשְׂכֹּרֶת* wages.

מַשְׂמֵרָה* nail.

מִשְׂפָּח breach of law.

מִשְׂרָה dominion.

מִשְׂרָפוֹת* burning.

מִשְׂרְפ(וֹ)ת מַיִם *n. place* Misrephoth-maim.

מַשְׂרֵקָה *n. place* Masrekah.

מַשְׂרֵת pan.

מָשׁ *n. pers.* Mash.

מַשָּׁא debt, usury.

מֵשָׁא *n. place* Mesha.

מַשְׁאָב* watering-channel.

מַשָּׁאָה* debt.

מַשֻּׁאָה → מְשׁוֹאָה.

מַשָּׁאָה* ruins.

מַשָּׁאוֹן deception.

מִשְׁאָל *n. place* Mishal.

מִשְׁאָלָה* request.

מִשְׁאֶרֶת* kneading-trough.

מְשׁוּבָה turning away, apostasy, faithlessness.

מְשֻׁבָּצוֹת settings; *Ps. 45.14 dub.*

מַשְׁבֵּר mouth of the womb.

מִשְׁבָּר* breakers.

מִשְׁבָּת* ruin.

מִשְׁגֶּה inadvertence.

מֹשֶׁה *q* draw out.
hi draw out.

מֹשֶׁה *n. pers.* Moses.

מַשֶּׁה* loan.

מְשׁוֹאָה devastation.

מַשֻּׁאוֹת ruins.

מְשׁוֹבָב *n. pers.* Meshobab.

מְשׁוּבָה → מְשֻׁבָה.

מְשֻׁגָּה* error.

מָשׁוֹט, מִשּׁוֹט* oar.

מְשׁוּקָה rd. Q (Isa. 42.24).

מָשַׁח q smear, anoint.

    ni be anointed.

מִשְׁחָה I anointing.

מִשְׁחָה* II portion.

מָשְׁחָה I anointing.

מָשְׁחָה II portion.

מַשְׁחִית coll. destroyers; destruction; Jer. 5.26 trap.

מִשְׁחָר early morning?

מַשְׁחֵת* destruction.

מִשְׁחָת* disfigurement.

מָשְׁחָת* defect.

מִשְׁטוֹחַ, drying-ground.

מִשְׁטַח*

מִשְׁטָר* writing.

מֶשִׁי fine fabric, silk?

מֵשִׁי →מוּשִׁי.

מְשֵׁיזַבְאֵל n. pers. Meshezabel.

מָשִׁיחַ anointed, anointed one.

מָשַׁךְ q draw, drag along; prolong, maintain; have patience, be stead-

    fast; draw (the bow); sound (the horn).

    ni be delayed.

    pu pt. long-drawn-out, tall; long protracted.

מֶשֶׁךְ I bag.

מֶשֶׁךְ II n. peop. Meshech.

מִשְׁכָּב lying, intercourse; couch; sick-bed.

מֹשְׁכוֹת fetters.

מִשְׁכָּן dwelling.

מָשַׁל I q compose/utter a proverb, parable.

    ni become like.

    pi constantly utter proverbs.

    hi compare.

    hitp become like, similar.

מָשַׁל II	*q* rule.
	hi cause to rule.
מָשָׁל I	saying, proverb; parable; lampoon, mocking-song.
מָשָׁל II	*n. place* Mashal.
מֹשֶׁל* I	the like.
מֹשֶׁל* II	dominion.
מִשְׁלוֹחַ, מִשְׁלֹחַ	sending; *w.* יָד possession.
מִשְׁלָח*	*w.* יָד undertaking, acquisition; *Isa. 7.25* pasture whither cattle are driven.
מִשְׁלַחַת	band; discharge.
מְשֻׁלָּם	*n. pers.* Meshullam.
מְשִׁלֵּמוֹת	*n. pers.* Meshillemoth.
מְשֶׁלֶמְיָה(וּ)	*n. pers.* Meshelemiah.
מְשֶׁלֶּמִית	*n. pers.* Meshillemith.
מְשֻׁלֶּמֶת	*n. pers. f.* Meshullemeth.
מְשַׁמָּה	devastation; *pl.* devastated area; horror.
מִשְׁמָן*	fatness; *pl.* robust people, fertile tracts of land.
מִשְׁמַנָּה	*n. pers.* Mishmannah.
מַשְׁמַנִּים	rich foods.
מִשְׁמָע* I	rumour.
מִשְׁמָע II	*n. pers.* Mishma.
מִשְׁמַעַת*	bodyguard; *Isa. 11.14* subjects.
מִשְׁמָר	guard, sentinel; detachment; *pl.* service; custody, confinement, prison; *Prov. 4.23* vigilance.
מִשְׁמֶרֶת	guard, sentinel; detachment; *pl.* service; observance; obligation, service.
מִשְׁנֶה	the second, second *(of part, rank, position, litter)*; double; duplicate, copy; *w.* עַל twice as much as.
מִשְׁסָּה	plundering, booty.
מִשְׁעוֹל	narrow defile.
מִשְׁעִי	cleansing?
מִשְׁעָם	*n. pers.* Misham.
מִשְׁעָן	support.
מַשְׁעֵן	support.
מַשְׁעֵנָה	support, staff.
מִשְׁעֶנֶת	support, staff.
מִשְׁפָּחָה	family, clan; association; species.

מִשְׁפָּט judgment, legal process; arbiter's decision, verdict, sentence; ruling; legal case, right, legal claim; > suitability, what is right; duty, obligation; manner; mode of life, custom, conduct; *II Kings 1.7* appearance.

מִשְׁפְּתַיִם saddle-bags.

מֶשֶׁק possession?

מַשָּׁק* attack.

מַשְׁקֶה cup-bearer; drink; well-watered region.

מִשְׁקוֹל weight.

מַשְׁקוֹף lintel.

מִשְׁקָל weight.

מִשְׁקֹלֶת, level.
מִשְׁקֶלֶת

מִשְׁקָע* clear water.

מִשְׁרָה* juice.

מֵישָׁרִים → מֵישָׁרִים.

מִשְׁרָעִי *gent.* Mishraite.

משׁשׁ *q* feel.
pi investigate by feel, search thoroughly; grope.
hi feel all round, let feel.

מִשְׁתֶּה drinking; revelry; drinks; banquet.

מֵת dead, corpse.

מַת* *pl.* men, people.

מַתְבֵּן heap of straw.

מֶתֶג bridle.

מָתוֹק sweet.

מְתוּשָׁאֵל *n. pers.* Methushael.

מְתוּשֶׁלַח *n. pers.* Methuselah.

מתח *q* spread out.

מָתַי when?

מַתְכֹּנֶת proportion, tally.

מַה־תִּלָּאָה > מֶה־תְּלָאָה.

מְתַלְּעוֹת jawbones.

מְתֹם uninjured, sound spot.

מַתָּן I gift, present.

מַתָּן II *n. pers.* Mattan.

מַתָּנָה I present, gift.

מַתָּנָה II *n. place* Mattanah.

מִתְנִי *gent.* Mithnite.

מַתְּנַי *n. pers.* Mattenai.

מַתַּנְיָה(וּ) *n. pers.* Mattaniah.

מָתְנַיִם loins, hips, small of the back.

מתק *q* be/become sweet; *Job 24.20* feast upon.

    hi make sweet; taste sweet.

מֹתֶק* sweetness.

מֶתֶק* sweet.

מִתְקָה *n. place* Mithkah.

מִתְרְדָת *n. pers.* Mithredath.

מַתָּת gift.

מַתַּתָּה *n. pers.* Mattattah.

מַתִּתְיָה(וּ) *n. pers.* Mattithiah.

נ

נָא I *particle of request or encouragement.*

נָא II raw.

נֹא *n. place* No, Thebes.

נֹאד leathern bottle.

נאה (נאו) *q* be lovely, beautiful.

נָאוֶה the seemly, proper.

נָאוֶה beautiful, lovely; seemly.

נִאוּפִים adultery.

נָאוֹת *pl. of* I נָוֶה.

נאם *q* speak.

נְאֻם saying.

נאף *q* commit adultery.

    pi commit adultery.

נַאֲפוּפִים* marks of adultery.

נַאֲפִים → נִאוּפִים.

נאץ *q* despise, reject.

    pi treat with contempt.

    hitpo pt. abused.

נְאָצָה humiliation.

נֶאָצָה* abuse.

נאק *q* groan.

נְאָקָה* groaning.

נאר *pi* abandon, annul; desecrate.

נֹב *n. place* Nob.

נבא *ni* appear as a prophet, speak as a prophet; be in ecstasy; *I Chron. 25.1–3* play in ecstatic state.

hitp behave as a prophet, rave; speak as a prophet.

נבב *q pt. pass.* hollow; *fig.* stupid.

נְבוֹ *n. deity* Nebo *(name of a Bab. god)*; *n. place* Nebo.

נְבוּאָה prophetic word; prophetic writing.

נְבוּזַרְאֲדָן *n. pers.* Nebuzaradan.

נְבוּכַדְנֶאצַּר, *n. pers.* Nebuchadnezzar; *Jer. 49.28*; *Ezra 2.1* rd. Q.
נְבוּכַדְנֶצַּר,
נְבוּכַדְרֶאצַּר

נְבוּשַׁזְ־בָּן *n. pers.* Nebushazban.

נָבוֹת *n. pers.* Naboth.

נבח *q* bark.

נֹבַח *n. pers., n. place* Nobah.

נִבְחַז *n. pers.* Nibhaz.

נבט *pi* look.

hi look, look up; see, look at, look towards; behold; regard; heed.

נְבָט *n. pers.* Nebat.

נָבִיא prophet.

נְבִיאָה prophetess.

נְבָיוֹת, נְבָיֹת *n. pers., n. peop.* Nebaioth.

נְבְכַדְנֶאצַּר, → נְבוּכַדְנֶאצַּר.
נְבְכַדְנֶצַּר

נֵבֶךְ* spring?; bottom?

נבל I *q* wither, break down.

נבל II *q* be foolish.

pi treat contemptuously.

נָבָל I foolish; godless.

נָבָל II *n. pers.* Nabal.

נֵבֶל I jar.

נֵבֶל, נֶבֶל II harp.

נְבָלָה folly, foolishness; sin.

נְבֵלָה corpse, carcass.

נִבְלוּת* private parts.

נְבַלָּט n. *place* Neballat.

נבע *q* gush.
    hi cause to gush, gush out.

נִבְשָׁן n. *place* Nibshan.

נֶגֶב arid land; south-land; south; n. *terr.* Negeb.

נגד *hi* bring forward, report, tell, inform; solve, explain.
    ho be told.

נֶגֶד in the sight of, before, opposite, straight ahead; corresponding
    to; *w.* לְ in front of, facing, towards, present to, before, with
    regard to; *w.* מִן away from, far from, opposite; *adv.* opposite,
    beyond, aside.

נגה *q* shine, gleam.
    hi light up.

I נֹגַהּ brightness, clear light.

II נֹגַהּ n. *pers.* Nogah.

נְגֹהָה* brightness.

נגח *q* gore.
    pi gore, butt, knock down.
    hitp clash.

נַגָּח liable to gore.

נָגִיד chief, leader.

נְגִינָה* string music; mocking-song; *stringed instrument?*

נגן *q* play *(stringed instrument)*.
    pi play *(stringed instrument)*.

נגע *q* touch, harm, hurt, strike; extend; reach; arrive.
    ni be defeated.
    pi strike, hit.
    pu be stricken.
    hi touch, reach; cause to touch; come up to, come to; attain,
       approach; *Lev. 5.7* afford, give.

נֶגַע blow, plague; mark.

נגף *q* knock, strike, strike dead.

ni be defeated.

hitp trip.

נֶגֶף plague, blow; collision.

נגר *ni* run, flow; *Ps. 77.3* be stretched out.

hi pour out; give over; *Micah 1.6* throw down.

ho be poured out.

נגשׂ *q* press, drive; exact; *pt.* tyrant.

ni oppress one another; be hard pressed, harassed.

נגשׁ *q* draw near, approach; present oneself; *Gen. 19.9 w.* הָלְאָה move out of the way; *Job 41.8* join together.

ni approach, draw near; *Amos 9.13* overtake.

hi bring, offer, produce, bring forward.

ho be brought, offered.

hitp approach.

נֵד dam, dike.

נֹד* *Ps. 56.9 unexplained.*

נדא *q or hi* divert.

נדב *q* prompt.

hitp volunteer; enlist, present oneself voluntarily; give voluntarily.

נָדָב *n. pers.* Nadab.

נְדָבָה free choice, voluntariness; freewill offering; *Ps. 68.10 w.* גֶּשֶׁם abundant rain.

נְדַבְיָה *n. pers.* Nedabiah.

נדד *q* flee, take to flight; wander about; *Isa. 10.14* flap up and down, beat.

poel flee away.

hi drive out.

ho be chased away, be blown away.

נְדֻדִים restlessness.

נדה *pi* exclude; imagine to be distant.

נֶדֶה gift, fee.

נִדָּה abhorrent thing, impurity; menstruation.

נדח *q* wield.

ni be scattered, driven away, banished; be diverted, misled; *Deut. 19.5* swing.

pu pt. banished.

hi scatter, drive asunder; divert; drive away; mislead, expel;

II Sam. 15.14 bring.

ho pt. scared away.

נָדִיב   willing, ready; noble.

נְדִיבָה*   dignity; *pl.* that which is noble.

I נָדָן*   sheath.

II נֵדֶן*   gift, reward for love-making.

נדף   *q* blow about, blow away, scatter.

     ni be blown away.

נדר   *q* make a vow, vow.

נֵדֶר, נֶדֶר   vow.

נֹהַּ   splendour?

I נהג   *q* drive, drive away, drive on; lead, lead out.

     pi lead away, lead; make to drive.

II נהג   *pi* moan.

נהה   *q* lament.

     ni lament.

נְהִי   lamentation.

נהל   *pi* conduct, transport; provide.

     hitp proceed.

נַהֲלָל   *n. place* Nahalal.

I נַהֲלֹל*   watering-place.

II נַהֲלֹל   *n. place* Nahalol.

נהם   *q* growl; groan.

נַהַם   growling.

נְהָמָה*   roaring; groaning.

נהק   *q* bray, cry.

I נהר   *q* stream.

II נהר°   *q* shine, beam.

נָהָר   stream, river; current; *frequently* Euphrates; *Dan. 10.4* Tigris.

נְהָרָה°   daylight.

אֲרַם נַהֲרַיִם ← נַהֲרַיִם.

נוא   *q rd. Q (Num. 32.7).*

     hi prevent, hinder.

נוב   *q* increase.

     pol make to grow, thrive.

נוֹב   *rd. Q (Isa. 57.19).*

נוֹבַי   *n. pers. rd. Q (Neh. 10.20)* Nebai.

נוּג*   distressed.

נוּד *q* sway; be/become aimless, homeless; show sympathy.
hi make homeless; shake.
hitpo sway to and fro; shake oneself; lament.

נוֹד *n. terr.* Nod.

נוֹדָב *n. pers. or n. peop.* Nodab.

I נוה *q* achieve the aim?

II נוה *hi* praise.

I נָוֶה pasturage; abode.

II נָוֶה* beautiful, lovely.

נָוֶה* abode.

נָוֹת *unexplained*.

נוח *q* settle, rest, repose; have rest, wait; *Isa. 7.2; Ps. 125.3* be
friendly, make an agreement.
hi rest; give repose, rest; still, satisfy; *Aram. forms:* put, place,
lay; lay aside, deposit; leave; leave behind; allow; leave
alone; let do; let act.
ho be given rest; *Aram. forms: pt.* left empty, vacant; *Zech. 5.11*
text corr.

נוֹחַ rest.

נוֹחָה *n. pers.* Nohah.

נוט *q* be terrified?, reel?

נָוִית *unexplained*.

נום *q* slumber.

נוּמָה somnolence.

נוּן, נֹון *n. pers.* Nun.

נוס *q* flee.
pol drive.
hi put to flight; take to flight.

נוע *q* shake, dangle; tremble; be vagrant, homeless.
ni be shaken.
hi make to stagger, shake; shake up; make homeless; *II Kings
23.18* disturb.

נוֹעַדְיָה *n. pers. m. and f.* Noadiah.

I נוּף   *hi* move to and fro, wield, brandish; present a wave-offering.
         ho be waved in consecration.
         pol brandish.

II נוּף   *q* sprinkle.
         hi shed.

נוֹף   loftiness?

נוֹצָה   pinions, plumage.

נוק   *hi rd.* וַתֵּינָקֵהוּ (*Ex. 2.9*).

נושׁ   *q Ps. 69.21 text corr.*

נזה   *q* spurt.
         hi cause to spurt, sprinkle.

נָזִיד   that which has been boiled, dish.

נָזִיר   prince; one consecrated, Nazirite; *Lev. 25.5,11* unpruned
         vine.

נזל   *q* trickle, flow, overflow; *pt. pl. also* floods.
         hi cause to flow.

נֶזֶם   ring.

נֶזֶק°   trouble.

נזר   *ni* dedicate oneself; abstain, fast; display propriety.
         hi dedicate oneself; abstain; *Lev. 15.31* hold back.

נֵזֶר   consecration; headband, diadem.

נֹחַ   *n. pers.* Noah.

נַחְבִּי   *n. pers.* Nahbi.

נחה   *q* lead, guide.
         hi direct, guide.

נְחוּם   *n. pers.* Nehum.

נַחוּם   *n. pers.* Nahum.

נְחוּמִים   → נִחֻמִים.

נָחוֹר   *n. pers.* Nahor.

נָחוּשׁ   bronze.

נְחוּשָׁה   bronze, copper.

נְחִילָה*   *musical direction*; flute-playing?

נְחִירַיִם*   nostrils.

נחל   *q* get as a possession; take possession of; assign as a possession;
         own property.
         pi assign, allocate as a possession; put in possession of.

hitp get possession; obtain possession for oneself; get as a possession by allocation; bequeath.

hi give as a possession; place in one's inheritance; hand down as an inheritance.

ho be made possessor, heir.

נַחַל   valley of a stream, watercourse, stream; *Job 28.4* shaft.

נַחֲלָה   possession, share in possession, inheritance.

נַחֲלִיאֵל   *n. place* Nahaliel.

נְחֶלָמִי   *gent.* Nehelamite.

נחם   *ni* allow oneself to be sorry, repent; take comfort, allow oneself to be comforted; observe the period of mourning; *Isa. 1.24* take vengeance.

pi comfort.

pu be comforted.

hitp allow oneself to feel sorry; take comfort; take vengeance.

נַחַם   *n. pers.* Naham.

נֹחַם   pity.

נֶחָמָה*   comfort.

נְחֶמְיָה   *n. pers.* Nehemiah.

נִחֻמִים   comfort.

נַחֲמָנִי   *n. pers.* Nahamani.

נַחְנוּ   we.

נֶחְנְתְּ   *pf. ni of* אנח.

נָחוּץ   *q pt. pass.* urgent.

נחר   *q* snort.

pi snort.

נַחַר*   snorting.

נַחֲרָה*   snorting.

נַחֲרַי   *n. pers.* Naharai.

נחשׁ   *pi* seek an omen, divine; *Gen. 30.27* know from omens; *I Kings 20.33* take as a good omen.

נַחַשׁ   enchantment.

I נָחָשׁ   serpent.

II נָחָשׁ   *n. pers.* Nahash.

נְחֻשָׁה   → נְחוּשָׁה.

נַחְשׁוֹן   *n. pers.* Nahshon.

I נְחֹשֶׁת   copper, bronze; bronze fetter.

II נְחֹשֶׁת*   menstruation.

נְחֻשְׁתָּא   *n. pers. f.* Nehushta.

נְחֻשְׁתָּן   *serpent-idol* Nehushtan.

נחת°   *q* descend; *Prov. 17.10* affect more deeply.

     ni sink.

     pi press down, bend *(bow)*; smooth.

     hi lead down.

I   נַחַת°   descending.

II   נַחַת   rest, calmness; *Isa. 30.15* covenant loyalty; *Prov. 29.9* recon-
     ciliation.

III   נַחַת   *n. pers.* Nahath.

נָחֵת*   descending.

נטה   *q* stretch out; pitch, stretch, spread out > lengthen; bend,
     incline, bend towards, press against; turn aside, turn
     towards.

     ni be stretched; be long extended.

     hi stretch out, stretch oneself out; spread out; pitch; extend;
     incline; pervert; divert, lead astray, seduce; convey;
     prevent, push aside, drive aside, repulse; deviate, turn
     aside.

     ho pt. outspread, repulsed.

נְטוֹפָתִי   *gent.* Netophathite.

נָטִיל*   weighing out.

נְטִיפָה   → נְטִפָה.

נְטִישׁוֹת   tendrils.

נטל   *q* impose; *Isa. 40.15* weigh.

     pi lift up.

נֵטֶל   burden.

נטע   *q* plant, implant; drive in.

     ni be implanted.

נֶטַע   planting, plant.

נְטָעִים   plants.

נְטָעִים   *n. place* Netaim.

נטף   *q* drop, drip.

     hi make to drip; make to flow *(words)*, drivel.

נָטָף   drops, drops of resin.

נְטֹפָה   *n. place* Netophah.

נְטִפָה*   earring.

נְטֹפָתִי   → נְטוֹפָתִי.

נטר I°   *q* guard, keep.

נטר II   *q* be angry, have a grudge against.

נטש   *q* leave, leave to another, deposit, abandon; disregard, desist from, forgo; *Gen. 31.28* give opportunity; *I Sam. 30.16 pt. pass.* scattered; *Isa. 21.15* draw; *Ezek. 29.5* leave to one's fate; *Hos. 12.15* let weigh upon; *I Sam. 4.2 unexplained.*

    ni roam; grow luxuriantly; hang slack; lie disregarded.

    pu be neglected.

נִי*   lamentation.

נִיב   fruit.

נִיד   condolence.

נִידָה   object of aversion.

נִיחוֹחַ, נִיחֹחַ   soothing.

נִין   *ni* sprout?

נִין   offspring; descendants.

נִינְוֵה   *n. place* Nineveh.

נִיסָן   Nisan *(name of a month, March/April)*.

נִיצוֹץ   spark.

ניר   *q* bring into cultivation.

נִיר I   lamp; lasting existence.

נִיר II   newly broken ground.

נֵיר   → I נֵר.

נכא   *ni* be whipped out.

נָכָא*   shattered.

נָכֵא*   dejected.

נְכֹאת   ladanum resin.

נֶכֶד   descendants.

נכה   *ni* be struck down.

    pu be battered down.

    hi strike, dash to pieces, strike down, kill, smite, pierce, wound.

    ho be beaten, struck down, smitten, conquered.

נָכֶה*   crippled; dejected.

נֵכֶה*   striking?, stricken?

נְכֹה, נְכוֹ   *n. pers.* Neco.

נָכוֹן I   blow.

נָכוֹן II   n. pers., n. place? Nacon.

נֹכַח   over against; straight ahead; opposite, before, in the sight of; w. אֶל directly towards; w. ? directly in front of, on behalf of; w. עַד as far as opposite.

נָכֹחַ*   straight, right; the straight, the right, straight away.

נכל   q act deceitfully.

pi act craftily.

hitp behave craftily.

נֵכֶל*   craftiness.

נְכָסִים   treasures, riches; wealth.

נכר I   ni dissemble.

pi misunderstand; make unrecognizable.

hitp disguise oneself, pretend.

נכר II   ni be recognized.

pi regard, consider carefully.

hi look at carefully, examine; recognize, acknowledge; know, understand; wish to know; w.פָּנִים show partiality.

hitp make oneself known.

נֹכֶר*, נֵכֶר   misfortune.

נֵכָר   foreignness, foreign land.

נָכְרִי   alien, foreign; foreigner; Isa. 28.21 surprising.

נְכֹת*   w.בֵּית treasure-house.

נלה   rd.כְּבַלֹּתְךָ (Isa. 33.1).

נְמִבְזָה   rd.נִבְזָה (I Sam. 15.9).

נְמוּאֵל   n. pers. Nemuel.

נְמוּאֵלִי   gent. Nemuelite.

נְמָלָה   ant.

נָמֵר   leopard.

נִמְרֹד   n. pers. Nimrod.

נִמְרָה   n. place Nimrah.

נִמְרוֹד   → נִמְרֹד.

נִמְרִים   n. place Nimrim.

נִמְשִׁי   n. pers. Nimshi.

נֵס   signal-pole, standard, sign; sail.

נְסִבָּה   turn of events, disposing.

נְסֵה   imv. q of נשׂא.

נסה   *pi* put to the test, try, attempt; give something a trial.

נסח   *q* tear down, tear out.

    ni be driven out.

נָסִיךְ*   drink-offering; cast image; one consecrated, leader, prince.

נסך I   *q* pour out; consecrate; cast *(cast image)*.

    ni be installed.

    pi pour out.

    hi pour out.

    ho be poured out.

נסך II   *q* weave.

נֶסֶךְ, נֵסֶךְ   drink-offering; cast image.

נסס   *q* falter.

    hitpo glitter, sparkle; *Ps. 60.6 dub.*

נסע   *q* pull out; set out, march on; *Num. 11.31* burst out.

    ni be pulled up, snapped.

    hi pull up, quarry *(stones)*; make to set out, rush out; *II Kings 4.4* remove.

נִסְרֹךְ   *n. deity* Nisroch *(name of an Assyr. god).*

נֵעָה   *n. place* Neah.

נֹעָה   *n. pers. f.* Noah.

נְעוּרִים   early life, youth.

נְעִיאֵל   *n. place* Neiel.

נָעִים   pleasant, lovely, charming; *Job 36.11* delight.

נעל   *q* tie up, lock; tie on *(sandals).*

    hi provide with footwear.

נַעַל   *f.* sandal.

נעם   *q* be pleasant, lovely, charming.

נַעַם   *n. pers.* Naam.

נֹעַם   kindness, pleasantness.

נַעֲמָה   *n. pers. f.*, *n. place* Naamah.

נָעֳמִי   *n. pers. f.* Naomi.

נַעֲמִי   *gent.* Naamite.

נַעֲמָן   *n. pers.* Naaman.

נַעֲמָנִים   *w.* נִטְעֵי Adonis-gardens.

נַעֲמָתִי   *gent.* Naamathite.

נַעֲצוּץ   thorn-bush.

נֶ֫עַר I *q* growl.

נֶ֫עַר II *q* shake.

ni shake oneself free; be shaken off.

pi shake into; shake out; shake off.

hitp shake oneself free.

נַ֫עַר boy, lad, young man; servant, retainer; *pl. also* young people; *Gen. 24; 34; Deut. 22 rd. Q; Zech. 11.16 dub.*

נֹ֫עַר youth.

נַעֲרָה I young girl; maidservant; young married woman; prostitute?

נַעֲרָה II *n. pers. f., n. place* Naarah.

נְעָרוֹת* youth.

נַעֲרַי *n. pers.* Naarai.

נְעַרְיָה *n. pers.* Neariah.

נְעָרִים → נְעוּרִים.

נַעֲרָן *n. place* Naaran.

נְעֹ֫רֶת tow.

נֹף *n. place* Noph, Memphis.

נֶ֫פֶג *n. pers.* Nepheg.

נָפָה* yoke; mountain-ridge.

נְפוּשְׁסִים *n. pers. rd. Q (Neh. 7.52)* Nephishesim.

נפח *q* blow, blow upon; fan; pant.

pu be fanned.

hi cause to pant.

נֹ֫פַח *n. place* Nophah.

נְפִילִים giants.

נְפִיסִים *n. pers. rd. Q (Ezra 2.50)* Nephusim.

נָפִישׁ *n. pers.* Naphish.

נֹ֫פֶךְ *semi-precious stone* turquoise?, malachite?

נפל *q* fall, be inferior, collapse; be downcast; be nullified; fall down, throw oneself down; dismount; desert, defect; *Isa. 26.18* be born.

hi cause to fall, bring down, fell; cast; knock out; discontinue; bear.

hitp attack; prostrate oneself.

pil rd. נָפַל *(Ezek. 28.23).*

נֵ֫פֶל miscarriage.

נְפִלִים → נְפִילִים.

נפץ   *q* shatter; be shattered, scatter.
     pi shatter.
     pu pt. crushed.

נֶפֶץ   cloudburst.

נפשׁ   *ni* draw breath, breathe freely.

נֶפֶשׁ   throat; breath, breathing; being; life; soul *(not in the Greek sense)*, person, self; human beings, people; desire, feeling, mood, will; dead person.

נֵפֶת   high ground?

נֹפֶת   honey from the comb.

נֶפְתּוֹחַ   *n. place* Nephtoah.

נִפְתּוּלִים*   struggles.

נַפְתֻּחִים   *n. peop.* Naphtuhim.

נַפְתָּלִי   *n. pers., n. peop.* Naphtali.

I נֵץ   falcon.

II נֵץ*   blossom.

נָצָא   *q* fly?

נצב   *ni* take one's stand, be stationed, stand; *pt. also* governor.
     hi set up, erect; set apart, fix, establish.
     ho be set up.

נָצָב   handle, hilt.

I נצה   *q Lam. 4.15* set out?

II נצה   *ni* struggle.
     hi struggle.

III נצה   *q* be devastated.
     ni be devastated.

נִצָּה   blossom.

I נֹצָה*   filth.

II נֹצָה   → נוֹצָה.

נְצוּרִים   *rd.* בֵּין צוּרִים *(Isa. 65.4).*

נצח   *ni pt.* lasting, persistent.
     pi direct, supervise; *I Chron. 15.21* accompany?; *pt. also liturgical direction* choirmaster?, director?

I נֶצַח, נֵצַח   splendour; enduring; *adv.* continually, for ever; *w.* לְ continually, for ever.

II נֶצַח*   spurt of blood.

נָצִיב I   pillar; outpost, garrison; governor.

נָצִיב II   n. place Nezib.

נְצִיחַ   n. pers. Neziah.

נְצִירֵי   rd. Q (Isa. 49.6).

נצל   ni save oneself, be saved.

    pi plunder; extricate, save.

    hi snatch away, take away; save.

    ho be snatched.

    hitp rid oneself of.

נִצָּנִים   flowers.

נצץ   q sparkle.

    hi blossom.

נצר   q guard, preserve, keep, observe; pt. also watchman; pt. pass.
    preserved, something kept in reserve.

נֵצֶר   sprout, shoot.

נקב   q bore, pierce; point > fix, designate; distinguish; Lev. 24.11,16
    blaspheme.

    ni be specified.

נֶקֶב I   perforated piece of jewellery?

נֶקֶב II   → אֲדָמִי הַנֶּקֶב.

נְקֵבָה   woman, female.

נָקֹד   speckled.

נֹקֵד   sheep-breeder.

נְקֻדָּה*   (glass)bead.

נִקֻּדִים   bread-crumbs; something baked.

נקה   q Jer. 49.12 inf. abs. in conjunction with ni.

    ni be free, exempt; be guiltless, innocent; remain unpunished;
    Isa. 3.26 be deprived.

    pi pronounce to be guiltless, acquit; leave unpunished.

נְקוֹדָא   n. pers. Nekoda.

נָקִי, נָקִיא   exempt, free; free from responsibility, guilt; guiltless.

נִקָּיוֹן   cleanness, bareness; innocence.

נָקִיק*   cleft.

נקם   q take vengeance, avenge oneself; avenge.

    ni be avenged; avenge oneself; procure vengeance.

    pi avenge.

ho be avenged; come under vengeance.

hitp avenge oneself.

נָקָם vengeance.

נְקָמָה vengeance, vindictiveness.

נקע *q* turn away from, be disgusted.

I נקף *pi* cut off.

II נקף *q* revolve.

hi move round; encircle, surround, besiege; *Lev. 19.27* trim round about; *Isa. 15.8* penetrate throughout; *Job 1.5* be completed (in sequence).

נֹקֶף beating.

נִקְפָּה rope.

נקר *q* gouge, pick out.

pi gouge, bore out.

pu be bored out.

נְקָרָה* hole.

נקשׁ *q* become entangled?

ni be caught, ensnared.

pi lay snares.

hitp lay snares.

I נֵר lamp.

II נֵר *n. pers.* Ner.

נִר → I נִיר.

נֵרְגַל *n. deity* Nergal *(name of a city-god).*

נֵרְגַל שַׁר־אֶצֶר *n. pers.* Nergalsarezer.

נֵרְדְּ nard.

נֵרִיָּה(וּ) *n. pers.* Neriah.

נשא *q* lift, raise, pick up, lift high; lift up, give utterance; carry, bear, carry away; take, take away, forgive; bring; number, count; *w.* פָּנִים receive kindly, show consideration for, show partiality, favouritism, *pt. pass. also* esteemed; *w.* נֶפֶשׁ long for, desire; *w.* לֵב be willing, be presumptuous.

ni raise oneself; be elevated, lifted up, be/become exalted; be carried, carried off.

pi raise, lift up; carry, assist; *w.* נֶפֶשׁ long.

hi make to carry.

hitp rise up.

נשׁג   *hi* reach, overtake; be able to afford; prosper; come true, come upon.

נְשׂוּאָה*   burden.

נָשִׂיא I   chief, prince.

נָשִׂיא* II   damp fog.

נשׂק   *ni* be kindled.

     hi kindle.

נשׁא I   *q* lend; practise usury; *pt. also* creditor.

     hi lend.

נשׁא II   *ni* be duped.

     hi dupe, deceive; attack, invade.

נשׁב   *q* blow.

     hi cause to blow; drive off.

נשׁה I   *q* forget.

     ni be forgotten.

     pi cause to forget.

     hi cause to forget.

נשׁה II   → נשׁא I.

נָשֶׁה   region of the hips.

נְשִׁי*   debt.

נְשִׁיָּה   forgetting.

נָשִׁים   *pl. of* אִשָּׁה.

נְשִׁיקָה*   kiss.

נשׁך I   *q* bite.

     pi bite.

נשׁך II   *q* demand interest.

     hi exact interest.

נֶשֶׁךְ   interest.

נִשְׁכָּה   room, cell.

נשׁל   *q* loosen; take off; detach, drive away; detach itself, fall off.

     pi drive away.

נשׁם   *q* pant.

נְשָׁמָה   blowing, breath, breathing; *pl.* beings, souls.

נשׁף   *q* blow, blow upon.

נֶשֶׁף   twilight.

נשק I   *q* kiss.

       ni kiss.

       hi be in close contact.

נשק II   *q* arm oneself.

נֶשֶׁק, נֵשֶׁק   equipment, weapons.

נֶשֶׁר   eagle, vulture.

נשת   *q* dry up, be parched.

       ni be dried up, be parched.

נִשְׁתְּוָן   letter.

נְתוּנִים   rd. Q *(Ezra 8.17)*.

נתח   *pi* cut into pieces.

נֵתַח   piece.

נָתִיב   path.

נְתִיבָה   path.

נָתִין*   temple-servant.

נתך   *q* gush forth.

       ni gush forth; be melted.

       hi pour out, empty out; melt.

       ho be melted.

נתן   *q* give, proffer, grant, bring, offer, repay, give in exchange, give up, deliver up, hand over, transmit, proclaim, allow, commission; set, place, put; make, cause to be, cause to find; מִי יִתֵּן o that!; *Ps. 81.3* beat *(drum)*; *Lev. 17.10*; *Dan. 9.3* turn *(the face)*; *Neh. 9.17* take *(it into one's head)*; *Jer. 12.8* raise *(the voice)*.

       ni be given, commissioned, given up, made, put, granted, placed.

       ho be given.

נָתָן   n. pers. Nathan.

נְתַנְאֵל   n. pers. Nethanel.

נְתַנְיָה(וּ)   n. pers. Nethaniah.

נְתַן־מֶלֶךְ   n. pers. Nathan-melech.

נתס   *q* break up.

נתע°   *ni* be knocked out.

נתץ   *q* tear down, demolish, destroy, knock out.

       ni be torn down, destroyed.

       pi tear down.

pu be torn down.

ho be shattered.

נתק   *q* tear away; cut off.

ni be torn off, cut off; be drawn out.

pi tear apart, tear out.

hi separate, single out, cut off.

ho be cut off.

נֶתֶק   itch.

נתר   *q* leap up.

pi leap.

hi cause to start up; cause to leap up > loosen, release; *Job 6.9* withdraw.

נֶתֶר   natron.

נתשׁ   *q* tear up; drive out.

ni be torn up.

ho be torn up.

ס

סְאָה   *grain-measure* seah *(between 7.3 and 15 l).*

סְאוֹן   boot.

סאן   *q* tramp along.

סאסא   scare away.

סבא   *q* tipple, drink, be a drunkard.

*סֹבֶא   beer (made from wheat).

סְבָא   *n. peop., n. terr.* Seba.

סְבָאִים   *n. peop.* Sabeans.

סבב   *q* rotate, turn; look about; turn away from; go round) make the round, walk round; surround, flow round, encircle, make a detour; step aside; go off to, come towards; roam about; *I Sam. 16.11* sit at table; *Zech. 14.10* be transformed.

ni turn, bend; encircle, surround; be given into the possession of.

pi transform, change.

po walk round, flow round, stand around, encompass; roam through, roam about.

hi turn, turn towards; turn back, turn away, turn round, turn away from; change; bring; cause to go around; *II Chron. 14.6* erect all round.

ho turn; be turned, changed, set.

סִבָּה   turn of events, disposing.

סָבִיב   vicinity; all round, round about; on every side; *pl.* surroundings, cycle, all round.

סבך   *q pt. pass.* entwined.

     pu be entwined.

סְבַךְ   undergrowth, thicket.

סֹבֶךְ*   undergrowth, thicket.

סִבְּכַי   *n. pers.* Sibbecai.

סבל   *q* carry.

     pu pt. laden.

     hitp drag oneself along.

סֵבֶל   burden, forced-labour.

סֹבֶל*   burden.

סַבָּל   porter.

סִבְלוֹת   carrying of burdens, forced-labour.

סִבֹּלֶת   *Ephraimite pronunciation of* שִׁבֹּלֶת.

סִבְרַיִם   *n. place* Sibraim.

סַבְתָּא, סַבְתָּה   *n. peop., n. terr.* Sabtah.

סַבְתְּכָא   *n. peop., n. terr.* Sabteca.

סגד°   *q* bow down.

סָגוֹר   enclosure.

סָגוּר   *w.* זָהָב pure, solid gold; *I Kings 6.20f.* gold-leaf.

סְגֻלָּה   possession.

סֶגֶן*, סָגָן*   governor, official, chief.

סגר   *q* shut, close, shut in; *pt. pass. also* → סָגוּר.

     ni be shut; shut oneself in; be shut out.

     pi hand over.

     pu be shut up.

     hi shut up; isolate; hand over, abandon; *Job 11.10* imprison.

סַגְרִיר   heavy rain.

סַד°   stocks.

סָדִין undergarment.
סְדֹם n. place Sodom.
סְדַר* ° order.
סַהַר roundness.
סֹהַר w. בַּיִת prison.
סוֹא n. pers. So?, n. place Sais?
סוּבָא* rd. K (Ezek. 23.42).
I סוּג q deviate, be disloyal.
   ni draw back, fall away, become disloyal.
   hi displace.
   ho be driven out.
II סוּג ° q pt. pass. fenced round.
סוּג rd. Q (Ezek. 22.18).
סוּגַר cage.
סוֹד assembly, circle; joint consultation, confidential conversation;
   decision; secret.
סוֹדִי n. pers. Sodi.
סוּחַ n. pers. Suah.
סוּחָה refuse.
סוֹטַי n. pers. Sotai.
I סוּךְ pilp spur on, incite.
   hi make unapproachable, shut off.
II סוּךְ q anoint; anoint oneself.
   hi anoint oneself.
   ho be rubbed in.
סוֹלְלָה → סֹלְלָה.
סְוֵנֵה n. place Syene, Aswan.
סוּס rd. Q (Jer. 8.7) swift, swallow.
I סוּס rd. סִיס (Isa. 38.14) swift, swallow.
II סוּס horse.
סוּסָה* mare.
סוּסִי n. pers. Susi.
סוּף q cease, come to an end.
   hi put an end to.
סוֹף° end, rearguard.
I סוּף reed, aquatic plants.
II סוּף n. place Suph.
I סוּפָה storm, storm-wind.

סוֹפָה II   *n. place* Suphah.

סוֹפֵר   → סָפַר.

סוֹפֶרֶת   → סֹפֶרֶת.

סוּר   *q* leave, deviate, turn aside; go away, depart, keep away from; turn; fall away; put up at.

     pol reduce to confusion.

     hi remove, take away; take off, cut off; withdraw; keep away, divert; abolish, do away with; revoke; have brought.

     ho be taken away; *Isa. 17.1 w.* מֵ cease to be.

סוּר* I   cast off, degenerate, disloyal.

סוּר II   *n. place* II Kings *11.6* Sur.

סוּת   *hi* lead astray, instigate, incite; distract.

סוּת*   garment.

סחב   *q* drag about, draw away.

סְחָבוֹת   rags.

סחה   *pi* sweep away.

סְחִי   refuse.

סָחִישׁ   corn growing wild.

סחף   *q* wash away.

     ni be swept away.

סחר   *q* journey up and down; *pt.* merchant, buying-agent.

     pealal beat violently.

סַחַר   gain, profit.

סֹחֵרָה*   trading partner.

סֹחֵרָה   rampart?

סֹחֶרֶת   sohereth stone.

סֵט   transgression?

סָטַי   → סוֹטַי.

סִיג   dross of silver; *Prov. 26.23* glaze.

סִיוָן°   Sivan (*name of a month, May/June*).

סִיחוֹן, סִיחֹן   *n. pers.* Sihon.

סִין   *n. place, n. terr.* Sin.

סִינִי   *gent.* Sinite.

סִינַי   *n. place* Sinai.

סִינִים   *n. terr.* Sinim.

סִיסְרָא   *n. pers.* Sisera.

סִיעָא, סִיעֲהָא · · *n. pers.* Sia.

I סִיר · · cooking-pot, tub.

II סִיר* · · *pl.* thorns, bushes *(thorny burnet)*.

סִירָה* · · thorn, hook, fishing tackle.

סָךְ · · throng?

סֹךְ* · · hut; lurking-place.

סֻכָּה · · canopy of leaves, hut, booth; lurking-place.

סֻכּוֹת · · *n. place* Succoth.

סַכּוּת · · *rd.* סַכּוּת *(Amos. 5.26) n. deity* Sakkuth *(Saturn)*.

סֻכּוֹת בְּנוֹת · · *n. deity* Sarpanitu *(name of a Bab. deity)*.

סֻכִּיִּים · · *n. peop.* Sukkiim.

סְכִים · · *Jer. 39.3 text corr.*

סכך · · *q* cover, screen; wrap oneself; *Ps. 139.13* weave.

· · · · *poel* intertwine.

· · · · *hi* cover; *w.* רֶגֶל relieve nature.

סֹכֵךְ · · blockade, barricade.

סְכָכָה · · *n. place* Secacah.

סכל · · *ni* behave foolishly.

· · · · *pi* make to appear foolish.

· · · · *hi* act foolishly.

סָכָל · · foolish.

סֶכֶל · · foolishness, fool.

סִכְלוּת · · foolishness.

I סכן · · *q* yield profit; *pt.* administrator, attendant.

· · · · *hi* be in the habit of, be conversant with; agree.

II סכן · · *ni* be endangered.

III סכן · · *pu* be set up.

סכסך · · *pilp of* I סוּךְ.

I סכר · · *ni* be stopped up.

· · · · *pi* hand over.

II סכר · · *q* buy, bribe.

סכת · · *hi* keep silent.

סַכֹּת · · → סֻכּוֹת.

סַל · · basket.

סִלָּא · · → II סלה.

סִלָּא · · *n. place* Silla.

סַלָּא · · → סַלּוּא.

סלד *pi* leap.

סֶלֶד *n. pers.* Seled.

I °סלה *q* reject.

    pi reject.

II סלה *pu* be paid for.

סֶלָה *liturgical direction* Selah.

סַלּוּ *n. pers.* Sallu.

סָלוּא *n. pers.* Salu.

סַלּוּא *n. pers.* Sallu.

סַלּוֹן thorn.

סלח *q* forgive *(only of God)*.

    ni be forgiven.

סַלָּח ready to forgive.

סַלַּי *n. pers.* Sallai.

סְלִיחָה forgiveness.

סַלְכָה *n. place* Salecah.

סלל *q* throw up, pile up.

    pilp think highly of.

    hitpo act haughtily.

סֹלְלָה siege-mound.

סֻלָּם staircase.

*סַלְסִלָּה tendril.

I סֶלַע rock, crag.

II סֶלַע *n. place* Sela.

סָלְעָם locust.

סלף *pi* twist, ruin; *Job 12.19* dry up.

סֶלֶף crookedness, falseness.

°סלק *q* ascend.

סֹלֶת wheat groats.

*סַם paste, fragrance.

סַמְגַּר־נְבוּ *n. pers.* Samgar-nebo.

°סְמָדַר perule.

סמך *q* support, lay, provide; throw oneself; *pt. pass.* supported, firm,
    unshakeable.

    ni support oneself, brace oneself.

    pi refresh.

סְמַכְיָהוּ *n. pers.* Semachiah.

סֶמֶל image, idol?

סמן *ni Isa. 28.25 dub.*

סמר *q* shiver.

pi bristle.

סָמָר bristling.

סְנָאָה *n. pers.* Senaah.

סְנָאָה → סְנוּאָה.

סַנְבַלַּט *n. pers.* Sanballat.

סְנֶה thorn-bush.

סֶנֶּה *n. place* Seneh.

סְנוּאָה *n. pers.* Senuah.

סַנְוֵרִים blindness.

סַנְחֵרִב, סַנְחֵרִים *n. pers.* Sennacherib.

סַנְסַנָּה *n. place* Sansannah.

סַנְסִנָּה* cluster of dates.

סְנַפִּיר fin.

סָס moth.

סִסְמַי *n. pers.* Sismai.

סעד *q* support, strengthen; fortify, take refreshment.

סעה *q* be rushing.

סָעִיף* I cleft, fissure.

סָעִיף* II branch.

סעף *pi* hew down.

סֵעֵף* wavering?, base?

סְעַפָּה* branch.

סְעַפִּים crutches.

סער *q* be stormy.

ni become agitated.

pi blow away.

poel fly away.

pu be blown away, driven away.

סַעַר storm.

סְעָרָה storm.

סַף I basin, cup.

סַף II threshold.

סַף III *n. pers.* Saph.

ספד *q* lament, lament for the dead; *Isa. 32.12* beat *(the breast)* in lamentation.

ni be lamented.

סָפָה *q* snatch away, carry off; vanish away; *Num. 32.14; Isa. 30.1* rd. סְפֶת(לְ).

ni be carried off, perish.

hi rd. אֹסְפֶה *(Deut. 32.23).*

סָפַח *q* attach.

ni join.

pi admix.

pu come together.

hitp have a share in.

סַפַּחַת scab, eruption.

סִפַּי *n. pers.* Sippai.

I *סָפִיחַ* downpour.

II סָפִיחַ after-growth.

סְפִינָה° ship.

סַפִּיר lapis lazuli.

סֵפֶל bowl.

סָפַן *q* cover, panel; *Deut. 33.21* reserve.

סִפֻּן ceiling.

סָפַף *hitpo* stay at the threshold.

סָפַק *q* clap, strike, strike oneself; *Jer. 48.26* fall with a splash into.

סֶפֶק mockery?

סָפַר *q* count, reckon; measure; *Ezra 1.8* count out; *pt. also* clerk.

ni be counted.

pi count, recount, reckon; make known, relate.

pu be related.

סֵפֶר inscription; document, letter, scroll; kind of writing.

סֹפֵר clerk; secretary; scribe.

I סְפָר° census.

II *סְפָר* *n. place* Sephar.

סְפָרַד *n. place* Sepharad.

סְפָרָה* scroll.

סְפַרְוַיִם *n. place* Sepharvaim.

סְפַרְוִים *gent.* of Sepharvaim.

סְפָרוֹת numbers?

סֹפֶרֶת *n. pers.* Sophereth.

סָקַל   *q* stone.

     ni be stoned.

     pi throw stones; clear of stones.

     pu be stoned.

סַר   sullen.

סָרָב°*   obstinate.

סַרְגּוֹן   *n. pers.* Sargon.

סֶרֶד   *n. pers.* Sered.

סַרְדִּי   *gent.* Sardite.

סָרָה I   desisting.

סָרָה II   obstinacy, disobedience, apostasy.

סִרָה   *n. place* Sirah.

סָרוּחַ   pendent; *Amos 6.4* lying indolently.

סרח I   *q* hang down; spread.

סרח II   *ni* be spilt.

סֶרַח   what is overhanging.

סִרְיֹן*   armour.

סָרִיס   court official; eunuch.

סֶרֶן*   axle.

סְרָנִים   princes.

סַרְעַפָּה°*   branch.

סרף   *pi* burn.

סִרְפַּד   *steppe-plant?*, nettle?

סרר   *q* be stubborn, obstinate.

סְתָו°   winter, rainy season.

סְתוּר   *n. pers.* Sethur.

סתם   *q* stop up, block; keep secret; בְּסָתֻם secretly.

     ni be stopped up, closed.

     pi stop up.

סתר   *ni* hide, be hidden.

     pi hide.

     pu pt. kept secret.

     hi hide, cover, keep secret.

     hitp keep oneself hidden.

סֵתֶר   hiding-place; cover, shelter; *w.* בְּ *also* secretly.

סִתְרָה   cover, shelter.

סִתְרִי   *n. pers.* Sithri.

ע

I עֵב   trellis?

II עֵב   cloud, clouds.

III *עֲב   thicket.

עבד   *q* work, till; serve; be a slave; perform, do; make to perform,
do; do service; worship; *I Kings 12.7* do as someone wishes.
ni be tilled, cultivated.
pu be worked.
hi cause to work, subject to work; enslave, hold in servitude,
make subject to; *Isa. 43.23f.* distress.
ho let service be paid to.

I עֶבֶד   slave, servant, subject.

II עֶבֶד   *n. pers.* Ebed.

°*עֲבַד   deed.

עֹבֵד   → עוֹבֵד.

עַבְדָּא   *n. pers.* Abda.

עֹבֵד(־)אֱד(וֹ)ם   *n. pers.* Obed-edom.

עַבְדְּאֵל   *n. pers.* Abdeel.

עֲבֹדָה   work, forced labour, service; worship; *Ex. 12.25f.; 13.5*
rite.

עֲבֻדָּה   domestics, servants.

עַבְדּוֹן   *n. pers., n. place* Abdon.

עַבְדִּי   *n. pers.* Abdi.

עַבְדִּיאֵל   *n. pers.* Abdiel.

עֹבַדְיָה(וּ)   *n. pers.* Obadiah.

עֶבֶד־מֶלֶךְ   *n. pers.* Ebed-melech.

עֲבֵד נְגוֹ,
עֲבֵד נְגוֹא   *n. pers.* Abed-nego.

°*עַבְדֻת   servitude.

עבה   *q* be thick.

עֲבוֹדָה   → עֲבֹדָה.

עֲבוֹט   pledge.

I עֲבוּר   *w.* בְּ on account of, for the sake of, for, in order that, in order
to.

II עֲבוּר   *Josh. 5.11f.* produce.

עֲבוֹת   → עֲבֹת.

I עבט   *q* borrow; take a pledge.

     hi lend on pledge.

II עבט   *pi* change.

עַבְטִיט   debt secured by pledge.

עֳבִי   thickness; *II Chron. 4.17* mould?

I עבר   *q* pass, go one's way, pass through; pass over; pass by; pass on, pass away; go across, cross, go beyond, outstrip, go on ahead; *w.* אַחֲרֵי follow; *w.* מִן elude, *Ps. 81.7* let go; *w.* מָתּוֹךְ disappear among; *Num. 34.4* extend; *pt. also* current, liquid.

     ni be crossed.

     pi draw across; *Job 21.10* mount.

     hi make to pass over; make to cross, bring across; make to pass by, let pass; overlook, let slip; make over; present *(offering)*; issue, sound, circulate; lead past, lead through; take away, remove; take down; turn away, keep away, take off.

II עבר   *hitp* be angry, impassioned.

I עֵבֶר   opposite side; side, edge, bank > on the other side of.

II עֵבֶר   *n. pers.* Eber.

עֲבָרָה   crossing, ford.

עֶבְרָה   boiling up, arrogance; anger, rage.

עִבְרִי   *gent.* Hebrew.

עֲבָרִים   *n. place* Abarim.

עֶבְרֹן   *n. place* Ebron.

עַבְרֹנָה   *n. place* Abronah.

עבשׁ   *q* dry up.

עבת   *pi* twist?

עָבֹת   branch; branching.

עֲבֹת   cord, rope, twine.

עֹג   → עוֹג.

ענב   *q* have desire.

עֵנָב   → עוּגָב.

עֲנָבָה*   desire.

עֲנָבִים   love.

196

עֻגָּה flat cake of bread.

עֲנוֹל → עֲנָל.

עֲנוּר thrush.

עֲנִיל ring, earring.

עָנֹל round.

עֵגֶל bull-calf.

I עֶגְלָה young cow.

II עֶגְלָה n. pers. f. Eglah.

עֲגָלָה wagon, cart.

עֶגְלוֹן n. pers., n. place Eglon.

עֶגְלַיִם → עֵין עֶגְלַיִם.

עֶגְלַת שְׁלִשִׁיָּה n. place Eglath-shelishiyah.

עגם q have sympathy.

עגן° ni be withdrawn.

I עַד unlimited future; always, for ever, everlasting; *Job 20.4* מִנִי עַד since time began.

II עַד up to, until; during; on.

III עַד prey.

עֵד witness.

עֹד → עוֹד.

עִדּוֹא n. pers. Iddo.

עֹדֵד → עוֹדֵד.

I עדה° q stalk.
    hi strip off.

II עדה q adorn, adorn oneself.

עָדָה n. pers. f. Adah.

I עֵדָה assembly, congregation; troop, band.

II עֵדָה witness.

עִדָּה* menstruation.

עִדּוֹ(א) n. pers. Iddo.

עֵדוּת testimony, reminder; commandment, law; *II Kings 11.12*; *Ps. 132.12* royal protocol.

עֵדֹוֹת* pl. of עֵדוּת.

עֲדִי adornment.

עִדִּיא n. pers. rd. K or Q (*Neh. 12.16*).

עֲדִיאֵל n. pers. Adiel.

עֲדָיָה(וּ) n. pers. Adaiah.

עֲדִים pl. of עִדָּה.

I עָדִין* voluptuous.

II עָדִין n. pers. Adin.

עֲדִינָא n. pers. Adina.

עֲדִיתַיִם n. place Adithaim.

עַדְלַי n. pers. Adlai.

עֲדֻלָּם n. place Adullam.

עֲדֻלָּמִי gent. Adullamite.

עדן hitp luxuriate.

I עֵדֶן* delight; II Sam. 1.24 ornament.

II עֵדֶן n. pers., n. terr. Eden.

עֹדֶן n. terr. Eden.

עֲדֶן hitherto.

עַדְנָא n. pers. Adna.

עֲדֶנָה still.

עֶדְנָה sexual pleasure.

עַדְנָה n. pers. Adnah.

עַדְנַח n. pers. Adnah.

עַדְעָדָה n. place Adadah.

עדף q be in excess.

    hi have a surplus.

I עדר q be assembled, set in order.

II עדר ni be weeded.

III עדר ni be missing.

    pi leave lacking.

I עֵדֶר flock, herd.

II °עֵדֶר n. pers. Eder.

III עֵדֶר n. place Eder.

°עֶדֶר n. pers. Eder.

°עַדְרִיאֵל n. pers. Adriel.

עֲדָשִׁים lentils.

עֵדֻת → עֵדוּת.

עֵדֹת* pl. of עֵדוּת.

עַוָּא n. place Avva.

עוב hi becloud.

עוֹבֵד n. pers. Obed.

עוֹבָל n. pers. Obal.

עוג q bake.

עוֹג n. pers. Og.

עֻגָב   flute.

עוּד   *pi* surround.

pol aid.

hi affirm, admonish, warn; be witness; call to witness.

ho be warned.

hitpol raise oneself.

עוֹד   duration, lasting; continually, always, still; once more, again; moreover, besides; while.

עוֹדֵד   *n. pers.* Oded.

עוה   *q* do wrong, go astray.

ni be troubled; *I Sam. 20.30 dub.*

pi disturb, disrupt.

hi pervert, distort; go astray, do wrong; *Jer. 3.21 w.* דֶּרֶךְ go on crooked paths.

עַוָּה   ruins.

עַוָּה   *n. place* Ivvah.

עוז   *q* seek refuge.

hi save, bring into safety.

עוֹז   → עֹז.

עֲוִיל   boy, lad.

עַוִּים   *n. peop.*, *n. place* Avvim.

עַוִּית   *n. place* Avith.

עוּל I   *pi* act wrongfully.

עוּל II   *q* suckle.

עוּל   sucking child.

עַוָּל   evildoer, criminal.

עָוֶל   wrong.

עוֹלָה   perversity, wickedness.

עוֹלָה I   perversity, wickedness.

עוֹלָה II   → עֹלָה I.

עוֹלֵל, עוֹלָל   child.

עוֹלֵלוֹת   → עֹלֵלוֹת.

עוֹלָם   long time, duration, eternity; for all time, for ever, continually, eternally; time to come; remote past, ancient, long since.

עוֹן   *q rd. Q (I Sam. 18.9).*

עָוֹן   transgression, sin; guilt; punishment.

עוֹעִים   staggering.

I עוּף *q* fly, fly away; *Prov. 23.5 rd. Q.*
   pol fly, soar; wield.
   hi cause to fly; *Prov. 23.5* direct (upon).
   hitpol fly away.

II עוּף *q* become dark.
עוֹף *coll.* birds.
עוֹפַי *n. pers. rd.* Q *(Jer. 40.8)* Ephai.
עוֹפֶרֶת → עֹפֶרֶת.
עוּיִן *q* plan.
עוּיִן *n. pers., n. terr.* Uz.
עוּק → עיק.

I עוּר *pi* blind.

II עוּר *ni* be bare.

III עוּר *q* bestir oneself; be active, awake.
   ni be roused; come into action, be wakened.
   pol bring into action, waken; rouse, stir up; let oneself be roused;
     wield.
   polp Isa. 15.5 raise.
   hi awaken, stir up, rouse, bring into action; let be awakened,
     summon; bestir oneself; *Hos. 7.4* poke.
   hitpol summon one's energies, rouse oneself.

עוֹר skin, hide; leather.
עִוֵּר blind; one-eyed.
עוֹרֵב → עֹרֵב.
עִוָּרוֹן blindness.
עַוֶּרֶת blindness.
עוּשׁ *q* come to aid?

I עוּת *pi* pervert, falsify, misguide.
   pu pt. bent.
   hitp stoop.

II עוּת *q* support?
עַוָּתָה* oppression.
עֻתַי *n. pers.* Uthai.
עַז strong; obstinate, defiant; shameless.
עַז might; strength.
עֹז strength, power, might; protection, refuge.

עֵז   she-goat; *pl. also* goats' hair.

עֻזָּא   *n. pers.* Uzza; → פֶּרֶץ עֻזָּא.

עֲזָאזֵל   *n. pers.* Azazel *(desert demon)*.

I עזב   *q* leave, dismiss; not follow *(counsel)*; leave behind, leave to another; leave over; let go; leave lying; give up; let loose, release, let do as one pleases; remit; *Gen. 24.27; Ruth 2.20* withhold, let fail; *Job 9.27 w.* פָּנִים change the expression.

ni be forsaken, neglected; be left to another.

pu be forsaken, deserted.

II עזב   *q* pave? *(Neh. 3).*

עִזְבוֹנִים*   wares.

עַזְבּוּק   *n. pers.* Azbuk.

עַזְגָּד   *n. pers.* Azgad.

עַזָּה   *n. place* Gaza.

עֻזָּה   *n. pers.* Uzzah.

עֲזוּבָה   *n. pers. f.* Azubah.

עֱזוּז   strength, might, power.

עִזּוּז   powerful; *coll.* heroes.

עַזּוּר   → עַזּוּר.

עזז   *q* be strong; show oneself strong; be defiant.

hi w. (בְּ)פָנִים assume a defiant, insolent expression.

עֲזָז   *n. pers.* Azaz.

עֲזַזְיָהוּ   *n. pers.* Azaziah.

עֻזִּי   *n. pers.* Uzzi.

עֻזִּיָּא   *n. pers.* Uzzia.

עֲזִיאֵל   *n. pers.* Aziel.

עֻזִּיאֵל   *n. pers.* Uzziel.

עֻזִּיאֵלִי   *gent.* Uzzielite.

עֻזִּיָּה(וּ)   *n. pers.* Uzziah.

עֲזִיזָא   *n. pers.* Aziza.

עַזְמָוֶת   *n. pers., n. place* Azmaveth.

עַזָּן   *n. pers.* Azzan.

עָזְנִיָּה   vulture.

עזק   *pi* hoe.

עֲזֵקָה   *n. place* Azekah.

עזר   *q* help, aid, support; come to aid.

ni find/receive help.

hi help.

עֵזֶר I   help; helper.

עֶזֶר II   *n. pers.* Ezer.

עֶזֶר   *n. pers.* Ezer.

עַזֻּר   *n. pers.* Azzur.

עֶזְרָא   *n. pers.* Ezra.

עֲזַרְאֵל   *n. pers.* Azarel.

עֶזְרָה I   help, aid; helpers.

עֶזְרָה II   *n. pers.* Ezrah.

עֲזָרָה   barrier, enclosure; outer court.

עֶזְרִי   *n. pers.* Ezri.

עַזְרִיאֵל   *n. pers.* Azriel.

עֲזַרְיָה(וּ)   *n. pers.* Azariah.

עַזְרִיקָם   *n. pers.* Azrikam.

עֶזְרָת   help.

עַזָּתִי   *gent.* Gazite.

עֵט   stylus.

עטה I   *q* cover, cover up; wrap oneself up in something.

hi wrap up, envelop.

עטה II   *q* seize; *Jer. 43.12* delouse.

עָטוּף*   weakened, feeble.

עֲטִין*   trough?, intestines?

עֲטִישָׁה*   sneeze.

עֲטַלֵּף   bat.

עטף I   *q* cover oneself; wrap up; *Job 23.9* turn aside.

עטף II   *q* become weak.

ni languish.

hi be feeble.

hitp feel weak; despair.

עטר   *q* surround, encircle.

pi crown.

hi bestow garlands, diadems.

עֲטָרָה I   garland, diadem.

עֲטָרָה II   *n. pers. f.* Atarah.

עֲטָר(וֹ)ת   *n. place* Ataroth.

עַטְרֹת שׁוֹפָן   *n. place* Atroth-shophan.

עִי   *n. place* Ai.

עִי   ruins, heap of ruins.

עַיָּא   *n. place* Aija.

עֵיבָל   *n. pers.*, *n. place* Ebal.

עַיָּה   *n. place* Aijah.

עִיּוֹן   *n. place* Ijon.

עֵיוֹת   *n. place rd. Q (I Chron. 1.46).*

עִיט   *q* fall upon; scream at, round angrily upon.

עַיִט   bird of prey; *also coll.* birds of prey.

עֵיטָם   *n. place* Etam.

עִיִּים   *n. place* Ijim.

עֵילוֹם   *rd.* עוֹלָם *(II Chron. 33.7).*

עִילַי   *n. pers.* Ilai.

עֵילָם   *n. pers.; n. peop., n. terr. m. and f.* Elam.

עַיִם   → בַּעֲיִם.

עִין   *q* eye with mistrust.

עַיִן   eye; appearance, gleam; what is visible; spring.

עֵין(־)גֶּדִי   *n. place* En-gedi.

עֵין(־)גַּנִּים   *n. place* En-gannim.

עֵין־דֹּאר   *n. place* En-dor.

עֵין דּוֹר, עֵין־דֹּר   *n. place* En-dor.

עֵין הַקּוֹרֵא   *n. place* En-hakkore.

עֵין הַתַּנִּין   *n. place* Dragon Spring.

עֵינוֹן   → חֲצַר עֵינוֹן.

עֵין חַדָּה   *n. place* En-haddah.

עֵין חָצוֹר   *n. place* En-hazor.

עֵין חֲרֹד   *n. place* En-harod.

עֵינַיִם   *n. place* Enaim.

עֵינָם   *n. place* Enam.

עֵין מִשְׁפָּט   *n. place* En-mishpat.

עֵינָן   *n. pers.* Enan; → חֲצַר עֵינָן.

עֵין עֶגְלַיִם   *n. place* En-eglaim.

עֵין(־)רֹגֵל   *n. place* En-rogel.

עֵין רִמּוֹן   *n. place* En-rimmon.

עֵין שֶׁמֶשׁ   *n. place* En-shemesh.

עִינֹת*   *rd. Q (Hos. 10.10).*

עֵין תַּפּוּחַ   *n. place* En-tappuah.

עִיף   *q* be weary; *Jer. 4.31* succumb.

עָיֵף   weary, exhausted.

עֵיפָה I darkness.

עֵיפָה II n. pers. m. and f., n. peop., n. terr. Ephah.

עֵיפָתָה darkness.

עִיק q sway?
hi make to sway?

עִיר I town, (permanent) settlement, occupation; fig. population (of a town).

עִיר II agitation, fear.

עִיר III n. pers. Ir.

עִיר IV *, עַיִר ass, young ass; male ass.

עִירָא n. pers. Ira.

עִירָד n. pers. Irad.

עִיר הַהֶרֶס n. place City of the Sun.

עִיר הַמֶּלַח n. place City of Salt.

עִיר הַתְּמָרִים n. place City of Palm Trees.

עִירוּ n. pers. Iru.

עֵירוֹם → עֵירֹם.

עִירִי n. pers. Iri.

עִירָם n. peop.? Iram.

עֵירֹם naked, unclothed; nakedness.

עִיר נָחָשׁ n. place Ir-nahash.

עִיר שֶׁמֶשׁ n. place Ir-shemesh.

עַיִשׁ f. lioness (constellation).

עַיַּת n. place Aiath.

עַכְבּוֹר n. pers. Achbor.

עַכָּבִישׁ spider.

עַכְבָּר mouse.

עַכּוֹ n. place Acco.

עָכוֹר n. place Achor.

עָכָן n. pers. Achan.

עכס pi jingle (with anklets).

עֶכֶס anklet.

עַכְסָה n. pers. f. Achsah.

עכר q make taboo, untouchable, taboo.
ni become taboo, untouchable.

עָכָר n. pers. Achar.

עָכְרָן n. pers. Ochran.

עַכְשׁוּב horned viper?

עַל height, what is above; on, over; at, by; concerning; on account of, because of; against, over against; together with; w. כְּ in accordance with; w. מִן down from, away from, off from; up over; w. כֵּן thereon, therefore, for that reason.

עֹל yoke.

עֻלָּא n. pers. Ulla.

עַלְבוֹן →אֲבִי־עַלְבוֹן.

עִלֵּג* stammerer.

עלה q ascend, mount, go up, climb (up); come (up); become intense *(battle)*; withdraw *(army)*.

ni rise; be exalted; be led up; withdraw; w. עַל־שְׂפַת לָשׁוֹן get talked about.

hi bring up, lead up; present *(offering)*; bring upon someone; make high, set high; send up, cause to go up (into), grow, raise; overlay *(gold)*; set up *(lamp)*; raise *(levy for forced labour)*; take away, cause to die; w. גֵּרָה chew the cud.

ho be offered, be led away, be entered.

hitp rise.

עָלֶה leaves.

I עֹלָה burnt-offering.

II עֹלָה perversity, wickedness.

I עַלְוָה obstinacy.

II עַלְוָה n. peop.? Alvah.

עֲלוּמִים* youth, youthful vigour.

עַלְוָן n. pers. Alvan.

עֲלוּקָה leech.

עלז q rejoice, exult.

עָלֵז exultant.

עֲלָטָה darkness.

עֵלִי n. pers. Eli.

עֱלִי pestle.

עִלִּי* upper.

עֲלָיָה n. peop.? Aliah.

עֲלִיָּה upper room.

עֶלְיוֹן upper; highest.

עַלִּיז* exultant; unrestrained, wanton.

עֲלִיל° crucible?

עֲלִילָה deed, action; w. דְּבָרִים deed which gets talked about.

עֲלִילִיָּה deed.

עַלְיָן n. pers. Alian.

עֲלִיצֻת* rejoicing, exultation.

I עלל poel deal with, do to; glean.

    poal be inflicted on.

    hitp treat (harshly), indulge in wantonness.

    hitpo perpetrate.

II עלל° poel push in.

עֹלֵל → עוֹלֵל

עֹלֵלוֹת gleaning.

עלם q pt. pass. that which is hidden.

    ni be hidden, cunning.

    hi hide, cover.

    hitp hide oneself; withdraw.

עֹלָם → עוֹלָם.

עֶלֶם young man.

עַלְמָה young woman (until the birth of her first child); Ps. 46.1; 1 Chron. 15.20 musical direction with girls' voices?

עַלְמוֹן n. place Almon.

עָלֶמֶת n. pers., n. place Alemeth.

עלם q enjoy.

    ni beat joyously.

    hitp take pleasure, luxuriate.

עלע pi gulp?

עלף pu be wrapped up, covered; faint.

    hitp wrap oneself up; faint.

עֻלְּפֶה rd. עֻלְּפוּ Ezek. 31.15.

עלץ q rejoice, be glad.

עֲלָתָה wickedness.

עַם, עָם kinsman, fellow-tribesman, relative, relatives; tribe, nation, people, persons; w. הָאָרֶץ coll. citizens with full rights; pl. w. הָאָרֶץ heathen nations.

עִם with, at; as well as, as, comparable to; as long as, at the same time; w. מִן away from, before; on the part of; w. זֶה nevertheless.

עֲמֹד *q* take up position, place oneself, present oneself, come forward; stand (forth), dwell; stay, come to a halt, remain, be preserved, stand firm, stop, cease; do service, attend; *Eccles. 8.3* engage in; *Esther 3.4* be allowed; *Ezra 10.14* *w.* ? represent.

hi make to stand, place, post; leave in place, let remain; appoint; erect, restore, set up; confirm; *w.* אֲדָמָה allot land; *w.* דָּבָר *and* ? make a decision to; *w.* פָּנָיו stare straight ahead.

ho be made to stand.

עֹמֶד* place.

עָמָד* with.

עֶמְדָּה* location, stay.

I עֻמָּה* *w.* ? close by, beside; corresponding to, just as; *I Kings 7.20* close beside.

II עֻמָּה *n. place* Ummah.

עַמּוּד tent-support, pillar, column, post.

עַמּוֹן *n. peop.* Ammon, Ammonites.

עַמּוֹנִי *gent.* Ammonite.

עָמוֹס *n. pers.* Amos.

עָמוֹק *n. pers.* Amok.

עַמִּיאֵל *n. pers.* Ammiel.

עַמִּיהוּד *n. pers.* Ammihud.

עַמִּיזָבָד° *n. pers.* Ammizabad.

עַמִּיחוּר *n. pers.* Ammihur.

עַמִּינָדָב *n. pers.* Amminadab.

עָמִיר (mown) corn.

עַמִּישַׁדָּי *n. pers.* Ammishaddai.

עָמִית* fellow, associate.

עָמַל *q* toil, labour.

I עָמָל toil, trouble; gain; misfortune, mischief.

II עָמָל *n. pers.* Amal.

עָמֵל toiling, laborious; labourer.

עֲמָלֵק *n. pers.* Amalek; *n. peop.* Amalekites.

עֲמָלֵקִי *gent.* Amalekite.

I עמם *q* be equal to.

II עמם *ho* become dim.

עֲמָמִים *pl. of* עַם.

עִמָּנוּ אֵל   *n. pers.* Immanuel.

עַמּוֹנִי   → עַמּוֹנִי.

עמס   *q* load, pick up, carry.

hi lay on.

עֲמַסְיָה   *n. pers.* Amasiah.

עָמְעָד   *n. place* Amad.

עמק   *q* be deep, mysterious.

hi make deep; *in conjunction with another verb* deeply.

עֵמֶק   valley bottom, flat valley floor, plain.

עֹמֶק   depth.

עָמֹק   deep, deepened; mysterious, unfathomable.

עָמֵק*   deep, unintelligible.

עֵמֶק בְּרָכָה   *n. place* Valley of Beracah.

עֵמֶק הָאֵלָה   *n. place* Vale of Elah.

עֵמֶק קָצִיץ   *n. place* Emek-keziz.

עֵמֶק רְפָאִים   *n. place* Vale of Rephaim.

עֵמֶק שָׁוֵה   *n. place* Valley of Shaveh.

עמר I   *pi* gather.

עמר II   *hitp* treat brutally.

עֹמֶר I   (cut) corn.

עֹמֶר II   grain-measure omer *(between 2.2 and 4.5 l)*.

עֲמֹרָה   *n. place* Gomorrah.

עָמְרִי   *n. pers.* Omri.

עַמְרָם   *n. pers.* Amram.

עַמְרָמִי   *gent.* Amramite.

עֲמָשָׂא   *n. pers.* Amasa.

עֲמָשַׂי   *n. pers.* Amasai.

עֲמַשְׁסַי   *n. pers.* Amashsai.

עֲנָב   *n. place* Anab.

עֵנָב   grape.

ענג   *pu pt.* pampered.

hitp pamper oneself, enjoy thoroughly, revive oneself; make fun of.

עֹנֶג   pleasure, joy.

עָנֹג   pampered, spoiled.

עָנַד   *q* wind around.

עֲנָה I *q* reply, answer; take up discourse; give to understand; give a favourable hearing, furnish; testify, bear witness.

ni let oneself be moved to answer, receive an answer.

hi pay heed.

עֲנָה II *q* submit, be wretched; be humiliated, humbled.

ni bow down; be/become humbled.

pi oppress, violate, humble; *w.* נֶפֶשׁ humble, mortify oneself; rape, abuse; overcome; *Ps. 105.18* force.

pu be humbled; humble oneself, mortify oneself.

hi oppress.

hitp humbly submit, subject oneself; *Ps. 107.17* be afflicted.

עֲנָה III *q* toil.

hi divert?, compensate?

עֲנָה IV *q* sing, celebrate in song; howl.

pi sing, celebrate in song.

עֹנָה* marital intercourse.

עֲנָה *n. pers.* Anah.

עָנָו* lowly, humble, meek.

עַנּוּ *rd. Q (Neh. 12.9).*

עַנּוּב *n. pers.* Anub.

עֲנָוָה humility; *Ps. 18.36* condescension.

עַנְוָה clemency.

עֲנוֹק *n. pers.* Anok.

עֲנוּשִׁים fines.

עֲנוֹת → בֵּית־עֲנוֹת.

עֱנוּת affliction.

עָנִי unfortunate, wretched, poor; humble.

עֳנִי affliction, misery; *I Chron. 22.14* trouble, hardship.

עֻנִּי *n. pers.* Unni.

עֲנָיָה *n. pers.* Anaiah.

עָנִים *n. place* Anim.

עִנְיָן task, occupation; happening.

עָנֵם *n. place* Anem.

עֲנָמִים *n. peop.* Anamim.

עֲנַמֶּלֶךְ *n. deity* Anammelech.

עָנַן *pi* cause to appear.
poel conjure, practise sorcery.

I עָנָן clouds, cloud-mass.

II עָנָן *n. pers.* Anan.

עֲנָנָה cloud.

עֲנָנִי *n. pers.* Anani.

עֲנַנְיָה *n. pers., n. place* Ananiah.

עָנָף branch *also coll.*

עָנֵף* many-branched.

ענק *q* put round the neck.
hi put on the neck, present.

I עֲנָק neck-chain, necklace.

II עֲנָק *n. peop.* Anak, Anakim.

עָנֵר *n. pers., n. place* Aner.

ענשׁ *q* impose a fine, punish.
ni be fined; must suffer for.

עֹנֶשׁ fine.

עֲנָת *n. pers.* Anath.

עֲנָתוֹת *n. pers., n. place* Anathoth.

עַנְּתוֹתִי *gent.* Anathothite.

עֲנָתֹת *n. place* Anathoth.

עַנְּתֹתִי → עַנְּתוֹתִי.

עֲנָתֹתִיָּה *n. pers.* Anthothijah.

עָסִיס grape-juice.

עסם *q* trample down.

עֳפִי*° thick foliage.

עפל *pu* be puffed up, presumptuous.
hi presume.

I עֹפֶל *II Kings 5.24* hill; *n. place* Ophel.

II עֹפֶל* ulcer.

עָפְנִי *n. place* Ophni.

עַפְעַפִּים* beams; flashing eyes.

עפר *pi* throw at.

עָפָר surface soil, loose earth, dust; soil; rubble; coating, plaster.

עֵפֶר *n. pers.* Epher.

עֹפֶר young, fawn.

עָפְרָה *n. pers., n. place* Ophrah.

עֲפְרָה   *n. place* Aphrah.

עֶפְרוֹן, עֶפְרֹן   *n. pers., n. place* Ephron.

עֹפֶרֶת   lead.

עֲפָתָה   darkness.

עֵץ   tree *also coll.*; wood; *pl. also* logs, wood-pile; pole, shaft.

I עצב   *pi* fashion.

     hi portray.

II עצב   *q* rebuke, hurt, grieve.

     ni be grieved, fret; hurt oneself.

     pi vex, grieve.

     hi vex.

     hitp be vexed, grieved.

עָצָב*   image, idol.

עַצָּב*   workman.

I עֶצֶב   creature.

II עֶצֶב   pain; offence; that which is hard-won.

I עֹצֶב*   idol.

II עֹצֶב   pain, hardship.

עִצָּבוֹן   difficulty, hardship.

עַצֶּבֶת   pain; *Ps. 147.3* wound.

עצה   *q* narrow.

עָצֶה   tail-bone.

I עֵצָה   counsel; resolution, plan; community, circle; *Zech. 6.13* agreement.

II עֵצָה*   *Ps. 106.43* disobedience.

III עֵצָה   *Jer. 6.6* wood.

עָצוּם   strong, mighty; numerous.

עֶצְיוֹן(־)גֶּבֶר,   *n. place* Ezion-geber.
עֶצְיוֹן גֶּבֶר

עצל   *ni* delay.

עָצֵל   idle, lazy.

עַצְלָה   laziness, idleness.

עַצְלוּת   laziness, idleness.

עַצְלְתַיִם   laziness.

I עצם   *q* be strong, mighty, numerous.

     pi gnaw the bones of.

     hi make strong.

עָצַם II   *q* shut.

     pi shut.

עֶצֶם I   bone, bones; *pl. also* corpse; being > precisely, just, even.

עֶצֶם II   *n. place* Ezem.

עֹצֶם   abounding might; bones.

עָצְמָה*   crime; suffering.

עָצְמָה   strength, abounding might.

עַצְמוֹן   *n. place* Azmon.

עֲצֻמוֹת*   proofs.

עֶצֶן*   *II Sam. 23.8 text corr.*

עָצַר   *q* hold back, hinder, detain; shut up, arrest; retain; close, withhold, restrain; keep within bounds, rule; עָצוּר וְעָזוּב *significance uncertain* slave and freeman?, unclean and clean?, minor and of age?

     ni cease; be closed; be detained.

עֶצֶר   possession?

עֹצֶר   closedness; oppression.

עֲצָרָה, עֲצֶרֶת   festival.

עָקַב   *q* seize by the heel, cheat.

     pi hold back.

עָקֵב   heel, hoof; *fig.* rearguard; *pl. also* footprints; *Ps. 49.6* adversary.

עֵקֶב   to the end, to the last > result, reward > in return for the fact that; *w.* עַל because of.

עָקֹב   rugged; deceitful; *Hos. 6.8* tracked?

עָקְבָּה   cunning.

עָקַד   *q* bind.

עָקֹד   striped.

עָקֹד   → בֵּית עֵקֶד (הָרֹעִים).

עָקָה*   oppression.

עַקּוּב   *n. pers.* Akkub.

עִקֵּל   *pu pt.* perverted, distorted.

עֲקַלְקַל*   devious.

עֲקַלָּתוֹן   twisting.

עָקָן   *n. pers.* Akan.

עָקַר   *q* uproot, weed out.

ni be destroyed.

pi hamstring.

עָקָר barren.

I עֵקֶר offspring.

II עֵקֶר *n. pers.* Eker.

עַקְרָב scorpion, lash.

עֶקְרוֹן *n. place* Ekron.

עֶקְרוֹנִי *gent.* Ekronite.

עקשׁ *ni* go by devious ways.

pi distort, pervert.

hi declare guilty.

I עִקֵּשׁ distorted, perverted, false.

II עִקֵּשׁ *n. pers.* Ikkesh.

עִקְּשׁוּת distortion, falseness.

I* עָר enemy?

II עָר *n. terr.* Ar.

עֵר *n. pers.* Er.

I ערב *q* go bail, give security, intervene on behalf of; give in pledge, mortgage; exchange.

hitp make a wager.

II ערב *hitp* have dealings with, mingle with, be involved in.

III ערב *q* be pleasant, be pleasing.

IV ערב *q* become evening; vanish.

hi do late.

I עֶרֶב evening; *du. w.* בֵּין in the evening.

II עֶרֶב *I Kings 10.15 Jer. 25.24 dub.*

III עֶרֶב mixed race, mixture.

I עֵרֶב mixed race, mixture.

II עֵרֶב *(weaving)* woven material?, woof?

I עֲרָב desert.

II עֲרָב *n. peop.* Arabs.

עָרֵב pleasant.

I עֹרֵב raven.

II עֹרֵב *n. pers.* Oreb.

עָרֹב noxious insects, dog-fly.

I* עֲרָבָה Euphrates poplar.

II עֲרָבָה steppe, desert; הָעֲרָבָה Jordan depression, Arabah *(as far as the Gulf of Aqabah)*, *w.* יָם Dead Sea.

עֲרֻבָּה security; token.

עֵרָבוֹן pledge.

עַרְבִי, עֲרָבִי *gent.* Arab.

עַרְבָתִי *gent.* Arbathite.

עָרַג *q* long for, desire.

עֲרָד *n. pers.*, *n. place* Arad.

עָרָה *ni* be poured out.

pi lay bare, remove the covering; pour out.

hi expose; *Isa. 53.12* give up.

hitp expose oneself; *Ps. 37.35* be expansive.

עָרָה* rush?

עֲרוּגָה* bed.

עָרוֹד wild ass.

עֶרְוָה nakedness, exposedness, genital (area), sex organ; *w.* דָּבָר indecency.

עָרוֹם naked, unclothed; scantily clad.

עָרֹם → עֵירֹם.

עָרוּם clever; crafty.

עֲרוֹעֵר *n. place* Aroer.

עָרִיץ* slope.

עֵרִי *n. pers.* Eri; *gent.* Erite.

עֶרְיָה nakedness, bareness.

עֲרִיסָה* dough.

עֲרִיפִים* drizzle.

עָרִיץ powerful, violent; potentate, tyrant.

עֲרִירִי childless.

עָרַךְ *q* arrange in order, prepare, set in order, hold in readiness; draw up (for battle), form up; confront > compare; be equivalent; lay before, put forward.

hi value.

עֵרֶךְ layer, row; equipment, accessories; valuation; *Ps. 55.14* כְּעֶרְכִּי such as I.

עָרַל *q* leave unharvested.

ni display the foreskin.

עָרֵל uncircumcised.

עָרְלָה foreskin; *also fig.*

עָרַם I *ni* be dammed up.

עֲרַם II   *q* be/become clever, cunning.

     hi w. סוֹד plan a cunning attack.

עָרֹם   → עָרוֹם.

עֵירֹם   → עֵירֹם.

עָרְמָה   shrewdness; treachery.

עֲרֵמָה   heap.

עַרְמוֹן   plane-tree.

עֵרָן   *n. pers.* Eran.

עֵרָנִי   *gent.* Eranite.

עֲרָעוֹר   *rd.* עֲרוֹעֵר *(Judg. 11.26).*

עַרְעֵר   → עֲרוֹעֵר.

עַרְעָר   naked, destitute; juniper.

עֲרֹעֵרִי   *gent.* Aroerite.

עֲרַף I   *q* drop.

עֲרַף II   *q* break (the neck), break down.

עֹרֶף   nape, neck; back.

עָרְפָּה   *n. pers. f.* Orpah.

עֲרָפֶל   darkness, dark cloud.

ערץ   *q* frighten; be afraid.

     ni pt. fearful.

     hi fear.

ערק   *q* gnaw, gnaw off.

עַרְקִי   *gent.* Arkite.

ערר   *q* strip oneself.

     poel lay bare.

     pilp lay bare, demolish.

     hitpalp be demolished.

עֶרֶשׂ   *f.* bed, couch.

עֵשֶׂב   herb, herbage.

עָשׂה I   *q* make, manufacture, produce; perform, do, act, practise; work, be active, acquire; carry out, observe; prepare; fix; take steps; accomplish; *w.* בְּ cope with; *Eccles. 3.12* טוֹב enjoy oneself.

     ni be made, manufactured, prepared, carried out, observed, used, shown; be done, committed; proceed.

     pu be made.

II עָשֹׂה	*q Ezek. 23.21* squeeze, press.
	pi Ezek. 23.3,8 squeeze, press.
עֲשָׂהֵ־אֵל,	*n. pers.* Asahel.
עֲשָׂהאֵל	
עֵשָׂו	*n. pers.* Esau.
עָשׂוֹר	ten; tenth.
עֲשִׂיאֵל	*n. pers.* Asiel.
עֲשָׂיָה	*n. pers.* Asaiah.
עֲשִׂירִי	tenth; tenth part.
עשׁק	*hitp* quarrel.
עֵשֶׂק	*n. place* Esek.
עשׂר	*q* exact the tithe.
	pi collect/give the tithe.
	hi collect/give the tithe.
עֶשֶׂר	ten.
עֶשֶׂר	ten.
עָשׂוֹר	→ עָשׂוֹר.
עֲשָׂרָה	ten.
עֲשָׂרָה	ten.
עִשָּׂר(וֹ)ן	tenth.
עֲשִׂירִי	→ עֲשִׂירִי.
עֶשְׂרִים	twenty, twentieth.
עֲשֶׂרֶת	ten.
I עָשׁ	moth; pus?
II עָשׁ	*Job 9.9* Leo *(constellation)*.
עָשׁוֹק	oppressor.
עֲשׁוּקִים	oppression.
עָשׂוֹת	wrought.
עַשְׂוָת	*n. pers.* Ashvath.
עָשִׁיר	rich, rich man.
עשׁן	*q* smoke.
I עָשָׁן	smoke.
II עָשָׁן	*n. place* Ashan.
עָשֵׁן	smoking.
עשׁק	*q* oppress, wrong; extort.
	pu pt. abused.
עֹשֶׁק	oppression, extortion.
עֵשֶׁק	*n. pers.* Eshek.

עָשְׁקָה oppression.

עֲשֻׁקִים ← עֲשׁוּקִים.

עשׁר q be/become rich.

hi make rich, become rich.

hitp pretend to be rich.

עֹשֶׁר riches.

עשׁשׁ q become weak; disintegrate.

I עשׁת q become plump?

II °עשׁת *hitp* think of.

עֶשֶׁת plaque.

°עַשְׁתּוּת thought?

עַשְׁתֵּי *w.* עָשָׂר eleven, eleventh.

°עֶשְׁתֹּנֶת* thought, plan.

עַשְׁתָּרוֹת ← עַשְׁתָּרֹת.

עַשְׁתֹּרֶת *n. deity f.* Astarte.

עַשְׁתֶּרֶת* increase.

עַשְׁתָּרֹת *n. place* Ashtaroth.

עַשְׁתְּרָתִי *gent.* Ashterathite.

עֵת *m. and f.* time, moment, period; *pl. also* course of events, new eras.

עַתָּ ← עַתָּה.

עתד *pi* carry out.

hitp be destined.

עַתָּה now, at present; now then!, so now?

עָתוּד* ready; store.

עַתּוּד* ram, goat; *fig.* leader.

עַתִּי in readiness.

עַתַּי *n. pers.* Attai.

עָתִיד ready; *pl. also* events in store; stores.

עֲתָיָה *n. pers.* Athaiah.

עָתִיק choice.

עַתִּיק* removed, weaned; ancient *(Aram.)*.

עָתָךְ *n. place* Athach.

עַתְלַי *n. pers.* Athlai.

עֲתַלְיָה(וּ) *n. pers. f.* Athaliah; *Ezra 8.7; I Chron. 8.26 n. pers. m.*

עתם *ni* be laid waste?

עָתְנִי *n. pers.* Othni.

עָתְנִיאֵל *n. pers.* Othniel.

עתק   *q* move away; *Ps. 6.8* become dim?; *Job 21.7* grow old *(Aram.).*
       hi journey on; displace; leave in the lurch; collect.

עָתָק   forward, insolent.

עָתֵק   splendid?, inherited from of old?

עֵת קָצִין*   *n. place* Eth-kazin.

I עתר   *q* pray, entreat.
       ni be moved by entreaty, give a favourable hearing, have mercy.
       hi pray, entreat.

II עתר   *ni* be plentiful?
       hi heap up?

עָתָר*   *Ezek. 8.11* fragrance; *Zeph. 3.10* worshipper?

עֶתֶר   *n. place* Ether.

עֲתֶרֶת   abundance?

פ

פֹּא → פֹּה.

פאה   *hi* shatter.

I פֵּאָה   side, edge; *du.* temples.

II פֵּאָה   *Neh. 9.22* piece, portion.

III פֵּאָה   *Amos 3.12* magnificence.

I פאר   *pi* strip bare.

II פאר   *pi* beautify, glorify.
       hitp make oneself glorious, boast; *Ex. 8.5 w.* עַל deign to appoint.

פְּאֵר   head-dress.

פֹּארָה*   shoot, branch.

פֻּארָה   branches.

פָּארוּר   glow.

פָּארָן   *n. terr.* Paran.

פַּג*   unripe fig.

פִּגּוּל   unclean flesh.

פגע   *q* meet (with someone), encounter; reach; fall upon, attack;
       w. בְּ urge someone, entreat; touch *(border).*
       hi let fall upon; intercede; *w.* בְּ urge someone strongly.

פֶּגַע   happening, chance.

פַּגְעִיאֵל   *n. pers.* Pagiel.

פנר   *pi* be weak, weary.

פֶּגֶר   corpse; *coll.* corpses.

פנשׁ   *q* encounter, meet.
     ni meet.
     pi encounter.

פדה   *q* ransom, redeem; deliver; *Num. 18.15-17* let be redeemed.
     ni be ransomed; be delivered.
     hi let be ransomed.
     ho be ransomed.

פְּדַהְאֵל   *n. pers.* Pedahel.

פְּדָהצוּר,   *n. pers.* Pedahzur.
פְּדָה־צוּר

פְּדוּיִם*   ransom.

פָּדוֹן   *n. pers.* Padon.

פְּדוּת   deliverance.

פְּדָיָה(וּ)   *n. pers.* Pedaiah.

פִּדְיוֹם   ransom.

פִּדְיוֹן, פִּדְיֹן   ransom money.

פַּדָּן   *n. terr.* Paddan.

פרע   *q dub.*

פֶּדֶר   suet.

פֶּרֶת   → פְּדוּת.

פֶּה   mouth *(man, animal)*, jaws, beak; opening, entrance; edge *(sword)*; utterance, command; *w.* שְׁנַיִם two portions, two thirds; *w.* כְּ according to, corresponding to, as much as, accordingly (as); *w.* לְ according to, corresponding to, *in conjunction w. inf.* whenever, only when; *w.* עַל according to.

פֹּה, פוֹ   here, hither.

פּוּאָה   *n. pers.* Puah.

פוג   *q* be/become cold, weak.
     ni be enfeebled, powerless.

פּוּגָה*   slackening.

פֻּוָּה, פֻּוָה   *n. pers.* Puvah.

פוח   *q* blow.

hi snort, hurl out, utter; *Cant. 4.16* make fragrant.

פּוֹט *n. peop.* Put.

פּוּטִיאֵל *n. pers.* Putiel.

פּוֹטִיפַר *n. pers.* Potiphar.

פּוֹטִי פֶרַע *n. pers.* Potiphera.

פּוּךְ eye-paint; cement.

פּוֹל beans.

פּוּל *n. pers.*, *n. peop.* Pul.

פּוּן *q* be helpless?

פּוּנָה *rd.* הַפָּנָה (*II Chron. 25.23*).

פּוּנִי *gent.* Punite.

פּוּנֹן *n. place* Punon.

פּוּעָה *n. pers. f.* Puah.

פּוּץ *q* be scattered; be driven out, overflow.
ni be scattered; *II Sam. 18.8 rd. Q* spread.
hi scatter, disperse; be scattered; *Job 18.11* pursue; *Job 40.11*
let overflow.

פּוּק *q* reel.
hi wobble; obtain; let attain, grant.

פּוּקָה stumbling.

פּוּר *hi* break, frustrate.

פּוּר lot; *pl.* festival of Purim.

פּוּרָה wine-press.

פּוֹרָתָא *n. pers.* Poratha.

I פּוֹשׁ *q* trample, paw the ground.

II פּוֹשׁ *ni* be scattered.

פּוּתִי *gent.* Puthite.

פַּז pure gold.

I פָּזז *ho pt.* set with gold.

II פָּזז *q* be agile.
pi leap.

פָּזַר *q pt. pass.* scattered.
ni be scattered.
pi scatter, spread abroad.
pu pt. scattered.

I פַּח clapnet.

II פַּח* plate.

פָּחַד   *q* tremble, be afraid; *Isa. 60.5* leap.

       pi be afraid; *Prov. 28.14* be God-fearing.

       hi make to shake.

I   פַּחַד   trembling, terror; *Job 39.16 w.* בְּלִי unconcerned; *w.* יִצְחָק Fear of Isaac?, Kinsman of Isaac? *(title of a God)*.

II *פַּחַד   loin, thigh.

*פַּחְדָּה   fear.

פֶּחָה   governor; deputy.

פָּחֹז   *q pt.* insolent, undisciplined.

פַּחַז   frothing over.

*פַּחֲזוּת   telling lies.

פָּחַח   *hi* be captive?

פֶּחָם   charcoal.

פַּחַת   pit.

פַּחַת מוֹאָב   *n. pers.* Pahath-moab.

פְּחֶתֶת   penetration (by rotting).

פִּטְדָה   *yellow precious stone* chrysolite?

פְּטוּרִים   *rd. Q (I Chron. 9.33)* exempt from duty.

פַּטִּישׁ   sledge-hammer.

פָּטַר   *q* elude; free from duty, let flow freely; *I Kings 6* פְּטוּרֵי צִצִּים festoons of flowers?, buds?

       hi w. בְּשָׂפָה make a wry mouth (in scorn).

פֶּטֶר   firstborn.

*פִּטְרָה   firstborn.

פִּי   → פֶּה.

פִּי־בֶסֶת   *n. place* Pi-beseth.

פִּיד   misfortune, ruin.

פִּי הַחִירֹת   *n. place* Pi-hahiroth.

פֵּיוֹת   *pl. of* פֶּה.

פִּיחַ   soot.

פִּיכֹל   *n. pers.* Phicol.

פִּילֶגֶשׁ   → פִּלֶגֶשׁ.

פִּים   *unit of weight* pim *(between 7.17 and 7.77 g)*.

פִּימָה   fat.

פִּינְחָס   *n. pers.* Phinehas.

פִּינֹן   *n. peop.?* Pinon.

פִּיפִיּוֹת   with double edges.

פִּישׁוֹן *n. river* Pishon.

פִּיתוֹן *n. pers.* Pithon.

פַּךְ jug.

פכה *pi* trickle.

פֹּכֶרֶת הַצְּבָיִים *n. pers.* Pochereth-hazzebaim.

I פלא *ni* be too hard, too difficult; be extraordinary, marvellous; *pt. pl. f. also* marvels, wonders, marvellous acts, *Job 37.5* wondrously, *Dan. 8.24* in monstrous fashion, *Dan. 11.36* unheard-of things.

> *hi* make marvellous, do wondrously; act/deal wondrously with; *inf. abs. also* wondrously.

> *hitp* show oneself marvellous.

II פלא *pi* fulfil *(vow)*.

> *hi* perform *(vow)*.

פֶּלֶא extraordinary thing, marvel, wondrous thing; *Lam. 1.9* in horrible fashion; *Dan. 12.6* wondrous event.

פִּלְאִי *rd. Q (Judg. 13.18)* wondrous.

פַּלֻּאִי *gent.* Palluite.

פִּלְאִיָה *rd. Q (Ps. 139.6)* wondrous.

פְּלָאיָה *n. pers.* Pelaiah.

פלג *ni* be divided.

> *pi* cut open, channel.

I פֶּלֶג canal, channel, stream.

II פֶּלֶג *n. pers.* Peleg.

פְּלַגָּה* division; watercourse.

פְּלֻגָּה* division.

פִּלֶגֶשׁ *f.* concubine; *Ezek. 23.20 m.* lecher.

פְּלָדָה* steel?

פִּלְדָּשׁ *n. pers.* Pildash.

פלה *ni* be distinguished, select.

> *hi* treat specially; distinguish.

פַּלּוּא *n. pers.* Pallu.

פְּלֹנִי → פְּלֹנִי.

פלח *q* furrow.

> *pi* rupture; cut up; give birth to, drop.

פֶּלַח *f.* slice; millstone; *w.* דְּבֵלָה figs pressed in a disc.

פִּלְחָא *n. pers.* Pilha.

פלט   *q* escape.

     pi bring to safety, deliver; *Job 21.10* give birth, bring forth; *Job 23.7* establish *(right)*.

פֶּלֶט   *n. pers.* Pelet.

פְּלֵטָה   → פְּלֵיטָה.

פַּלְטִי   *n. pers.* Palti; *gent.* Paltite.

פִּלְטַי   *n. pers.* Piltai.

פַּלְטִיאֵל   *n. pers.* Paltiel.

פְּלַטְיָה(וּ)   *n. pers.* Pelatiah.

פְּלָיָה   *n. pers.* Pelaiah.

פָּלִיט   one who escapes, fugitive *also coll.*

*פָּלֵיט   one who escapes, fugitive.

פְּלֵיטָה   what has escaped, remains over; escape, deliverance.

*פָּלִיל   judge.

פְּלִילָה   decision.

פְּלִילִי   calling for judgment.

פְּלִילִיָּה   judgment.

I פֶּלֶךְ   spindle-whorl.

II פֶּלֶךְ   district, region.

I פלל   *pi* judge, decide; *Gen. 48.11* expect; *Ezek. 16.52* become substitute for.

     hitp arbitrate.

II פלל   *hitp* pray, petition.

פָּלָל   *n. pers.* Palal.

פְּלַלְיָה   *n. pers.* Pelaliah.

פַּלְמוֹנִי   such and such a one.

פְּלֹנִי   a certain one, someone; *w.* אַלְמֹנִי such and such.

I פלס   *pi* prepare; *Ps. 58.3* prepare the way.

II פלס   *pi Prov. 5* note, observe.

פֶּלֶס   scales.

פלץ   *hitp* shake.

פַּלָּצוּת   shaking.

פלש   *hitp* roll.

פְּלֶשֶׁת   *n. terr.* Philistia.

פְּלִשְׁתִּי   *gent.* Philistine.

פֶּלֶת   *n. pers.* Peleth.

פְּלֵתִי   *gent.* Pelethite.

־פֶּן   lest, so that not; *Prov. 25.8* otherwise.

פֶּנַּג *kind of food, unexplained.*

פנה *q* turn, turn towards, follow a direction; pay heed; expect; turn
round, turn back; go on; apply oneself attentively; dawn,
decline *(time of day)*; turn *(the back)*; be directed, face.

   pi remove, clear up, make clear, prepare.

   hi turn *(intrans.)*, turn round, retreat; turn *(the back)*, turn
(trans.).

   ho turn; be directed, face.

*פָּנֶה face, countenance; appearance, expression; self; look; inten-
tion; visible side, surface, front, edge *(sword)*; *Joel 2.20* van;
w. מִלְחָמָה battle-front; (הַ)פָּנִים (לֶחֶם) שֻׁלְחַן table for shewbread; before, earlier, formerly.

   פְּנֵי *w.* אֶל to the front of, along; *w.* אֶת before; *w.* בְּ before,
against; *w.* לְ before *(time, place)*, in front of, quicker than; מִלִּפְנֵי
before, away from, starting from, because of; *w.* מִן before, away
from, on before, on the part of, because of, *Job 17.12* compared
with; *w.* עַל before, in view of, facing, over against, at the expense of.

פִּנָּה corner, corner-tower, battlement; leader.

פְּנוּאֵל *n. pers.*, *n. place* Penuel.

פִּנְחָם → פִּינְחָם.

פְּנִיאֵל *n. place* Peniel.

פְּנִיִּים *rd. Q (Prov. 3.15)*.

פָּנִים *pl. of* פָּנֶה.

פְּנִימָה inside, within; *w.* לְ on the inside, into the interior; *w.* מִן
within.

פְּנִימִי inner.

פְּנִינִים corals.

פְּנִנָּה *n. pers. f.* Peninnah.

פנק *pi* pamper.

*פַּס *pl.* multi-coloured?, ankle-length?

פסג *pi* go through?

פִּסְגָּה *n. place* Pisgah.

פַּס דַּמִּים *n. place* Pas-dammim.

*פָּסָה abundance?

פסח *q* be lame, limp; pass over, spare.

ni become lame.

pi limp around *(cultic dance)*.

פֶּסַח   passover; sacrifice of passover.

פָּסֵחַ   *n. pers.* Paseah.

פִּסֵּחַ   lame.

פָּסִיל*   idol.

פָּסַךְ   *n. pers.* Pasach.

פסל   *q* hew.

פֶּסֶל   idol.

פסס   *q* cease, disappear.

פִּסְפָּה   *n. pers.* Pispah.

פעה   *q* groan.

פָּעוּ   *n. place* Pau.

פְּעוֹר   *n. deity, n. place* Peor.

פָּעִי   *n. place* Pai.

פעל   *q* make, practise, commit, perpetrate, work; do, do to, accomplish, carry out; *Job 36.3 pt.* maker.

פֹּעַל   deed, labour, work; doing, working; wages, acquisition.

פְּעֻלָּה*   labour, deed; reward, wages, punishment.

פְּעֻלְּתַי   *n. pers.* Peullethai.

פעם   *q* impel.

ni be agitated.

hitp be disquieted.

פַּעַם   *f.* foot, step, pace; *Isa. 41.7* anvil; time, occurrence; *Neh. 13.20* once; הַפַּעַם this time, at last; פַּעַם—פַּעַם now—now; כְּפַעַם(־)בְּפַעַם as always.

פַּעֲמוֹן   bell.

פַּעֲנֵחַ   → צָפְנַת פַּעֲנֵחַ.

פער   *q* open wide.

פָּעֲרַי   *n. pers.* Paarai.

פצה   *q* gape, open wide; *Ps. 66.14* open; *Ps. 144 Aram.* rescue.

I פצח   *q* be glad.

II פצח   *pi* shatter.

פְּצִירָה   sharpening.

פצל   *pi* strip, peel.

פְּצָלוֹת   strips.

פצם   *q* split.

פָּצַע   *q* wound, crush.

פֶּצַע   wound.

פָּצַץ   *poel* shatter.

      pilp dash in pieces.

      hitpo be shattered.

פַּצֵּץ   → בֵּית פַּצֵּץ.

פִּצֵּץ   *n. pers.* Pizzez.

פָּצַר   *q* urge someone strongly, press.

      hi be rebellious.

פַּק   shaking.

פָּקַד   *q* seek, seek out, search; attend to, come to the aid of; miss, long for; enrol, muster; appoint, install, set, enjoin, commission; call to account, requite; *II Kings 5.24* deposit; *Num. 4.32* entrust.

      ni be missed, be missing, go missing; be summoned, be appointed, be called to account; befall; be affected.

      pi muster.

      pu be summoned; be determined.

      hi order, commission, appoint, commit; deposit, bring into custody, entrust; *Lev. 26.16* ordain; *I Sam. 29.4* assign; *Isa. 10.28* leave behind.

      ho be commissioned, appointed; be entrusted, deposited; *Jer. 6.6* be called to account.

      hitp be numbered, mustered.

      hotpaal be numbered, mustered.

פְּקֻדָּה   office, service, division for service; guard, care; sentry; administration; requital, visitation; muster, census; *Num. 16.29* fate; *Isa. 15.7* what remains over; *Jer. 52.11* w. בַּיַת prison.

פִּקָּדוֹן   deposit, store.

פְּקִדֻת   w. בַּעַל commander of the guard.

פְּקוֹד   *n. peop.*, *n. terr.* Pekod.

פְּקוּדִים*   *Ex. 38.21* calculation of costs.

פִּקּוּדִים*   directions.

פָּקַח   *q* open; *Ps. 146.8* open the eyes.

      ni be opened.

פֶּקַח *n. pers.* Pekah.

פִּקֵחַ having sight.

פְּקַחְיָה *n. pers.* Pekahiah.

פְּקַח־קוֹחַ opening.

פָּקִיד deputy, overseer, officer.

פְּקָעִים° gourd-shaped ornaments.

פַּקֻּעֹת° gourds.

פַּר young (male) ox, young bull.

פרא *hi* flourish?, bear fruit?

פֶּרֶא wild ass *or* zebra.

פִּרְאָם *n. pers.* Piram.

פַּרְבָּר forecourt.

פרד *q pt. pass.* outspread.

ni divide, part; be separated, isolated.

pi go aside.

pu pt. separated.

hi separate, isolate; disperse.

hitp be separated, be dispersed.

פֶּרֶד mule.

פִּרְדָּה she-mule.

פְּרֻדוֹת seeds?

פַּרְדֵּס orchard, park.

פרה *q* be fruitful, produce fruit.

hi make fruitful.

פָּרָה I cow.

פָּרָה II *n. place* Parah.

פָּרָה → פֶּרֶא.

פֻּרָה *n. pers.* Purah.

פְּרוּדָא *n. pers.* Peruda.

פְּרוּזִים *rd. Q (Esther 9.19).*

פָּרוּחַ *n. pers.* Paruah.

פַּרְוָיִם *n. place* Parvaim.

פַּרְוָר* forecourt.

פָּרוּר pot, cooking-pot.

פֵּרוֹת → חֲפֹר פֵּרוֹת.

פֶּרֶז*, פְּרָז* *Hab. 3.14 text corr.*

פְּרָזוֹן inhabitants of the open country?

פְּרָזוֹת open country.

פְּרָזִי inhabitant of the open country; open country.

פְּרִזִּי *gent.* Perizzite.

I פרח *q* sprout, bud, blossom; break out *(skin-disease)*, burst open *(boil)*.

hi cause to sprout, blossom; flourish.

II °פרח *q pt.* flying?

פֶּרַח bud, flower *(also as ornament)*.

פִּרְחַח brood?

פרט *q* bawl?

פֶּרֶט fallen grapes.

פְּרִי fruit *(also in the broadest sense)*.

פְּרִידָא *n. pers.* Perida.

פָּרִיץ burglar, robber; *Isa. 35.9* tearing.

פֶּרֶךְ ill-treatment.

פָּרֹכֶת curtain.

פרם *q* tear in pieces.

פַּרְמַשְׁתָּא *n. pers.* Parmashta.

פַּרְנָךְ *n. pers.* Parnach.

פרס *q* break.

hi have hoofs, divided hoofs.

פֶּרֶס vulture?

פָּרַס *n. peop.* Persians; *n. terr.* Persia.

פַּרְסָה foot; hoof.

פַּרְסִי *gent.* Persian.

פרע *q* let hang loose, unbind; release, abandon oneself to, ignore; *pt. pass. also* unbridled.

ni become unbridled, degenerate.

hi let be negligent; cause the spread of degeneracy.

I פֶּרַע loose hair of the head.

II פֶּרַע → פְּרַע פֹּטִי.

פַּרְעֹה Pharaoh.

I פַּרְעֹשׁ flea.

II פַּרְעֹשׁ *n. pers.* Parosh.

פִּרְעָתוֹן *n. place* Pirathon.

פִּרְעָת(וֹ)נִי *gent.* Pirathonite.

פַּרְפַּר *n. river* Pharpar.

פרץ *q* breach, tear down, break in, break through; overflow, spread; make a gap, a breach (in opposing ranks); urge someone.

ni pt. frequent.

pu pt. torn down.

hitp break away.

פֶּרֶץ I   bursting, gap, breach, bursting out.

פֶּרֶץ II   *n. pers.* Perez.

פַּרְצִי   *gent.* Perezite.

פְּרָצִים   *n. place* Perazim.

פֶּרֶץ עֻזָּא,   *n. place* Perez-uzzah.
פֶּרֶץ עֻזָּה

פרק   *q Ps. 7.3* tear?; *Aram.* tear off, rescue.

pi pull off, rend.

hitp pull off; be torn off.

פֶּרֶק   parting of ways; spoil.

פָּרָק*   crumbled thing.

פרר I   *hi* break, destroy, annul, frustrate, invalidate; burst *(fruit)*.

ho be shattered, annulled, frustrated.

פרר II   *q Isa. 24.19 inf. abs. in conjunction with hitpo.*

poel rouse.

pilp shake.

hitpo rock to and fro.

פרשׂ   *q* spread, stretch, spread out; *Isa. 33.23* make to shiver; *Micah 3.3; Lam. 4.4* → פרס.

ni be scattered.

pi spread, scatter.

פרשׁ   *q* give instructions.

ni rd. נִפְרָשׁ'ת *(Ezek. 34.12).*

pu be determined; *pt.* section by section.

hi secrete poison?, sting?

פֶּרֶשׁ I   contents of stomach.

פֶּרֶשׁ II   *n. pers.* Peresh.

פָּרָשׁ   horseman; steed.

פַּרְשֶׁגֶן°   copy.

פַּרְשְׁדֹן*   loophole.

פָּרָשָׁה*   exact statement.

פרשׁז   spread.

פַּרְשַׁנְדָתָא *n. pers.* Parshandatha.

פְּרָת *n. river* Euphrates.

פֹּרָת *q pt. f. of* פרה.

פַּרְתְּמִים nobles.

פשׂה *q* spread.

פשׂע *q* step.

פֶּשַׂע step.

פשׂק *q* open wide.

    pi spread wide.

פַּשׂ *rd.* פֶּשַׁע *(Job 35.15).*

פשׁח *pi* tear in pieces.

פַּשְׁחוּר *n. pers.* Pashhur.

פשׁט *q* take off, strip off; undress, shed the skin; make straight for.

    pi strip.

    hi take off, strip, strip off; flay.

    hitp strip off.

פשׁע *q* break (with), transgress, revolt, rebel.

    ni pt. treated faithlessly.

פֶּשַׁע offence, revolt, rebellion; *Micah 6.7* atonement?

°פֵּשֶׁר explanation, interpretation.

*פֵּשֶׁת flax, linen; פִּשְׁתֵּי הָעֵץ stalks of flax.

פִּשְׁתָּה flax, linen; wick.

פַּת morsel, bit.

*פֹּת forehead; front, façade.

פִּתְאוֹם →פִּתְאֹם.

פְּתָאִים *pl. of* פֶּתִי.

פִּתְאֹם instantly, suddenly, unexpectedly.

°פַּת־בַּג food, board, table.

°פִּתְגָם decree, order, sentence.

פתה I *q* be inexperienced, simple; be deluded, allow oneself to be led astray.

    ni let oneself be deluded.

    pi delude, lead astray, seduce; persuade; deceive, defraud.

    pu allow oneself to be led astray, be seduced; allow oneself to be persuaded.

II פתה°   *q* open wide?

     hi provide ample space.

פְּתוּאֵל   *n. pers.* Pethuel.

פִּתּוּחַ   engraving, carving.

פְּתוֹר   *n. place* Pethor.

פְּתוֹת*   piece, morsel.

I פתח   *q* open, uncover; strip; conquer *(city)*; draw *(sword)*; solve *(riddle)*; offer for sale *(corn)*.

     ni be opened; open; be set free, released; *Job 32.19* be vented.

     pi open, loosen, untie; open up; break open; *Gen. 24.32* unharness.

     hitp loosen.

II פתח   *pi* engrave, carve.

     pu pt. engraved.

פֶּתַח   opening, entrance, door, gate.

פֵּתַח   disclosure, communication.

פִּתָּחוֹן*   opening.

פְּתַחְיָה   *n. pers.* Pethahiah.

I פֶּתִי   inexperienced, simple.

II פֶּתִי   simplicity.

פְּתִיגִיל   fine garment, gorgeous gown.

פְּתַיּוּת   simplicity.

פְּתִיחָה*   drawn sword.

פָּתִיל   thread, cord, rope.

פתל   *ni Gen. 30.8* wrestle, struggle; *pt.* cunning, wily.

     hitp show oneself cunning, wily.

פְּתַלְתֹּל   false, corrupt.

פִּתֹם   *n. place* Pithom.

פֶּתֶן°   cobra.

פֶּתַע   instant; *adv.* instantly, in a moment.

פתר   *q* explain, interpret.

פַּתְרוֹס   *n. terr.* Pathros (Upper Egypt).

פַּתְרֻסִים   *n. peop.* Pathrusim (inhabitants of Upper Egypt).

פִּתְרוֹן*   explanation, interpretation.

פַּתְשֶׁגֶן°   copy.

פתת   *q* crumble.

צ

צֵא *Isa. 30.22* filth *or imv. of* יצא away with!

צֵאָה* excrement.

צֹאָה excrement, filth, loathsome thing.

צֹאִי* filthy.

צֶאֱלִים thorny lotus.

צֹאן *coll.* small cattle; *I Sam. 25.2* sheep.

צַאֲנָן *n. place* Zaanan.

צֶאֱצָאִים offspring, descendants.

I צָב covered wagon, wagon.

II צָב *Lev. 11.29* thorn-tailed lizard.

צבא *q* wage war, do duty.
   hi muster.

I צָבָא army, host; military service; forced-labour; service in the cult;
   pl. hosts.

II צָבָא* *parallel form of* II צְבִי gazelle.

צָבָא → צִיבָא.

צְבָאָה* female gazelle.

צְבֹאִים *n. place* Zeboiim.

צֹבֵבָה *n. pers.* Zobebah.

צבה *q* swell up.
   hi make to swell up.

צֹבֶה → צוֹבָא.

צָבֶה* *q pt. of* צבא.

צָבֶה* swollen up.

צָבוֹעַ hyena.

צבט *q* pass.

I צְבִי ornament, glory.

II צְבִי gazelle.

צִבְיָא *n. pers.* Zibia.

צִבְיָה *n. pers. f.* Zibiah.

צְבִיָּה female gazelle.

צְבֹיִ(י)ם → צְבֹאִים.

צֶבַע coloured cloth.

צִבְעוֹן *n. pers.* Zibeon.

צְבֹעִים   *n. place* Zeboim.

צבר   *q* heap up, store up.

צִבֻּר*   heap.

צֶבֶת*   bundle of heads of corn.

I צַד   side, flank, hip.

II צַד*   snare.

צְדָד*   *n. place* Zedad.

I צדה   *q* lie in wait for.

II צדה°   *ni* be devastated.

צֵדָה   → צֵידָה.

צָדוֹק   *n. pers.* Zadok.

צְדִיָּה   evil intention, premeditation.

צַדִּים   *n. place* Ziddim.

צַדִּיק   innocent, righteous, just; godly, right, correct.

צָדֹנִי   → צִידֹנִי.

צָדְנִית   → צִידֹנִי.

צדק   *q* be innocent, be righteous, prove to be right, be just.
     ni be reinstated in its rights.
     pi make to appear righteous; consider oneself in the right; declare to be in the right; *w.* נֶפֶשׁ prove oneself righteous.
     hi declare innocent; treat as innocent; declare righteous; dispense justice, attribute right, help to procure rights.
     hitp justify oneself.

צֶדֶק   what is right, correct; righteousness; justice; victory.

צָדֹק   → צָדוֹק.

צְדָקָה   right conduct, justice; godliness; innocence; legal claim, right; victory, goodness; *pl. also* just cause, just deeds, acts of justice, deeds of victory, uprightness, godliness.

צִדְקִיָּה(וּ)   *n. pers.* Zedekiah.

צהב   *ho pt.* gleaming red.

צָהֹב   gleaming red.

I צהל   *q* neigh; shout with joy.
     pi make shrill.

II צהל *hi* make to shine.

צהר *hi* press out oil.

צֹהַר roof.

צָהֳרַיִם midday, noontide.

צַו, צָו *zaw meaning dub.; mimicking?, name of letter of alphabet?*

צַוָּאר neck, nape.

צוֹבָא, צוֹבָה *n. place., n. terr.* Zobah.

צוד *q* hunt, lie in wait for; spy on.
pol catch.

צוה *pi* appoint, order, summon; charge, command.
pu receive command, be charged.

צוח *q* cry.

צְוָחָה cry.

צוּלָה abyss (of sea).

צום *q* fast.

צוֹם fasting, time of fasting.

צוּעָר *n. pers.* Zuar.

צוֹעֵר → צֹעַר.

צוף *q* flow.
hi cause to flood; make to float.

I צוּף liquid honey.

II צוּף *n. pers.* Zuph.

צוֹפַח *n. pers.* Zophah.

צוֹפַי *n. pers.* Zophai.

צוֹפִים *element of n. place* Ramathaim-zophim.

צוֹפַר *n. pers.* Zophar.

I צוץ *q* blossom.
hi blossom; *Ps. 132.18* radiate.

II צוץ *hi* glance.

I צוק *hi* oppress, press hard.

II צוק *q* pour.

צוֹק affliction.

צוּקָה affliction.

I צור *q* tie up; clasp, surround, besiege; *Judg. 9.31* unite, stir up; *Isa. 29.3 w.* מַצָּב post sentries around; *Cant. 8.9* bar.

צוּר II *q* show hostility, press hard.

צוּר III *q* trace out; fashion, mould.

צוּר I boulder, rock.

צוּר II pebble, feldspar.

צוּר III *n. pers.* Zur.

צוֹר → צֹר II.

צֻוָּר* → צַוָּאר.

צוּרָה* plan; form.

צוּרִיאֵל *n. pers.* Zuriel.

צוּרִישַׁדַּי, *n. pers.* Zurishaddai.
צוּרִי(־)שַׁדַּי

צַוְּרֹנִים* necklace.

צוּת *hi* kindle.

צַח brilliant, radiant; *Isa. 18.4; Jer. 4.11* Zah *(name of month, summer?)*.

צְחָא → צִיחָא.

צָחֶה* parched.

צחח *q* gleam, be white.

צְחִחִים *rd. Q (Neh. 4.7)*.

צָחִיחַ* glaring, bare surface; *Neh. 4.7* open place?

צְחִיחָה bare, scorched region.

צַחֲנָה* stench, putrefaction.

צַחְצָחוֹת bare, scorched region.

צחק *q* laugh.

pi fondle, jest; make fun of, make merry; disport oneself.

צְחֹק laughter, mockery.

צַחַר *n. place?* Zahar.

צָחֹר* white?, sandy-coloured?

צֹחַר *n. pers.* Zohar.

צִי* I ship.

צִי II demon.

צִיבָא° *n. pers.* Ziba.

ציד *hitp* take as provision.

צַיִד I hunting, game.

צַיִד II food, provision.

צַיָּד* hunter.

צֵידָה provision.

צִידוֹן, צִידֹן *n. pers., n. place* Sidon.

צִידוֹנִי, צִידֹנִי *gent.* Sidonian.

צִיָּה drought; dry, waterless region.

צִיּוֹן dry, waterless region.

צִיּוֹן *n. place* Zion.

צִיּוּן stone mark, monument, road-mark.

צִיחָא *n. pers.* Ziha.

צִינֹק iron collar.

צִיעֹר *n. place* Zior.

צִיף rd. Q *(I Chron. 6.20).*

I צִיץ *coll.* blossom, flowers; plate worn on forehead.

II צִיץ → הַצִּיץ.

צִיצָה* flower.

צִיצִת tuft of hair; tassel.

צִיקְלַג → צִקְלַג.

צִיר *hitp dub.*

I צִיר envoy.

II צִיר* *pl.* labour-pains, convulsions.

III צִיר* *Isa. 45.16* image, form; *Ps. 49.15* rd. K.

IV צִיר* *Prov. 26.14* pivot-cup.

צֵל shadow.

צלה *q* roast.

צִלָּה *n. pers. f.* Zillah.

צְלוּל rd. K *(Judg. 7.13)* flat cake.

צלח *q* be fit, strong, effective; be of use; succeed, have success; *w.* רוּחַ take possession of.

hi have success; let succeed, give success.

צְלֹחִית° bowl.

צַלַּחַת, צֵלַחַת* bowl.

צָלִי roasted meat.

I צלל *q* ring; tremble.

II צלל *q* sink.

III צלל *q* grow shadowy, dark.

hi give shade.

צִלְלוֹ, צִלְלֵי *forms of* צֵל.

צְלָלִים

צֶלֶם statue, model, image.

צַלְמוֹן *n. pers., n. place* Zalmon.

צַלְמָוֶת darkness.

צַלְמֹנָה n. *place* Zalmonah.

צַלְמֻנָּע n. *pers.* Zalmunna.

צלע *q* limp, be lame.

צֶלַע stumbling.

I צֵלָע rib; side; side-chamber, annexe; door-leaf; board; beam.

II צֵלָע n. *place* Zela.

צָלָף n. *pers.* Zalaph.

צְלָפְחָד n. *pers.* Zelophehad.

צֶלְצַח n. *place* Zelzah.

צְלָצַל cricket.

צִלְצָל* harpoon.

צֶלְצְלִים cymbals.

צֶלֶק n. *pers.* Zelek.

צִלְּתַי n. *pers.* Zillethai.

צמא *q* be thirsty.

צָמָא thirst.

צָמֵא thirsty, parched.

צִמְאָה thirst.

צִמָּאוֹן thirsty, waterless territory.

צמד *ni* associate oneself with.

pu pt. fastened.

hi harness.

צֶמֶד pair; yoke *(square measure, area which can be ploughed by a pair of oxen in a day)*.

צַמָּה* veil.

צִמֻּקִים bunches of dried grapes.

צמח *q* sprout.

pi sprout, grow again.

hi make to sprout; cause to sprout.

צֶמַח sprouting, growth; plant, shoot.

I צָמִיד bracelet.

II צָמִיד cover.

צַמִּים *trapping equipment* snare?

צְמִיתֻת *w.* לְ irrevocably.

צמק *q* dry up, shrivel.

צִמֻּקִים → צִמֻּקִים.

צֶמֶר wool.

צְמָרִי *gent.* Zemarite.

צְמָרַיִם *n. place* Zemaraim.

צַמֶּרֶת tree-top.

צמת *q* silence, annihilate.
ni be silenced, annihilated.
pil silence, annihilate.
hi silence, annihilate.

צְמִיתֻת → צְמִתֻת.

צֵן* thorn, hook.

צִן *n. place* Zin.

צֹנֶא* *rd.* צֹאנְכֶם *(Num. 32.24).*

צֹנֶה small cattle.

I צִנָּה* coldness.

II צִנָּה large, upright shield.

צִנּוֹת *Amos 4.2 pl. of* צֵן.

צָנוּעַ* humble.

צָנוּף *rd. Q (Isa. 62.3).*

צִנּוֹר cataract; *II Sam. 5.8 dub.*

צנח *q Josh. 15.18; Judg. 1.14* clap the hands?, bend down?; *Judg. 4.21* strike?, pierce?

צְנִינִם thorns.

צָנִיף head-band.

צְנִיפָה* head-band.

צָנֵם* withered, shrivelled.

צְנָן *n. place* Zenan.

צְנִנִים → צְנִינִם.

צנע *hi* walk humbly.

צנף *q* wrap together.

צְנֵפָה bundle.

צִנְצֶנֶת receptacle; jar.

צַנְתָּרוֹת*° pipes?

צעד *q* step.
hi make to march.

צַעַד step; walking.

צְעָדָה marching; *Isa. 3.20* step-chain.

צעה *q* be bowed with fetters; sprawl *(prostitute)*; stride along;

Jer. 48.12 pt. cellarman.

pi tilt, pour out.

צָעוּר* rd. Q (Jer. 14.3; 48.4).

צָעִיף veil, wrapper.

I צָעִיר small; young; lowly; Jer. 14.3 underling.

II צָעִיר* n. place Zair.

צְעִירָה smallness; youth.

צען q pull down.

צֹעַן n. place Zoan.

צַעֲנַנִּים n. place Zaanannim.

צַעֲצֻעִים casting?

צעק q cry; cry for help.

ni be called together, mustered.

pi cry.

hi call together, summon.

צְעָקָה outcry, lamentation, cry for help.

צער q be/become small, insignificant; Zech. 13.7 pt. shepherd-boy.

צֹעַר n. place Zoar.

צפד q contract, shrivel.

I צפה q keep watch, be on the look out; lie in wait.

pi look out.

II צפה q spread out.

pi plate; overlay.

pu pt. overlaid.

צָפָה* discharge?

צְפוֹ n. pers. Zepho.

צִפּוּי plating.

I צָפוֹן north; Cant. 4.16 north wind.

II צָפוֹן n. place Zaphon.

צְפוֹן n. pers. Zephon.

I צְפוֹנִי northerner.

II צְפוֹנִי gent. Zephonite.

צְפוֹעֵי rd. Q (Ezek. 4.15) dung.

I צִפּוֹר f. bird; coll. birds.

II צִפּוֹר n. pers. Zippor.

צַפַּחַת vessel, flask?

צְפִי n. pers. Zephi.

צִפִּיָּה* look-out.

צִפְיוֹן   *n. pers.* Ziphion.

צַפִּיחִת   flat cake.

צָפִין*   *rd. Q (Ps. 17.14).*

צָפִיר   he-goat.

צְפִירָה   garland.

צָפִית   cushion.

צפן   *q* hide *(trans.),* shelter, store up; keep away; hide *(intrans.),*
    lie in wait for; *pt. pass. also* treasure.

    ni be hidden; be reserved, fixed.

    hi hide.

צְפַנְיָה(וּ)   *n. pers.* Zephaniah.

צָפְנַת פַּעְנֵחַ   *n. pers.* Zaphenath-paneah.

צֶפַע   (poisonous) snake, viper.

צִפְעָה*   leaf.

צִפְע(וֹ)נִי   (poisonous) snake, viper.

צפף   *pilp* chirp; twitter; whisper.

צַפְצָפָה   willow.

צפר   *q rd.* יְצָרְפֵם *(Judg. 7.3).*

צִפֹּר   → צִפּוֹר.

צֹפַר   → צוֹפַר.

צְפַרְדֵּעַ   frog; *coll.* frogs.

צְפָרָה   → צְפִירָה.

צִפֹּרָה   *n. pers. f.* Zipporah.

צִפֹּרֶן   nail *(finger, toe)*; point of graver.

צֶפֶת   capital.

צְפַת   *n. place* Zephath.

צְפַתָה   *n. place* Zephathah.

צָקוּן   *Isa. 26.16 dub.*

צִקְלַג   *n. place* Ziklag.

צָקְלֹן*   *dub.*

I צַר   narrow, limited; affliction, anguish; distress.

II צַר   oppressor, adversary, enemy.

III צַר   *Isa. 5.28* pebble.

צֵר   *n. place* Zer.

צֹר   → צוּר.

I צֹר   pebble; flint knife.

II צֹר   *n. place* Tyre.

צרב   *ni* be scorched.

צָרֵב*   scorching.

צָרֶבֶת   scorching; scar.

צְרֵדָה   n. place Zeredah.

I צָרָה   distress, affliction.

II צָרָה*   I Sam. 1.6 rival-wife.

צְרוּיָה   n. pers. f. Zeruiah.

צְרוּעָה   n. pers. f. Zeruah.

I צְרוֹר   bag, sack.

II צְרוֹר   stone, pebble.

III צְרוֹר   n. pers. Zeror.

צרח   q cry.

     hi raise the battle-cry.

צֹרִי   gent. Tyrian.

צֱרִי   mastic gum.

צֶרִי   n. pers. Zeri.

צְרִיָה   → צְרוּיָה.

צְרִיחַ   cave; cellar.

צֵרִים   pl. of I צֹר.

צֹרֶךְ*°   need.

צרע   q pt. pass. suffering from a skin eruption.

     pu pt. suffering from a skin eruption.

צְרָעָה   depression, demoralization.

צָרְעָה   n. place Zorah.

צָרְעִי   gent. Zorite.

צָרַעַת   skin eruption.

צָרְעָתִי   gent. Zorathite.

צרף   q smelt, refine, sift; pt. also goldsmith, silversmith.

     ni be refined.

     pi smelt, refine.

צֹרְפִי   goldsmiths' guild.

צָרְפַת   n. place Zarephath, Sarepta.

I צרר   q tie up, wrap up; shut up; be narrow, cramped; be distressed,
     oppressed; be grieved, anxious.

     pu pt. patched up.

     hi afflict; be in affliction.

II צרר   q show hostility to, make war upon; be rival-wife.

צְרֵרָה*   n. place Zererah.

צֶרֶת   n. pers. Zereth.
צֶרֶת הַשַּׁחַר   n. place Zereth-shahar.
צָרְתָן   n. place Zarethan.

ק

קָא*   vomit.
קָאַת, קָאָת   species of owl?
קַב   dry measure kab (between 1.2 and 2.5 l).
קבב   q wish (someone) ill, curse.
קֵבָה   rennet-bag, fourth stomach of ruminants; Num. 25.8 dub.
קֻבָּה   women's quarter.
קֻבִּין*   dub.
קְבוּרָה   grave; burial.
קבל°   pi accept, receive; undertake; choose.
     hi be opposite to.
קֹבֶל°*   siege-engine battering-ram?; II Kings 15.10 text corr.
קבע   q cheat?, rob?
קֻבַּעַת   cup.
קבץ   q gather; gather together.
     ni gather; be gathered.
     pi gather, gather together, harvest; w. פָּארוּר grow pale or redden.
     pu pt. gathered.
     hitp gather together.
קַבְצְאֵל   n. place Kabzeel.
קְבָצָה*   gathering.
קִבְצַיִם   n. place Kibzaim.
קבר   q bury.
     ni be buried.
     pi bury.
     pu be buried.
קֶבֶר   grave.
קִבְרוֹת הַתַּאֲוָה, קִבְרֹת הַתַּאֲוָה   n. place Kibroth-hattaavah.

קָדַד‎ *q* bow *(in homage)*.

קִדָּה‎ cassia.

קִדּוּמִים‎ *dub.*

קָדוֹשׁ‎ holy.

קָדַח‎ *q* flare up; kindle.

קַדַּחַת‎ inflammation; fever.

קָדִים‎ what is in front > east side, east; east wind.

קָדַם‎ *pi* lead the way; meet, advance towards; *Ps. 119.147f.; Jonah 4.2* forestall, do early *(Aram.)*.

hi Amos 9.10; Job 41.3 rd. pi.

קֶדֶם‎ in front; east; earlier, of old; antiquity, primeval times; *adv.* from of old.

קֵדֶם‎* east.

קַדְמָה‎* origin; former condition; former time; *Ps. 129.6 w.* שֶׁ‎ before, ere *(Aram.)*.

קָדְמָה‎* over against.

קֵדְמָה‎ *n. pers.* Kedemah.

קַדְמוֹן‎* eastern.

קַדְמוֹנִי‎ → I קַדְמֹנִי‎.

קְדֵמוֹת‎ *n. place* Kedemoth.

קַדְמִיאֵל‎ *n. pers.* Kadmiel.

I קַדְמֹנִי‎ eastern, former, earlier; *coll.* forefathers; *Isa. 43.18* former thing.

II קַדְמֹנִי‎ *gent.* Kadmonite.

קְדֵמֹת‎ → קְדֵמוֹת‎.

קָדְקֹד‎ crown of the head; parting.

קָדַר‎ *q* grow dark; be/become turbid, dirty; wear mourning.

hi darken; cause to mourn.

hitp grow dark.

קֵדָר‎ *n. pers., n. peop.* Kedar.

קִדְרוֹן‎ *n. river* Kidron.

קַדְרוּת‎ darkness.

קְדֹרַנִּית‎ in mourning.

קָדַשׁ‎ *q* be holy.

ni show oneself holy; be hallowed.

pi declare holy; consecrate, dedicate; transmit holiness; regard as holy.

pu pt. consecrated, dedicated.

hi let be holy; consecrate, dedicate, offer; treat as holy.

hitp purify, sanctify oneself; show oneself holy.

קָדֹשׁ → קְדוֹשׁ.

I קָדֵשׁ   sacred, (cult) prostitute.

II קָדֵשׁ   *n. place* Kadesh.

קֶדֶשׁ   *n. place* Kedesh.

קֹדֶשׁ   holy thing; holiness; holy place; *pl. also* offerings.

קָדֵשׁ בַּרְנֵעַ   *n. place* Kadesh-barnea.

קהה   *q* become blunt.

pi become blunt.

קהל   *ni* assemble.

hi assemble, convoke.

קָהָל   assembly, convocation, congregation.

קְהִלָּה   assembly, congregation.

קֹהֶלֶת   preacher.

קְהֵלָתָה   *n. place* Kehelathah.

קְהָת   *n. pers.* Kohath.

קְהָתִי   *gent.* Kohathite.

קָו   line, measuring-line; *Isa. 18.2,7 rd.* קַו־קָו vigour.

קַו, קָו   kaw *meaning dub.; mimicking?, name of letter of alphabet?*

קְוֵא   *rd.* קֹוֵא *(II Chron. 1.16) n. terr.* Ko, Cilicia.

קוֹבַע   helmet.

קוֹדֶשׁ → קֹדֶשׁ.

I קוה   *q* wait for, hope.

pi wait for, hope, expect; lie in wait.

II קוה   *ni* gather.

*קָוֶה   *rd. Q (I Kings 7.23; Jer. 31.39; Zech. 1.16).*

קְוֵה   *rd.* קֹוֵא *(I Kings 10.28) n. terr.* Ko, Cilicia.

קוֹחַ → פְּקַח־קוֹחַ.

קוט   *q* loathe.

ni feel loathing.

hitpol loathe.

קוֹל   sound, noise, blast, stir, din; voice, call; listen!; *pl. also* thunder; *Gen. 45.16* report, news.

קוֹלָיָה   *n. pers.* Kolaiah.

קוּם *q* stand up, rise up, rebel; come to pass; endure; be valid;
　　belong to; *Lev. 27.14,17* stand; *I Sam. 4.15; I Kings 14.4*
　　be/become fixed; *pt. also* adversary.

　　pi Aram. ratify, regulate, confirm; raise up.

　　pol erect.

　　hi raise up, erect, appoint; make/command to rise; rouse; per-
　　form, observe, honour; bring about, provide; *Ps. 107.29*
　　make; *Ruth 4.5,10* revive.

　　ho be erected, performed, set.

　　hitpol rebel.

קוֹמָה　height, stature.

קוֹמְמִיּוּת　*adv.* erect.

קוֹנֵן　*pol of* קין.

קוֹעַ　*n. peop.* Koa.

קוֹף*　ape.

I קִין　*q* loathe; dread.

II קִין　*hi* tear asunder; split open.

I קוֹץ　thorn-bushes, thorns.

II קוֹץ　*n. pers.* Koz.

קְוֻצּוֹת*　locks.

קוּר　*q* dig.

קוּר*　thread.

קוֹרֵא　→ II קרא.

קוֹרָה　beam, rafters.

קוֹשׁ　*q* trap, lay snares.

קוּשָׁיָהוּ　*n. pers.* Kushaiah.

קַח　willow.

קַט　only?, little?

קֶטֶב, קֶטֶב*　sting; contagious disease, destruction.

קְטוֹרָה　smoke of sacrifice.

קְטוּרָה　*n. pers. f.* Keturah.

קָטַל°　*q* kill.

קֶטֶל°　murder.

קָטֹן　*q* be small, insignificant.

　　hi make small.

קֹטֶן* small one.

קָטֹן small, insignificant; young, youngest.

קָטָן I small, insignificant; young, younger, youngest.

קָטָן II *n. pers.* Katan.

קטף *q* pluck, break off.
ni be cut down.

קטר I *pi* send (sacrifice) up in smoke, burn incense.
pu pt. perfumed.
hi send up in smoke, burn incense.
ho go up in smoke, be offered.

קטר II *q pt. pass.* enclosed?, unroofed?

קְטָר smoke of sacrifice.

קִטְרוֹן *n. place* Kitron.

קְטֹרֶת smoke of sacrifice; incense.

קַטָּת *n. place* Kattath.

קיא *q* spew out; vomit.
hi spew out.

קיא what is vomited up, spewed out.

קיה → קיא.

קִיטוֹר, קִיטֹר smoke.

קִים* adversary.

קִימָה* standing up.

קין *pol* chant a dirge.

קַיִן I* spear.

קַיִן II *n. pers., n. place* Cain; *n. peop.* Kenites.

קִינָה I dirge.

קִינָה II *n. place* Kinah.

קֵינִי *gent.* Kenite.

קֵינָן *n. pers.* Kenan.

קיץ *q* spend the summer.
hi awake.

קַיִץ summer; summer-fruit.

קִיצוֹן* last, outermost one.

קִיקָיוֹן castor-oil plant.

קִיקָלוֹן disgrace.

קִיר I wall, city-wall.

קִיר II *n. place, n. peop.* Kir.

קִיר חֶרֶשׂ *n. place* Kir-heres.

קִיר חֲרֶשֶׂת *n. place* Kir-hareseth.

קֵירֹם *n. pers.* Keros.

קִישׁ *n. pers.* Kish.

קִישׁוֹן *n. river* Kishon.

קִישִׁי *n. pers.* Kishi.

קַל swift; light.

I קֹל frivolousness.

II קֹל → קוֹל.

קלֹה *rd. Q (II Sam. 20.14).*

I קלה *q* roast.

ni pt. burning.

II קלה *ni* be/become despised.

hi treat contemptuously.

קָלוֹן disgrace.

קַלַּחַת pot, cauldron.

קלט *q pt. pass.* incompletely developed.

קַלָּי *n. pers.* Kallai.

קָלִי, קָלִיא parched grain.

קֵלָיָה *n. pers.* Kelaiah.

קְלִיטָא *n. pers.* Kelita.

קלל *q* be/become small, insignificant; be light, swift.

ni be little; humble, lower oneself; be easy, too little; *Isa. 30.16* show oneself swift; עַל־נְקַלָּה superficially.

pi declare contemptible, accursed; curse.

pilp Ezek. 21.26 shake; *Eccles. 10.10* sharpen, whet.

pu be declared contemptible, accursed; be cursed.

hi lighten, make light, lighter; treat as insignificant, treat contemptuously.

hitpalp be shaken.

קָלָל burnished.

קְלָלָה curse.

קלס *pi* scoff at.

hitp mock, make fun of.

קֶלֶס mockery.

קַלָּסָה laughing-stock.

I קלע   *q* sling.
       pi sling.

II קלע   *q* carve.

I קֶלַע   sling.

II *קֶלַע   curtain.

*קַלָּע   slinger.

קַלֹּקֵל   meagre, poor.

קִלְּשׁוֹן   *w.* שָׁלֹשׁ three-pronged fork.

קָמָה   uncut grain.

קֹמָה   → קוֹמָה.

קְמוּאֵל   *n. pers.* Kemuel.

קָמוֹן   *n. place* Kamon.

קִמּוֹשׂ   weeds.

קֶמַח   flour.

קמט   *q* seize.
       pu be seized.

קמל   *q* wither?, be infested with insects?

קמץ   *q* take a handful.

*קֹמֶץ   handful; *Gen. 41.47* in abundance.

קֵן   nest; *pl. also* compartments.

קנא   *pi* be jealous; arouse jealousy; be zealous.
       hi provoke jealousy, anger.

קַנָּא   jealous.

קִנְאָה   zeal, ardour; passion; jealousy.

I קנה   *q* acquire, buy, ransom.
       ni be bought.
       hi buy.

II קנה   *q* create, give birth to.

קָנֶה   reed; cane, pipe, stalk; length of a reed *(6 cubits)*; bone of the upper arm; beam of a balance, scales.

קָנָה   *n. place, n. river* Kanah.

קַנּוֹא   jealous.

קְנַז   *n. pers., n. peop.?* Kenaz.

קְנִזִּי   *gent.* Kenizzite.

קֵנִי   → קֵינִי.

°קִנְיָן   possession, property; *Ps. 104.24* created thing?

קִנָּמוֹן   cinnamon.

קִנֵּן *pi* nest.
pu pt. nested.

קֵנָן* limit?

קְנָת *n. place* Kenath.

קסם *q* practise divination by casting lots; divine.

קֶסֶם divination by casting lots; *Prov. 16.10* decision.

קסם *poel* pluck off?, make to flake?

קֶסֶת writing equipment.

קְעִילָה, קְעִלָה *n. place* Keilah.

קַעֲקַע tattooing.

קְעָרָה dish.

קפא *q* congeal, thicken.
hi curdle.

יְקִפָּאוֹן *rd. Q (Zech. 14.6)* frost.

קפד *pi* roll up.

קִפֹּד hedgehog; owl.

קְפָדָה anguish, anxiety.

קִפּוֹד → קִפֹּד.

קִפּוֹז arrow-snake?

קפץ *q* draw together, shut.
ni be carried off?
pi leap.

קֵץ end, limit, goal; extreme; time of the end; *w.* לְ *or* מִן at the end of, after, . . . later.

קצב *q* cut off, shear.

קֶצֶב*, קֵצֶב fashion, shape; *Jonah 2.7* base.

קצה *q* cut down.
pi strike hard; cut off.
hi scrape off.

קָצֶה end, border, limit, extremity; point; *w.* מִן *also* endlessly, entirely, irretrievably.

קָצָה end, border, edge, extremity; *w.* מִן *also* at the extremity.

קֵצֶה end.

קָצוּ* end.

קָצוּר* shortened, small.

קְצוֹת* end; generality.

קְצָוֹת *pl. of* קָצֶה.

קֶצַח black cummin.

קָצִין I   chief, leader.

קָצִין II   → עֵת קָצִין *(Josh. 19.13)*.

קְצִיעָה* I   cinnamon-flower.

קְצִיעָה II   *n. pers. f.* Keziah.

קְצִין   → עֵמֶק קְצִין.

קָצִיר I   harvest, crop.

קָצִיר II   branch.

קצע I   *hi* scrape off.

קצע II   *pu pt.* cornered.
         ho pt. cornered.

קצף   *q* be/become angry.
         hi provoke to anger.
         hitp fly into a rage.

קֶצֶף I   anger.

קֶצֶף II   *Hos. 10.7* broken-off branch.

קְצָפָה   stump?, trunk?

קצץ   *q* cut off, clip.
         pi cut off, cut up; cut through, dash in pieces.
         pu pt. cut off.

קצר I   *q* harvest; *pt. also* reaper.
         hi rd. Q (Job 24.6).

קצר II   *q* be short, too short, shortened; be/become impatient, be
         angry.
         pi shorten.
         hi shorten.

קֹצֶר   *w.* רוּחַ impatience.

קָצָר*   short; *w.* אַפַּיִם short-tempered; *w.* יָד powerless; *w.* יָמִים short-
         lived; *w.* רוּחַ impatient.

קְצָת°   end, extremity; *w.* מִן at the end of, some.

קַר   cool, cold.

קֹר   cold.

קַר   → קִיר I.

קרא I   *q* call, invoke, name; appoint; summon; announce, proclaim;
         invite; recite, read, read aloud; *Jer. 36.18* dictate.
         ni be summoned, called out, invoked; be called, named; be
         read; *I Chron. 23.14* be classed among.

pu be called, named.

II קרא *q* meet, encounter, befall; *inf. also prep.* toward, against, opposite.

ni permit oneself to be met; happen to be; be met with.

hi bring upon.

I קֹרֵא partridge.

II קֹרֵא *n. pers.* Kore.

קרב *q* approach, come near; draw near, come forward.

ni be brought near; approach.

pi cause to come near, bring near, be near, draw near.

hi present, offer, bring; approach; bring near; bring forward.

קָרֵב approaching; drawing near.

קְרָב battle, war.

קֶרֶב inner self; body; inner parts; middle; *w.* בְּ amongst, in the midst of.

קָרֹב → קָרוֹב.

קִרְבָה* drawing near.

קָרְבָּן offering, gift.

קָרְבָּן* supply.

קַרְדֹּם* axe.

I קרה *q* meet, encounter, befall; happen.

ni permit oneself to be met, meet; happen to be.

hi bring to pass, dispose; choose for oneself.

II קרה *pi* lay the beams.

קָרֶה* *w.* לַיְלָה? pollution.

קָרָה cold.

קֹרָה → קוֹרָה.

קָרוֹב near; nearest one, friend, relative.

קרח *q* shave bald.

ni be shaved bald.

hi shave oneself bald.

ho pt. shaved bald.

קֵרֵחַ bald head.

קֶרַח frost, ice.

קָרֵחַ *n. pers.* Kareah.

קֹרַח *n. pers.* Korah.

קָרְחָה baldness.

קָרְחִי *gent.* Korahite.

קָרַחַת bald spot.

קְרִי *w.* הלך *and* עִם resist.

קָרִיא* summoned.

קְרִיאָה proclamation.

קִרְיָה city, town.

קְרִיּוֹת *n. place* Kerioth.

קִרְיַת אַרְבַּע *n. place* Kiriath-arba.

קִרְיַת־בַּעַל *n. place* Kiriath-baal.

קִרְיַת הָאַרְבַּע → קִרְיַת אַרְבַּע.

קִרְיַת הַיְּעָרִים → קִרְיַת יְעָרִים.

קִרְיַת חֻצוֹת *n. place* Kiriath-huzoth.

קִרְיָתַיִם *n. place* Kiriathaim.

קִרְיַת(־)יְעָרִים *n. place* Kiriath-jearim.

קִרְיַת־סַנָּה *n. place* Kiriath-sannah.

קִרְיַת־סֵפֶר *n. place* Kiriath-sepher.

קרם° *q* cover over with.

קרן *q* shine.

hi have horns.

קֶרֶן horn; *fig.* might; *Isa. 5.1* hillside; *Hab. 3.4* ray.

קֶרֶן הַפּוּךְ *n. pers. f.* Keren-happuch.

קַרְנַיִם *n. place* Karnaim.

קרס *q* bend down.

קֶרֶס* hook.

קֶרֶס → קֵירֹם.

קַרְסֹל* ankle.

קרע *q* rend, tear away, enlarge; *Ps. 35.15* revile.

ni be rent.

קְרָעִים rags, pieces of torn cloth.

קרץ *q* narrow, purse (the lips in scorn).

pu be pinched off, formed.

קֶרֶץ mosquito.

קַרְקַע I sea-bed, bottom, floor; roof.

קַרְקַע* II *n. place* Karka.

קַרְקַר *rd.* קָדְקֹד *(Num. 24.17)*.

קַרְקֹר *n. place* Karkor.

קֹרֵר I *hi* keep cool.

II קרר   *pilp* pull down?, make an uproar?

קֶרֶשׁ   board; *Ezek. 27.6* cabin wall.

קֶרֶת   town.

קַרְתָּה   *n. place* Kartah.

קַרְתָּן   *n. place* Kartan.

*קַשְׂוָה   jug.

קְשִׂיטָה   kesitah *(unit of value)*.

קַשְׂקֶשֶׂת   scale.

קַשׁ   straw; chaff.

*קִשֻּׁאָה   cucumber.

קשׁב   *q* be attentive.

     hi pay attention, listen to.

קֶשֶׁב   attentiveness, paying attention.

*קַשָּׁב   attentive.

*קַשֻּׁב   attentive.

קשׁה   *q* be heavy, hard, difficult.

     ni pt. distressed.

     pi suffer severely.

     hi make heavy, hard; harden; suffer severely.

קָשֶׁה   hard, hardened; severe, difficult.

קשׁח   *hi* harden; treat harshly.

°קֹשְׁטְ   truth.

°קֶשֶׁט   bow.

קְשִׁי   stubbornness.

קִשְׁיוֹן   *n. place* Kishion.

קשׁר   *q* bind; conspire, be in conspiracy; *pt. pass.* strong.

     ni be bound to; be closed.

     pi fasten, put on.

     pu pt. strong.

     hitp conspire.

קֶשֶׁר   conspiracy.

קִשֻּׁרִים   ribbons.

קשׁשׁ   *q* gather?

     poel gather.

     hitpo assemble.

קֶשֶׁת   bow; *w.* בֵּן arrow.

קַשָּׁת   archer.

ר

רָאה   *q* see, take for; become aware of, observe, look at; consider, experience, know, distinguish; find out, concern oneself about, visit; choose, select; watch.

ni let oneself be seen, be/become visible, show oneself, appear.

pu be seen.

hi cause to see, show; cause to experience.

ho be shown.

hitp look at one another, try one another's strength.

רֹאֶה   seer; *Isa. 28.7* vision.

רָאָה   red kite.

רְאוּבֵן   *n. pers., n. peop.* Reuben.

רְאוּבֵנִי,   *gent.* Reubenite; Reuben.

רְאוּבֵנִי

רַאֲוָה   *inf. q of* רָאה.

רְאוּמָה   *n. pers. f.* Reumah.

רְאִי   mirror.

רֳאִי   appearance; fair looks; spectacle; *w.* אֵל El-Roi.

רְאָיָה   *n. pers.* Reaiah.

רְאֵים   → רְאֵם.

רַאִישׁוֹן   *rd. Q (Job 15.7).*

רְאִית   *rd. Q (Eccles. 5.10)* seeing, sight.

ראם   *q* tower.

רְאֵם   wild ox.

רָאמוֹת I   corals?

רָאמוֹת II   *n. place* Ramoth.

רָאמֹת   → רָאמוֹת.

רָאשׁ   *pt. q of* רוֹשׁ.

רָאשׁ   → רֵישׁ.

רֹאשׁ I   head; top; beginning; the highest, supreme, best; chief, leader; total; division.

רֹאשׁ II   poisonous plant, poison.

רֹאשׁ III   *n. pers., n. terr.* Rosh.

רֵאשֶׁה* previous condition.

רֹאשֶׁה *w.* אֶבֶן coping-stone.

רִאשׁוֹן first; previous, earlier, former.

רֵאֲשׁוֹת → מְרַאֲשׁוֹת.

רֵאשִׁית beginning, starting-point; the first, best; first-fruit; *Deut. 33.21* portion of the first-born.

רִאשֹׁנִי* first.

I רַב numerous, many, great; abundant; chief; enough.

II רַב* missile.

רָב → רִיב.

רֹב number, abundance.

I רבב *q* be/become numerous, great.
pu pt. multiplied ten thousand-fold.

II רבב *q* shoot.

רְבָבָה great number > ten thousand.

רְבִבִים → רְבִיבִים.

רבד *q* prepare the couch.

I רבה *q* be/become numerous, great.
pi make numerous; rear; make a profit.
hi make numerous, great, increase; have many; הַרְבֵּה large number, much, exceedingly.

II רבה *q pt.* archer.

רַבָּה *n. place* Rabbah.

רְבּוֹ , רְבּוֹא° ten thousand.

רְבִיבִים showers.

רָבִיד necklace.

רְבִיעִי fourth; *f.* fourth part, *Ezek. 48.20* square; בְּנֵי רִבְּעִים descendants to the fourth generation.

רַבִּית *n. place* Rabbith.

רֻבַּךְ *ho pt.* mixed.

רִבְלָה *n. place* Riblah.

רַב־מָג → מָג.

רַב־סָרִים → סָרִים.

I רבע° *q* lie down; copulate.
hi make to copulate.

II רבע *q pt. pass.* square.
pu pt. square.

I רֶבַע quarter; side.

רֶבַע II   *n. pers.* Reba.

רֹבַע I   quarter.

רֹבַע II   dust.

רִבֵּעַ*   member of the fourth generation.

רְבִעִי   → רְבִיעִי.

רבץ   *q* lie down, lie; rest, stretch out.

     hi cause to lie down; set.

רֵבֶץ   resting-place.

רִבְקָה   *n. pers. f.* Rebecca.

רַב־שָׁקֵה   *Assyr. official title* chief cup-bearer.

רֶגֶב*   clod.

רגז   *q* quake, be troubled; be roused to anger; *Micah 7.17* come out
     trembling.

     hi set in commotion, agitate, disturb.

     hitp excite oneself, rage.

רֹגֶז   agitation, excitement; raging.

רַגָּז   trembling, quaking.

רָגְזָה   trembling.

רגל   *q* slander.

     pi slander; spy out; *pt.* spy.

     tiphal teach to walk.

רֶגֶל   foot, leg; *du. also euphemism for* private part; *pl. also* times;
     w. בְּ *also* behind.

רַגְלִי   on foot.

רֹגְלִים   *n. place* Rogelim.

רגם   *q* stone.

רֶגֶם   *n. pers.* Regem.

רִגְמָה*   throng?

רגן   *q* grumble.

     ni mutter, slander.

רגע   *q* be soothed, form a scab; *Isa. 51.15; Jer. 31.35; Job 26.12* stir
     up.

     ni be at rest.

     hi bring rest; come to rest, abide; do in an instant.

רָגֵעַ*   quiet, peaceful.

רֶגַע   tranquillity; moment; in an instant, suddenly; רֶגַע—רֶגַע at one
     time—at another; *pl. w.* לְ time and again.

°רנשׁ   *q* be restless.

°רֶגֶשׁ   agitation.

°*רִגְשָׁה   agitation.

רדד   *q* trample down, subjugate.
     hi have hammered out.

I רדה   *q* tread *(wine-press)*; rule.
     hi make to tread down.

II רדה   *q* scrape out; *Jer. 5.31 dub.*

רַדַּי   *n. pers.* Raddai.

*רְדִיד   wrapper.

רדם   *ni* be in deep sleep; be stupefied.

רדף   *q* pursue someone/something, persecute, follow.
     ni be persecuted; *pt.* that which has vanished.
     pi chase after.
     pu be driven away.
     hi pursue.

רהב   *q* assail, importune.
     hi trouble, confuse.

רַהַב   *chaos-monster* Rahab; *also name for Egypt.*

*רְהַב   hurrying?

רהה   *q rd.* תִּרְאוּ *(Isa. 44.8).*

°*רַהַט   drinking trough; *Cant. 7.6 dub.*

רוב   → רִיב.

רוֹב   → רֹב.

רוד   *q* roam about.
     hi become restless.

רוֹדָנִים   *n. peop.* Rodanim *(inhabitants of Rhodes).*

רוה   *q* drink one's fill.
     pi give someone his fill to drink, soak.
     hi give someone his fill to drink, revive.

רָוֶה   given his fill to drink, watered.

רוֹהֲגָּה   *n. pers. rd. Q (I Chron. 7.34)* Rohgah.

I רוח   *q* become spacious, easy.
     pu pt. spacious, roomy.

II רוח   *hi* smell, perceive, enjoy; take pleasure.

רֶוַח   space, interval; liberation.

רוּחַ   breathing, blowing, snorting; breath; air; wind, direction of the wind, quarter of the earth; empty, vain thing; spirit; disposition, mind, temper.

רְוָחָה respite; relief.

רְוָיָה overflowing.

רוֹם *q* be/become high, be lifted high; be exalted; arise; be overbearing, proud; *pt.* high, towering; uplifted; exalted; arrogant, proud; *Deut. 27.14* loud.

ni rise up; remove oneself.

pol bring up; cause to grow tall; make to billow, erect, lift high; exalt; extol, praise.

polal be/become raised high, exalted.

hi raise, lift high, exalt; lift up, set up; serve *(food)*; be left with, take away, remove; cease; offer, contribute.

ho be suspended; be removed.

hitpol rise up (in pride).

רֻם height; arrogance, pride.

רוֹם height.

רוּמָה *n. place* Rumah.

רוֹמָה *adv.* upright.

רוֹמָם* praise.

רוֹמְמֻת* exaltedness.

רוֹמַמְתִּי עֶזֶר → רֹמַמְתִּי עֶזֶר.

רון *hitpol* come to oneself?

רוע *polal* shout of joy be raised.

hi cry (aloud); raise the battle-cry; sound (the alarm); shout in triumph, acclaim.

hitpol shout in triumph.

רוץ *q* run, hurry; be eager; *Hab. 2.2 w.* קרא read easily; *pt. also* runner, messenger.

pol drive to and fro.

hi cause to run, drive away; fetch quickly, bring quickly.

רוק → ריק.

רור → ריר.

רוש *q* be poor, starving.

hitpol pretend to be poor.

רוש → II רֹאשׁ.

רוּת *n. pers. f.* Ruth.

רוה *q* make to waste away?

ni waste away.

רָזֶה* lean.

I רָזוֹן emaciation.

II רָזוֹן dignitary.

רְזוֹן *n. pers.* Rezon.

רָזִי infirmity.

רום *q* wink.

רזן *q pt.* dignitary.

רחב *q* become broader; open wide.

ni pt. wide, spacious.

hi make wide, spacious, enlarge; open wide; make room for.

רֹחַב breadth, width.

I רָחָב broad, wide, spacious; extensive; *w.* לֵב arrogant, presumptuous; *w.* נֶפֶשׁ greedy.

II רָחָב *n. pers. f.* Rahab.

I רְחֹב open place.

II רְחֹב *n. pers., n. place* Rehob.

רְחֹבוֹת *n. place* Rehoboth.

רְחֹבֹת → רְחֹבוֹת.

רְחַבְיָה(וּ) *n. pers.* Rehabiah.

רְחַבְעָם *n. pers.* Rehoboam.

רְחוֹב → רְחֹב.

רְחוּם *n. pers.* Rehum.

רַחוּם compassionate.

רָחוֹק far, far off, distant, remote; inaccessible, hard to understand; interval, distance.

רָחִיט *rd. Q (Cant. 1.17)* rafters.

רֵחַיִם hand-mill.

I רָחֵל ewe.

II רָחֵל *n. pers. f.* Rachel.

רחם *q* love.

pi love, have mercy, be compassionate.

pu meet with mercy, love.

רָחָם carrion-vulture.

I רַחַם *n. pers.* Raham.

רֶחֶם, רַחַם II   womb; *pl.* heart, compassion, pity.

רָחָמָה   carrion-vulture.

רַחֲמָה*   womb.

רַחֲמָנִי°*   motherly.

רחף   *q* tremble.
    pi hover.

רחץ   *q* wash, wash away, have a wash.
    pu be washed.
    hitp wash oneself.

רַחַץ*   washing.

רַחְצָה   dipping.

רחק   *q* be/remain far; separate oneself; keep away.
    ni be removed.
    pi remove far away; put an end to.
    hi remove (oneself); keep (oneself) away.

רָחֵק*   separating oneself.

רָחֹק   → רָחוֹק.

רחשׁ   *q* be stirred.

רַחַת   winnowing-fork.

רטב   *q* be/become wet.

רָטֹב   full of sap.

רטה   *q* hurl?

רֶטֶט   terror.

רטפשׁ   *rd.* יְטֻפַּשׁ *(Job 33.25)* become plump.

רטשׁ   *pi* dash in pieces.
    pu be dashed in pieces.

רִי   moisture.

ריב   *q* conduct a lawsuit, dispute; *Ex. 21.18* fight.
    hi dispute?, fight?

רִיב   lawsuit.

רִיבָה*   *pl.* lawsuit, contention.

רִיבַי   *n. pers.* Ribai.

רֵיחַ   odour, scent.

רֵים   wild ox.

רֵיעַ   → רֵעַ II.

רִיפוֹת   grain.

רִיפַת   *n. pers.* Riphath.

רִיק   *hi* pour out, empty; leave empty; *w.* חֶרֶב draw the sword.
      ho be decanted, purified *(by pouring from one vessel into another).*

רִיק   empty, vain, futile; what is empty.

*רֵיק   empty, vain; unsatisfied; wanton.

רֵיקָם   empty, with empty hands; without cause.

רִיר   *q* secrete.

רִיר   spittle, slime.

רִישׁ, רֵישׁ   poverty.

רִישׁוֹן   → רִאשׁוֹן.

רֹךְ   delicacy.

רַךְ   tender, sensitive, pampered, delicate; mild; *w.* לֵבָב faint-
      hearted.

רכב   *q* be mounted, ride.
      hi set on a mount, make to ride; transport *(corpse)* in state;
      Hos. 10.11 yoke; *II Kings 13.16* lay.

רֶכֶב   *coll.* band of chariots, war-chariots; train; chariot; upper mill-
      stone.

רַכָּב   charioteer, driver, horseman.

רֵכָב   *n. pers.* Rechab.

רִכְבָּה   riding.

*רֵכָבִי   *gent.* Rechabite.

רֵכָה   *n. place* Recah.

*רְכוּב   vehicle.

רְכוּשׁ   possession, goods; equipment; personal property; *Dan. 11.13*
      baggage-train.

רָכִיל   slander; slanderer.

רכךְ   *q* be tender, weak, timid.
      pu be softened.
      hi cause to be discouraged.

רכל   *q pt.* trader, merchant.

רָכָל   *n. place* Racal.

*רְכֻלָּה   trading; merchandise.

רכס   *q* tie on.

*רֶכֶס   rugged country.

*רֹכֶס   league?

רכשׁ   *q* gather, acquire.

רֶכֶשׁ   *coll.* team of horses; horses.

רְכֻשׁ   → רְכוּשׁ.

רָם *n. pers.* Ram.

רֵם → רוּם.

I רמה *q* throw; shoot.

II רמה *pi* betray; leave in the lurch; deceive.

I רָמָה hill-top.

II רָמָה *n. place* Ramah.

רִמָּה maggot.

I רִמּוֹן pomegranate, pomegranate tree.

II רִמּוֹן *n. pers., n. place* Rimmon; → בֵּית־רִמּוֹן.

רִמּוֹנוֹ *n. place* Rimmono.

רָמוֹת → II רָאמוֹת.

רָמֻת* heap of corpses?

רָמוֹת גִּלְעָד → רָמֹת גִּלְעָד.

רֹמַח lance.

רַמְיָה *n. pers.* Ramiah.

רְמִיָּה slackness, laziness; deception, deceit.

רַמִּים *rd.* אֲרַמִּים *(II Chron. 22.5)*.

רַמָּךְ* race-horse *(f.)*?

רְמַלְיָהוּ *n. pers.* Remaliah.

I רמם *q rd.* רָמוּ *(Job 24.24)*.

II רמם *q* go bad, become worm-infested.

רֹמַמְתִּי עֶזֶר *n. pers.* Romamti-ezer.

רִמֹּן → רִמּוֹן.

רמס *q* tread, trample down.
ni be trampled down.

רמשׂ *q* move; crawl; swarm.

רֶמֶשׂ animals; reptiles.

רָמֹת → II רָאמוֹת.

רֶמֶת *n. place* Remeth.

רָמֹת גִּלְעָד *n. place* Ramoth-gilead.

רָמָתִי *gent.* Ramathite.

רָמָתַיִם צוֹפִים *n. place* Ramathaim-zophim.

רֹן* rejoicing?

רנה *q* rattle.

I רִנָּה shrill cry; rejoicing; lamentation, supplication.

II רִנָּה *n. pers.* Rinnah.

רָנַן *q* cry shrilly; rejoice, shout with joy; wail.

pi rejoice, praise with shouts of joy.

pu shout of joy be raised.

hi cause to rejoice; rejoice.

רְנָנָה rejoicing, shout of joy.

רְנָנִים *f.* female ostriches.

רִסָּה *n. place* Rissah.

I רָסִיס* drop.

II רָסִיס* fragment; ruins.

I רֶסֶן bridle.

II רֶסֶן *n. place* Resen.

רסס *q* moisten.

רַע, רַע bad, inferior, decayed; ugly; wrong, evil, despicable; harmful, bringing misfortune.

I רֵעַ shouting.

II רֵעַ kinsman, fellow-countryman, friend; another; neighbour.

III רֵעַ°* will, intention, thought.

רֹעַ poor quality, ugliness; grief; evil.

רעב *q* be hungry.

hi make to suffer hunger.

רָעָב hunger; famine.

רָעֵב hungry.

רְעָבוֹן hunger.

רעד *q* quake.

hi tremble.

רַעַד quaking, trembling.

רְעָדָה quaking, trembling.

I רעה *q* graze; pasture, let graze, tend, *pt. also* shepherd; care for, concern oneself with.

hi tend.

II רעה *q* have dealings with.

pi be best man?

hitp have dealings with.

רָעָה evil, wickedness; wrong, disaster.

רֵעֶה friend, companion.

רֵעֶה* friend, companion.

רֹעָה   *rd.* רֹעַ *(Isa. 24.19)*; *rd.* רָעָה *(Prov. 25.19)*.

רְעוּ   *n. pers.* Reu.

רְעוּאֵל   *n. pers.* Reuel.

I רְעוּת*   friend, companion.

II רְעוּת°   striving, endeavour, snatching.

רְעִי   pasture.

רֵעִי   *n. pers.* Rei.

רַעְיָה*   friend, beloved.

רַעְיָה*   *rd. Q (Judg. 11.37)*.

רַעְיוֹן°   striving, endeavour, snatching.

רעל   *ho* be shaken?, be adorned (with veils)?

רַעַל   staggering.

רְעָלָה*   veil.

רְעֶלְיָה   *n. pers.* Reelaiah.

I רעם   *q* rage, roar.

    hi cause to rage, cause to roar, (cause to) thunder.

II רעם   *q* be agitated.

    hi agitate.

רַעַם   roaring, thunder.

רַעְמָא   → II רַעְמָה.

I רַעְמָה   mane.

II רַעְמָה   *n. pers., n. peop.* Raamah.

רַעַמְיָה   *n. pers.* Raamiah.

רַעַמְסֵס,   *n. place* Raamses, Rameses.
רַעְמְסֵס

רען   *pal* be rich in foliage, luxuriant.

רַעֲנָן   leafy, luxuriant; fresh.

I רעע   *q* be bad, evil, grudging, discontented.

    ni be badly treated, suffer harm.

    hi do harm (to), injure; behave corruptly.

II רעע°   *q* break in pieces, shatter.

    hitpo split asunder; *Prov. 18.24* break one another in pieces.

רעף   *q* drop; drip.

    hi let drip.

רעץ   *q* shatter.

רעשׁ   *q* be violently shaken; quake; *Ps. 72.16 dub.*

     ni quake.

     hi shake violently; make to jump.

רַעַשׁ   quaking, rumbling, rattle; vehemence.

רפא   *q* heal; *pt. also* physician.

     ni be healed, become healthy, sound.

     pi heal, make healthy; repair; provide for recovery; *Jer. 38.4* → רפה I.

     hitp let oneself recover.

רָפָא   *n. pers.* Rapha.

רְפָאוּת   healing.

רְפָאִים I   shades of the dead.

רְפָאִים II   *n. peop.* Rephaim; → עֵמֶק רְפָאִים.

רְפָאֵל   *n. pers.* Rephael.

רפד   *q* spread.

     pi spread; refresh.

רפה I   *q* become slack; desist; sink (down), decline; *w.* יָדַיִם be discouraged, lose courage; *Jer. 49.24* lose courage.

     ni pt. lazy.

     pi loosen *(girdle)*; let drop down; *w.* יָדַיִם discourage.

     hi let drop, forsake; withdraw *(hand)*; desist, leave alone.

     hitp show oneself indolent, lacking courage.

רפה II   *parallel form of* רפא.

רָפֶה   slack, weak; discouraged.

רָפַה   *n. pers.* Raphah; *n. peop.?*

רָפוּא   *n. pers.* Raphu.

רְפוּאָה*   healing.

רְפוֹת   → רִיפוֹת.

רֶפַח   *n. pers.* Rephah.

רְפִידָה*   back.

רְפִידִים,   *n. place* Rephidim.

רְפִידָם

רְפָיָה   *n. pers.* Rephaiah.

רִפָּיוֹן*   slackness.

רפס   → רפשׂ.

רַפְסֹדוֹת rafts.

רפף *poal* shake.

רפק *hitp* lean.

רפשׂ *q* muddy.

    ni pt. muddied.

    hitp dub.

רֶפֶשׁ slime.

רֶפֶת* stall?

רַץ* *dub.*

I רצא *q* run?

II רצא *parallel form of* I רצה.

רצד *pi* look with envy.

I רצה *q* take pleasure, delight; be favourably inclined, well-disposed
    towards, love; approve of; be pleased.

    ni be considered acceptable, received graciously.

    pi arouse charitable feeling in; beg from.

    hitp ingratiate oneself.

II רצה *q* pay for, pay off; have restituted.

    ni be paid off.

    hi receive payment, restitution for.

רָצוֹן favour, pleasure; will; wish; desire; inclination; whim; what is
    pleasant.

רצח *q* kill, murder.

    ni be killed.

    pi kill, murder.

רֶצַח murder.

רְצִיָא *n. pers.* Rizia.

רָצִין *pt. pl. (Aram.) q of* רוץ.

רְצִין *n. pers.* Rezin.

רצע *q* bore.

רצף *q pt. pass.* inlaid?, upholstered?

I רֶצֶף* glowing stone.

II רֶצֶף *n. place* Rezeph.

I רִצְפָּה glowing coal.

II רִצְפָּה *n. pers. f.* Rizpah.

רִצְפָּה pavement, mosaic floor.

רצץ *q* break in pieces, break; ill-treat.

  ni be broken.

  pi crush, oppress.

  poel oppress.

  hi crush.

  hitpo jostle.

רַק thin, lean; *adv.* only, merely.

רַק → רִיק.

רֹק spittle.

רקב *q* rot; be/become worm-eaten.

רָקָב bone-decay, caries; *Job 13.28 rd.* כְּרִקָב like a wine-skin.

רִקָּבוֹן rottenness.

רקד *q* jump, skip.

  pi skip, dance.

  hi make to skip.

*רַקָּה temple.

רַקּוֹן *n. place* Rakkon.

רקח *q* prepare, mix ointment.

  pu pt. mixed, prepared.

  hi prepare?

רֶקַח spice.

רֹקַח spice.

*רַקָּח ointment-mixer.

*רַקָּחָה ointment-mixer.

*רִקֻּחַ ointment.

רָקִיעַ firmament, vault of heaven.

רָקִיק flat cake.

רקם *q pt.* weaver using coloured yarns.

  pu be woven, formed.

רֶקֶם *n. pers.*, *n. place* Rekem.

רִקְמָה variegation, variegated fabric.

רקע *q* stamp, trample down flat; spread out.

  pi hammer out; overlay.

  pu pt. hammered out.

  hi hammer out, spread out.

*רִקֻּעַ that which has been hammered.

רקק *q* spit.

רַקַּת *n. place* Rakkath.

רָשׁ poor.

רִשְׁיוֹן authorization.

רֵשִׁית → רֵאשִׁית.

רֹשֶׁם °*q pt. pass.* entered.

רשׁע *q* be/become guilty.

    hi pronounce guilty, condemn; treat as guilty; incur guilt, become guilty.

רֶשַׁע wrong, guilt.

רָשָׁע guilty; evildoer; impious person.

רִשְׁעָה guilt.

רִשְׁעָתַיִם → פֻּשַׁן רִשְׁעָתַיִם.

I רֶשֶׁף blaze, flame; lightning flash; pestilence.

II רֶשֶׁף *n. pers. I Chron. 7.25* Resheph.

רשׁשׁ *poel* destroy.

    pu be/become shattered.

רֶשֶׁת net, lattice.

רַתּוֹק chain?

רתח *pi* bring to the boil.

    pu be brought to the boil, seethe.

    hi bring to the boil.

רֶתַח* *rd.* נְתָחֶיהָ *(Ezek. 24.5).*

רַתִּיקָה* *rd. Q (I Kings 6.21)* chain.

רתם *q* harness?

רֹתֶם broom.

רִתְמָה *n. place* Rithmah.

רתק *pu* be fettered.

רְתֻקוֹת chains.

רְתֵת terror.

ש

שְׂאֹר leaven.

I שְׂאֵת rising, uprising; exaltation, nobility.

II שְׂאֵת *f.* blotch, spot.

שְׂבָכָה trellis-work, net; lattice.

שְׂבָם   *n. place* Sebam.

שִׂבְמָה   *n. place* Sibmah.

שׂבע   *q* be/become satisfied, satisfy oneself; be/become sated; have enough, be sick of.

ni pt. sated.

pi sate.

hi sate.

שֹׂבַע   satiety; plenty, abundance.

שֹׂבַע   satiety, abundance.

שָׂבֵעַ   satisfied, sated; rich.

שָׂבְעָה   satiety, satiation.

שִׂבְעָה*   satiety, satiation.

שׂבר°   *q* inspect.

pi hope, wait.

שֵׂבֶר°*   hope.

שׂגא°   *hi* make great, give greatness; praise.

שׂגב   *q* become high; be inaccessible.

ni be high, inaccessible, protected; be exalted; be incomprehensible.

pi make high, inaccessible; protect, save; make great.

pu be/become protected.

hi be great.

שׂגה°   *q* become great, grow.

hi make great, increase.

שְׂגוּב   *n. pers.* Segub.

שַׂגִּיא°   great, exalted.

שָׂגִיב   *rd. Q (I Kings 16.34).*

שׂגשׂג   → II שׂוג.

שׂדד   *pi* plough; harrow.

שָׂדֶה   (open) country, field; territory, piece of ground; mainland.

שָׂדַי   country, field.

שִׂדִּים   *n. place* Siddim.

שְׂדֵרָה*   rank; *pl. also* precinct; *I Kings 6.9 architectural term.*

שֶׂה   sheep; goat.

שָׂהֵד°*   witness.

שָׂהֲדוּתָא   → *Biblical Aramaic part* שָׂהֲדוּ.

שַׂהֲרֹנִים crescents *(adornment)*.

שׂוֹא *inf. cs. of* נשׂא ? *(Ps. 89.10)*.

שׂוֹבֶךְ branches.

I שׂוּג → I סוּג.

II שׂוּג *pilp* raise?

שׂוּחַ *q dub*.

שׂוּט *q* deviate; get entangled.

שׂוּךְ *q* hedge round; hedge, block.

שׂוֹךְ* brushwood.

שׂוֹכָה* brushwood.

שׂוֹכֹה, שׂוֹכוֹ *n. place* Socoh.

שׂוּכָתִים *gent.* Sucathites.

שׂוֹם → שׂים.

I שׂוּר *q* strive, fight.

II שׂוּר *q* saw.

III שׂוּר *hi* appoint an official; → *also* שׂרר.

IV שׂוּר → סוּר.

שׂוֹרָה millet?

שׂוּשׂ *q* rejoice.

שֵׂחַ* thoughts.

שׂחה *q* swim.

    hi flood.

שָׂחוּ swimming.

שָׂחוּק → שְׂחֹק.

שׂחט *q* squeeze out.

שָׂחִיף* *Ezek. 41.16 dub*.

שׂחק *q* laugh, jest; mock; *Judg. 16.27* act clumsily.

    pi jest, play, dance; *Judg. 16.25* entertain; *II Sam. 2.14* hold a
       contest.

    hi mock.

שְׂחֹק laughter, jesting; laughing-stock.

שֵׂט* disloyal?

שׂטה *q* depart from; become unfaithful.

שׂטם *q* show enmity, persecute.

שׂטן *q* show enmity; oppose.

שָׂטָן opponent, adversary; Satan.

I שִׂטְנָה accusation.

שִׂטְנָה II   *n. place* Sitnah.

שִׂיא*   loftiness.

שִׂיאֹן   *n. place* Sion.

שִׂיב   *q* be/become grey, old.

שֵׂיב*   grey hair; old age.

שֵׂיבָה   grey hair; old age.

שִׂיג   bowel movement.

שִׂיד   *q* cover with lime, whitewash.

שִׂיד   lime.

שִׂיח   *q* be preoccupied, ponder; speak *(also complainingly)*.
     pol be concerned about, ponder.

שִׂיחַ I   bush.

שִׂיחַ II   business; trouble; complaint; *Ps. 104.34* meditation; *II Kings 9.11* babbling.

שִׂיחָה   meditation, devotion.

שִׂים   *q* place, put, lay; set up; appoint, determine, fix; give, make into; direct towards; *Gen. 45.7; II Sam. 14.7* ensure.
     hi dub.; Job 13.27 parallel form of סמם.
     ho be placed.

שִׂישׂ   → שׂושׂ.

שֵׂךְ*   thorn; splinter.

שֹׂךְ*   booth?

שֻׂכָּה*   harpoon.

שֹׂלָה   → שׂובה.

שֶׂכוּ   *n. place* Secu.

שֶׂכְוִי   cock.

שֶׂכְיָה   *n. pers.* Sachiah.

שְׂכִיָּה*   ship.

שַׂכִּין   knife.

שָׂכִיר   hired; day-labourer; *pl. also* mercenaries.

שָׂכַךְ   *q* cover.

שׂכל I   *q* have success.
     pi → סכל.
     hi understand, comprehend, have insight; give insight, teach; have success; act with insight, piety.

שׂכל II   *pi* cross.

271

שֵׂכֶל, שֶׂכֶל insight, understanding.

שִׂכְלוּת → סִכְלוּת.

שׂכר *q* enlist, engage; hire; *Gen. 30.16* buy.
  ni hire oneself out.
  hitp hire oneself out.

I שָׂכָר wages.

II שָׂכָר *n. pers.* Sacar.

שֶׂכֶר wages.

שְׂלָו quail.

שַׂלְמָא *n. pers.* Salma.

I שַׂלְמָה cloak.

II שַׂלְמָה *n. pers.* Salmah.

שַׂלְמוֹן *n. pers.* Salmon.

שְׂמֹאול, left side; left; north; northwards.
שְׂמֹאל

שׂמאל *hi* go to the left; *I Chron. 12.2* use the left hand.

שְׂמָאלִי left.

שׂמח *q* rejoice, be glad.
  pi cause to rejoice, make glad, let be glad.
  hi cause to exult.

שָׂמֵחַ joyful, glad.

שִׂמְחָה joy, gladness.

שְׂמִיכָה coverlet?

שַׂמְלָה *n. pers.* Samlah.

שִׂמְלָה cloak, outer garment; clothing.

שׂמם *hi II Kings 9.30; Job 13.27* smear, paint, colour.

שְׂמָמִית gecko.

שׂנא *q* hate, have an aversion to; scorn; *pt. also* enemy.
  ni be hated.
  pi hate; *pt. also* enemy.

שִׂנְאָה hatred, enmity.

שָׂנִיא* disregarded.

שְׂנִיר *n. place* Senir.

I שָׂעִיר he-goat; demon, in goat's form.

II שָׂעִיר* shower.

שֵׂעִיר   *n. place, n. terr.* Seir.

I* שְׂעִירָה   she-goat.

II* שְׂעִירָה   *n. place* Seirah.

שְׂעִפִּים   disquieting thoughts; musings.

I שָׂעַר   *q* shudder.

II שָׂעַר   *q* sweep away.

     ni be stormy *(impersonal)*.

     pi sweep away in the storm.

     hitp assail.

III שָׂעַר   *q* be acquainted with.

I שַׂעַר   shuddering.

II שַׂעַר   storm.

שָׂעִר   hairy.

שֵׂעָר   hair *(collective)*.

שַׂעֲרָה   a hair.

שְׂעָרָה   tempest.

שְׂעֹרָה   barley.

שְׂעֹרִים   *n. pers.* Seorim.

שָׂפָה   lip; language; shore, bank; edge.

שׂפח   *pi* make scabby.

שָׂפָם   moustache.

שְׂפָמוֹת   *n. place* Siphmoth.

שׂפן   *q pt. pass.* hidden.

I שׂפק   *q* clap *(the hands)*.

     hi Isa. 2.6 strike hands *(over a deal) or* II שׂפק.

II שׂפק   *q* suffice, be enough.

     hi Isa. 2.6 abound *or* I שׂפק.

שֶׂפֶק*   mockery?

שֵׂפֶק*   abundance.

שַׂק   haircloth; loin cloth worn in mourning, sack.

שׂקר   *ni* pay attention to?

שׂקר   *pi w.* עֵינַיִם cast seductive glances.

שַׂר   official, ruler, leader; noble, man of rank; chief, head; *also of heavenly beings.*

שַׂרְאֶצֶר,   *n. pers.* Sharezer.

שַׂר־אֶצֶר

שׂרג   *pu* be intertwined.

     hitp be intertwined.

שָׂרַד *q* escape.

שְׂרָד woven fabric.

שָׁשֵׁר red ochre.

שָׂרָה *q* strive.

I שָׂרָה lady, lady of noble rank.

II שָׂרָה *n. pers. f.* Sarah.

שְׂרוּג *n. pers.* Serug.

שְׂרוֹךְ sandal-thong > trifle.

שֶׂרַח *n. pers. f.* Serah.

שָׂרַט *q* make incisions.

ni lacerate oneself.

שֶׂרֶט incision.

שָׂרֶטֶת incision.

שָׂרַי *n. pers. f.* Sarai.

שָׂרִיג* tendril.

I שָׂרִיד survivor.

II שָׂרִיד *n. place* Sarid.

שְׂרָיָה(וּ) *n. pers.* Seraiah.

שִׂרְיֹן *n. place* Sirion.

שָׂרִיק* carded.

שָׂרַךְ *pi* run back and forth.

שַׂר־סְכִים *n. pers.* Sarsechim.

שָׂרַע *q pt. pass.* deformed.

hitp stretch oneself.

שַׂרְעַפִּים* disquieting thoughts; musings.

שָׂרַף *q* fire, burn.

ni be burned.

pu be burned.

I שָׂרָף serpent; seraph.

II שָׂרָף *n. pers.* Saraph.

שְׂרֵפָה firing; burning; scene of a fire; what has been burned.

שָׂרֹק* red; *pl.* fine grapes.

I שֹׂרֵק *variety of fine, bright red* grapes.

II שֹׂרֵק *n. place* Sorek.

שֹׂרֵקָה vine.

שׂוֹרֵר *q* rule, direct.

hi appoint an official.

hitp set oneself up as lord.

שָׂשׂוֹן joy, rejoicing.
שֵׁת uprising.
שֹׁתם *q* remain unheard.
שֹׁתר *ni* break out.

שׁ

שֶׁ , °שֶׁ , °שָׁ *relative particle*; that; because; *w.* כְּ as.
שֹׁא devastation?
שׁאב *q* draw (water).
שׁאג *q* roar, cry.
שְׁאָגָה roaring, crying.
I שׁאה *q* lie desolate.
    ni be devastated.
    hi lay waste.
II שׁאה *ni* rage.
III שׁאה *hitp* look at.
שֹׁאָה → שׁוֹאָה.
שׁאָוה *rd. Q (Prov. 1.27)*.
שְׁאוֹל Sheol, underworld.
שָׁאוּל *n. pers.* Saul.
שָׁאוּלִי *gent.* Saulite.
I שָׁאוֹן raging, din, roaring.
II שָׁאוֹן waste?, destruction?
שְׁאָט contempt.
שְׁאִיָּה desolation.
שׁאל *q* ask, inquire; desire, demand; request, wish; *pt. pass.* borrowed.
    ni request leave of absence for oneself.
    pi ask; beg.
    hi grant a request; lend.
שְׁאָל *n. pers.* Sheal.
שְׁאָלָה *rd.* שְׁאֹלָה *(Isa. 7.11)*.
שְׁאֵלָה request.
שְׁאַלְתִּיאֵל *n. pers.* Shealtiel.
שׁאן *pil* be untroubled.
שְׁאָן → בֵּיתשְׁאָן.

שַׁאֲנָן untroubled, secure; *II Kings 19.28; Isa. 37.29* arrogance *or rd.* שְׁאוֹנְךָ.

שָׁאֹסַיךָ *pt. q w. suffix of* שסה.

שָׁאַף *q* pant, long for; lie in wait for.

שָׁאַר *q* remain.

    ni be left over, remain over; remain behind, remain.

    hi leave over, leave behind; have left.

שְׁאָר rest, remainder.

שְׁאֵר flesh, body; blood-relation.

שַׁאֲרָה *rd.* שְׁאֵרָה (*Lev. 18.17*).

שֶׁאֱרָה *n. pers. f.* Sheerah.

שְׁאֵרִית rest, remainder; posterity.

שְׁאֵת desolation.

שְׁבָא *n. pers., n. peop., n. terr.* Sheba.

שְׁבָאִים *n. peop.* Sabaeans.

שְׁבִאֵל → שְׁבוּאֵל.

שְׁבָבִים splinters.

שׁבה *q* carry off captive.

    ni be carried off captive.

שְׁבוֹ *precious stone.*

שְׁבוּאֵל *n. pers.* Shebuel.

שָׁבוּעַ period of seven; week; שָׁבֻעוֹת(חַג) feast of weeks.

שְׁבוּעָה oath, curse.

שְׁבוּר fracture.

שְׁבוּת captivity; *w.* שׁוב *also* change the fortune.

שְׁבוּת *rd.* שְׁבִית.

I °שׁבח *pi* extol, praise; consider fortunate.

    hitp boast.

II שׁבח *pi* calm.

    hi calm.

שֵׁבֶט staff, stick; sceptre; dart; tribe.

שְׁבָט Shebat (*name of a month, January/February*).

שְׁבִי carrying off; captivity; captives.

*שָׁבְיָ carried off captive.

שׁוֹבִי *n. pers.* Shobi.

שׁוֹבַי *n. pers.* Shobai.

°*שָׁבִיב spark.

שִׁבְיָה carrying off; captivity; captives.

שְׁבִיל* path.

שְׁבִים* headband.

שְׁבִיעִי seventh.

שְׁבִית captivity; *w.* שׁוּב *also* change the fortune.

שָׁבִית *rd.* שְׁבִית *(Ezek. 16.53).*

שֹׁבֶל train, hem of skirt.

שַׁבְּלוּל snail?

I שִׁבֹּלֶת ear of corn; bunch.

II שִׁבֹּלֶת flood, stream.

שֶׁבְנָא *n. pers.* Shebna.

שֶׁבְנָה *n. pers.* Shebnah.

שְׁבַנְיָה(וּ) *n. pers.* Shebniah.

שבע *q pt. pass.* → שְׁבוּעָה.

ni swear; adjure.

hi cause to swear; adjure, urgently request.

I שֶׁבַע seven; *adv.* seven times; *du.* sevenfold.

II שֶׁבַע *n. pers., n. place* Sheba.

שִׁבְעָה *n. place* Shibah.

שִׁבְעָה → שְׁבוּעָה.

שִׁבְעָנָה *rd.* שִׁבְעָה *(Job 42.13)* seven.

שבץ *pi* weave in patterns.

pu pt. set.

שָׁבָץ cramp?, onset of weakness?

I שבר *q* break in pieces, shatter, crush; destroy; *Ps. 104.11* quench *(thirst).*

ni be broken in pieces, shattered; crack; break in pieces.

pi smash.

hi cause to break through.

ho be broken.

II שבר *q* buy; buy grain.

hi sell.

I שֶׁבֶר, שֵׁבֶר breaking, fracture; ruin; brokenness; *Judg. 7.15* elucidation, interpretation; *Ps. 60.4* fissure.

II שֶׁבֶר grain.

III שֶׁבֶר *n. pers.* Sheber.

שִׁבָּרוֹן collapse, ruin.

שְׁבָרִים *n. place? Josh. 7.5* quarry.

שׁבת *q* cease; come to a stop; stop work, rest; *w.* שַׁבָּת keep the
  sabbath; *Lam. 5.14* stay away.

  ni be brought to an end, disappear.

  hi cause to cease, bring to an end; do away with, remove; *Ex. 5.5*
  make to rest; *Deut. 32.26* wipe out; *Josh. 22.25* divert;
  Isa. 30.11 leave alone.

שֶׁבֶת cessation; loss of work.

שַׁבָּת sabbath; *Lev. 23.15; 25.8* week; *Lev. 26.34f., 43; II Chron.*
  36.21 sabbatical year.

שַׁבָּתוֹן celebration of the sabbath; day of rest.

שַׁבְּתַי *n. pers.* Shabbethai.

שׁגג *q* sin inadvertently.

שְׁגָגָה inadvertence.

שׁגה *q* stray; err; go astray; reel.
  hi misdirect, let deviate.

שָׁגֶה *n. pers.* Shageh.

שׁגח *hi* look, gaze.

שְׁגִיאָה* lapse.

שִׁגָּיוֹן dirge?

שׁגל *q* ravish.
  ni be ravished.
  pu be ravished.

שֵׁגַל *f.* royal consort.

שׁגע *pu pt.* mad, deranged.
  hitp behave as a madman.

שִׁגָּעוֹן recklessness, madness.

שֶׁגֶר offspring *(of animals)*.

שַׁד* breast.

שֵׁד* demon.

I שֹׁד breast.

II שֹׁד violent deed; devastation.

שׁדד *q* be violent, use violence; ravage, lay waste.
  ni be ravaged.
  pi maltreat; devastate.
  pu be ravaged.
  poel ravage.
  ho be devastated.

שִׂדָּה lady?

שַׁדַּי Shaddai *(title of God)*.

שְׁדֵיאוּר *n. pers.* Shedeur.

שַׁדִּין *rd.* יֵשׁ דִּין *(Job 19.29)*.

שְׁדֵמָה field; terrace.

שׂדף *q pt. pass.* dried up, scorched.

שְׁדֵפָה that which has been dried up, scorched.

שִׁדָּפוֹן blight *(on corn)*.

שַׁדְרַךְ *n. pers.* Shadrach.

I שֹׁהַם carnelian.

II שֹׁהַם *n. pers.* Shoham.

שָׁו *rd.* שָׁוְא *(Job 15.31)*.

שָׁוְא worthless, vain thing; deceit, falsity; *adv.* for nothing, in vain, idly.

שְׁוָא *n. pers.* Sheva.

שׁוֹאָה calamity; storm.

שׁוּב *q* turn back, return; turn; turn towards; turn away; do again, be/become again.

    pol bring back; lead astray; lead; restore.

    polal be restored; become apostate.

    hi bring back, lead back, let come back; give back; make restitution; pay back, requite; repulse; hinder; turn back *(hand)*; draw back, turn away; cancel, revoke; hold back, restrain, repel; answer, report, inform; restore; do again.

    ho be brought back, led back, given back.

שׁוּבָאֵל *n. pers.* Shubael.

I שׁוֹבָב apostate.

II שׁוֹבָב *n. pers.* Shobab.

שׁוֹבֵב apostate.

שׁוּבָה withdrawal *(from war)*.

שׁוֹבָךְ *n. pers.* Shobach.

שׁוֹבָל *n. pers.* Shobal.

שׁוֹבֵק *n. pers.* Shobek.

I שׁוה *q* be/become like; *pt. also* suitable; sufficient.

   ni rd. נִשְׁוָתָה *(Prov. 27.15)* be alike.

   pi make like, level, pacify.

   hi equate, compare.

   hitp? → *ni*.

II שׁוה *pi* set; lay.

   Job 30.22 rd. תְּשֻׁאָה.

שָׁוֶה* plain.

שָׁוֵה → עֵמֶק שָׁוֵה.

שׁוח *q* descend, sink.

שׁוּחַ *n. pers.* Shuah.

I שׁוּחָה pitfall; chasm.

II שׁוּחָה *n. pers.* Shuhah.

שָׁוחָט *rd. K (Jer. 9.7)*.

שׁוּחִי *gent.* Shuhite.

שׁוּחָם *n. pers.* Shuham.

שׁוּחָמִי *gent.* Shuhamite.

I שׁוט *q* range to and fro, wander about; *Ezek. 27* row.

   pol rove to and fro.

   hitpol wander about.

II שׁוט *q* despise.

I שׁוֹט whip, lash.

II שׁוֹט *Isa. 28.15, 18; Job 9.23* flood.

שׁוּל* train; hem.

שׁוֹלָל barefoot.

שׁוּלַמִּית *gent. f.* Shulammite.

שׁוּמִים garlic.

שׁוֹמֵר *n. pers.* Shomer.

שׁוּנִי *n. pers.* Shuni; *gent.* Shunite.

שׁוּנֵם *n. place* Shunem.

שׁוּנַמִּית *gent. f.* Shunammite.

שׁוע *pi* cry for help.

שֶׁוַע* cry for help.

I שׁוֹעַ noble, of high rank.

II שׁוֹעַ *n. peop.* Shoa.

I שׁוּעַ *dub*.

II שׁוּעַ *n. pers.* Shua.

שׁוּעָא *n. pers. f.* Shua.

שׁוְעָה* cry for help.

I שׁוּעָל fox.

II שׁוּעָל *n. pers.*, *n. place* Shual.

שׁוֹעֵר gate-keeper.

I שׁוּף *q Gen. 3.15bα* crush.

II שׁוּף *q* snap at.

שׁוֹפָךְ *n. pers.* Shophach.

שׁוּפָמִי *gent.* Shuphamite.

שׁוֹפָן → עֲטָרֹת שׁוֹפָן.

שׁוֹפָר ram's horn, horn.

שׁוֹק *pol* bestow abundantly.

hi overflow.

שׁוֹק thigh, hind leg.

שׁוּק street.

I שׁוּר *q* look, gaze; lie in wait.

II שׁוּר *q* descend; *pt.* caravan.

שׁוֹר ox, bull.

I שׁוּר° wall.

II שׁוּר* *Ps. 92.12* enemy?

III שׁוּר *n. place* Shur.

שׁוּרָה°* retaining wall.

שׁוֹרֵר* enemy.

שַׁוְשָׁא *n. pers.* Shavsha.

I שׁוּשַׁן lily, lotus flower; six-stringed.

II שׁוּשַׁן *n. place* Susa.

שׁוּשַׁק *rd.* Q *(I Kings 14.25).*

שׁוּת → שִׁית.

שׁוּתֶלַח *n. pers.* Shuthelah.

שׁזַף *q* glimpse; tan *(sun)*.

שׁזַר *ho pt.* twisted.

שַׁח downcast *(eyes)*.

שָׁחַד *q* offer a gift.

שֹׁחַד gift; bribe.

שָׁחָה *q* bend down.

hi weigh down.

hitpal bow, prostrate oneself.

שָׁחוֹר → שִׁיחוֹר.

שְׁחוֹר° blackness, soot.

שְׁחוּת* pit?

שׁחח *q* crouch, be brought low; be humbled, humiliated.
    ni be bowed, humbled; be muted; sound muffled.
    hi bring low, prostrate.

שׁחט I *q* slaughter, kill.
    ni be slaughtered.

שׁחט II *q pt. pass.* beaten?; alloyed?

שַׁחֲטָה *Hos. 5.2 text corr.*

שְׁחִי → שׁוּחִי.

שְׁחִיטָה* slaughtering.

שְׁחִין boil.

שָׁחִים corn growing wild.

שְׁחִית* pit.

שַׁחַל (young) lion.

שְׁחֵלֶת onycha.

שַׁחַף gull.

שַׁחֶפֶת consumption.

שַׁחַץ nobility.

שַׁחֲצוּמָה *n. place rd. Q (Josh. 19.22)* Shahazimah.

שׁחק *q* wear away, pulverize.

שַׁחַק layer of dust; cloud; clouds.

שׁחר I° *q* become black.

שׁחר II *q* be intent on something.
    pi be intent on something, seek; inflict.

שָׁחֹר° black.

שַׁחַר dawn; morning.

שַׁחֹר → שִׁיחוֹר.

שַׁחֲרוּת° black hair.

שְׁחַרְחֹר*° swarthy.

שְׁחַרְיָה *n. pers.* Shehariah.

שַׁחֲרַיִם *n. pers.* Shaharaim.

שׁחת *ni* be/become spoilt, depraved; be ravaged.
    pi ruin, destroy; act wickedly; create disaster.
    hi ruin, destroy; behave evilly, act wickedly.
    ho pt. tainted; defective.

שַׁחַת pit, pitfall; grave.

שִׁטָּה acacia.

שׁטח q spread out, scatter.
pi spread out.

שׁׁטֶט scourge.

שִׁטִּים n. place Shittim.

שׁטף q stream, flood; overflow, submerge; wash off.
ni be washed away, rinsed.
pu be rinsed.

שֶׁטֶף, שֶׁטֶף streaming, flood.

שׁטר q pt. official, clerk; overseer.

שִׁטְרַי n. pers. Shitrai.

שַׁי gift, present.

שְׁיָא n. pers. rd. Q (II Sam. 20.25).

שִׁיאׂן n. place Shion.

*שִׁיבָה II Sam. 19.33 stay?; Ps. 126.1 captivity?, fortune?

שׁיה q rd. תִּשֶּׁה (Deut. 32.18).

שִׁיזָא n. pers. Shiza.

שׁיח q melt, dissolve.
hitpol be dissolved.

שִׁיחָה pit.

שִׁיחׂר river; canal; also Nile.

שִׁיחׂר לִבְנָת n. canal Libnath canal.

שׁיט rd. Q (Isa. 28.15).

שַׁיִט oar.

שִׁילׂה → שָׁלׂה.

שִׁילׂו → שָׁלׂה.

שִׁילׂנִי → שִׁילׂנִי.

שׁׂילָל rd. Q (Micah 1.8).

שִׁילׂנִי gent. Shilonite.

שִׁימׂון n. pers. Shimon.

שׁין iphtael pt. pissing; w. בַּקִּיר pissing against the wall, male.

*שַׁיִן urine.

שִׁיר   *q* sing; sing of.

     pol sing; sing of; *pt. also* temple-singer.

     ho be sung.

שִׁיר   singing; song.

שִׁירָה   song.

שֵׁירָה*   bracelet.

שַׁיִשׁ   alabaster.

שִׁישָׁא   *n. pers.* Shisha.

שִׁישַׁק   *n. pers.* Shishak.

שִׁית   *q* place, put, lay; appoint, make (into something); prepare.

     ho be imposed.

שִׁית   garment, clothing.

שַׁיִת   weeds.

שׁכב   *q* lie down; lie.

     hi lay; let lie, let rest; *Job 38.37* tip > empty.

     ho be/become laid.

שִׁכְבָה*   covering; *w.* זֶרַע emission of semen.

שְׁכֹבֶת*   intercourse.

שׁכה*   *hi pt.* rutting?

שְׁכוֹל   childlessness.

שַׁכּוּל   bereft of offspring; childless.

שְׁכֻיל*   childless.

שִׁכּוֹר   drunk.

שׁכח   *q* forget.

     ni be forgotten; sink into oblivion.

     pi cause to be forgotten.

     hi cause to forget.

     hitp be forgotten.

שָׁכֵחַ*   forgetting.

שׁכך   *q* subside *(water)*; abate *(anger)*; crouch.

     hi cause to subside, silence.

שׁכל   *q* become childless.

     pi make childless; depopulate; cause miscarriage; have a miscarriage; suffer crop failure *(vine)*.

     hi pt. barren *or* miscarrying.

שְׁכֻלִים* childlessness.

שׁכם *hi* rise early; do something early, eagerly.

שְׁכֶם I neck, shoulder; ridge.

שְׁכֶם II *n. pers., n. place* Shechem.

שְׁכֶם *n. pers., n. place* Shechem.

שִׁכְמִי *gent.* Shechemite.

שׁכן *q* settle; remain, stay, dwell.

    pi let dwell; erect *(tent)*.

    hi let dwell; erect *(tent)*.

שָׁכֵן inhabitant, neighbour; neighbouring town; neighbouring people.

שְׁכַנְיָה(וּ) *n. pers.* Shecaniah.

שׁכר *q* become drunk; be drunk, intoxicated.

    pi make drunk, intoxicate.

    hi make drunk.

    hitp be drunken.

שֵׁכָר intoxicating liquor, strong drink.

שִׁכֹּר → שִׁכּוֹר.

שִׁכָּרוֹן I drunkenness, intoxication.

שִׁכָּרוֹן* II *n. place* Shikkaron.

שַׁל irreverence?

שֶׁל שֶׁ *w.* לְ.

שַׁלְאֲנַן *rd.* שַׁאֲנַן *(Job 21.23)*.

שׁלב *pu pt.* connected.

שָׁלָב* cross-piece, cross-bar.

שׁלג *hi* snow.

שֶׁלֶג I snow.

שֶׁלֶג II soapwort.

שׁלה *q* be at ease; *Job 27.8 dub.*

    ni be negligent.

    hi arouse false hopes in.

שֵׁלָה* I request.

שֵׁלָה II *n. pers.* Shelah.

שִׁלֹה *n. place* Shiloh.

שַׁלְהֶבֶת° flame.

שַׁלְהֶבֶתְיָה° *rd.* שַׁלְהֶבֶת יָה *(Cant. 8.6)* flames of Yahweh.

שָׁלֵו at ease, undisturbed, carefree; *Job 20.20 rd.* שַׁלְוָה.

שְׁלִי* untroubled state.

שָׁלוּ → שָׁלָה.

שַׁלְוָה ease, security, untroubled state.

שִׁלּוּחִים dismissal; dowry.

שָׁלוֹם unharmed state; well-being, prosperity; friendliness, peace, salvation.

שַׁלֻּם n. pers. Shallum.

שִׁלֻּם reward, requital.

שְׁלוֹמִית → שְׁלֹמִית.

שִׁלּוּן n. pers. Shallum.

שִׁילוֹנִי → שִׁילֹנִי.

שָׁלוֹשׁ → שָׁלֹשׁ.

שׁלח q stretch out; let loose, give full scope to, let go; dispatch, send.

ni be dispatched.

pi stretch out; let loose, give full scope to, let go; escort, accompany; send away, send out; set free; dispatch, send; *Jer. 38.6,11* let down.

pu be dispatched; be sent away; *Isa. 27.10* be forsaken; *Job 18.8 w.* בְּ fall into; *Prov. 29.15* be left to one's own devices.

hi let loose.

I שֶׁלַח javelin; *Cant. 4.13* shoot.

II שֶׁלַח *Neh. 3.15* conduit.

III שֶׁלַח n. pers. Shelah.

שִׁלֹחַ n. place Shiloah.

שְׁלֻחוֹת* shoots.

שִׁלְחִי n. pers. Shilhi.

שִׁלְחִים n. place Shilhim.

שִׁלֵּחִים → שִׁלּוּחִים.

שֻׁלְחָן leather mat *(spread on ground for meal)* > table.

שׁלט° q have power, win power; *Neh. 5.15* tyrannize.

hi let master; enable, permit.

שֶׁלֶט* circular shield.

שִׁלְטוֹן° that which has power.

שַׁלֶּטֶת° imperious.

שְׁלִי* quietness.

שִׁלְיָה* afterbirth.

286

שָׁלֵיו, שָׁלֵיו → שָׁלֵו.

שַׁלִּיט° governor, ruler.

I שָׁלִישׁ *Isa. 40.12; Ps. 80.6* third of a measure.

II שָׁלִישׁ* *I Sam. 18.6 musical instrument.*

III שָׁלִישׁ adjutant.

שְׁלִישִׁי third, third part; *Gen. 6.16* third story; *I Sam. 3.8* third time; *I Sam. 20.5* day after tomorrow.

שׁלך *hi* throw; cast off; throw away; reject, expel; overthrow, throw down.

ho be thrown; be thrown down; be overthrown.

שָׁלָךְ cormorant?

I שַׁלֶּכֶת felling.

II שַׁלֶּכֶת *name of a gate of the temple* Shallecheth.

שׁלל *q* plunder; *Ruth 2.16* pull out.

hitp be left despoiled.

שָׁלָל booty; gain.

שׁלם *q* remain whole, unscathed; be/become finished, completed; keep quiet.

pi make reparation; reward, requite; fulfil; *I Kings 9.25* complete; *Job 8.6* restore.

pu be repaid; receive reward; be fulfilled.

hi accomplish; hand over *(Aram.)*; be at peace; make peace, bring to be at peace.

ho live in peace.

שְׁלָם° agreement.

שֶׁלֶם concluding sacrifice.

I שָׁלֵם complete; unmolested, unhewn; peaceable.

II שָׁלֵם *n. place* Salem.

I שִׁלֵּם requital.

II שִׁלֵּם *n. pers.* Shillem.

שַׁלָּם → שַׁלּוּם.

שִׁלֵּם → שִׁלּוּם.

שִׁלֵּמָה* requital.

שְׁלֹמֹה *n. pers.* Solomon.

שְׁלֹמוֹת *n. pers.* Shelomoth.

שְׁלֹמִי *n. pers.* Shelomi.

שַׁלְמַי   *n. pers.* Shalmai.

שִׁלֵּמִי   *gent.* Shillemite.

שְׁלֻמִיאֵל   *n. pers.* Shelumiel.

שֶׁלֶמְיָה(וּ)   *n. pers.* Shelemiah.

שְׁלֹמִית   *n. pers. m. and f.* Shelomith.

שַׁלְמַן   *n. pers.* Shalman.

שַׁלְמַנְאֶסֶר   *n. pers.* Shalmaneser.

שַׁלְמֹנִים   gifts.

שֵׁלָנִי   *gent.* Shelanite.

שִׁילֹנִי   → שִׁילֹנִי.

שׁלף   *q* draw, take off.

שֶׁלֶף   *n. pers.* Sheleph.

שׁלשׁ   *pi Deut. 19.3* divide into three parts; *I Sam. 20.19* do on the
       third day; *I Kings 18.34* do for the third time.

       pu pt. threefold; *Gen. 15.9* three-year-old.

שָׁלֹשׁ   three.

שֶׁלֶשׁ   *n. pers.* Shelesh.

שָׁלִישׁ   → שָׁלִישׁ.

שָׁלִשָׁה   *n. terr.* Shalishah.

שִׁלְשָׁה   *n. pers.* Shilshah.

שִׁלְשׁוֹם   day before yesterday.

שִׁלֵּשִׁים   descendants of the third generation, (great-)grandchildren.

שִׁלְשֹׁם   → שִׁלְשׁוֹם.

שְׁאַלְתִּיאֵל   → שְׁאַלְתִּיאֵל.

שָׁם   here, there, thither; then, at that time.

I שֵׁם   name; reputation, fame; memory.

II שֵׁם   *n. pers.* Shem.

שַׁמָּא   *n. pers.* Shamma.

שֶׁמְאֵבֶר   *n. pers.* Shemeber.

שִׁמְאָה   *n. pers.* Shimeah.

שְׁמָאָם   *n. pers.* Shimeam.

שַׁמְגַּר   *n. pers.* Shamgar.

שׁמד   *ni* be destroyed, exterminated; be devastated, made unusable.
       hi destroy, exterminate; demolish.

שֶׁמֶד   *n. pers.* Shemed.

I שַׁמָּה   terrible thing, appalling thing; dismay; *Ps. 46.9* acts arousing
       dismay.

שַׁמָּה II *n. pers.* Shammah.

שַׁמְהוּת *n. pers.* Shamhuth.

שְׁמוּאֵל *n. pers.* Samuel.

שְׁמוֹנֶה → שְׁמֹנֶה.

שַׁמּוּעַ *n. pers.* Shammua.

שְׁמוּעָה news, report; revelation.

שָׁמוּר *n. pers. rd. K (I Chron. 24.24)* Shamur.

שַׁמּוֹת *n. pers.* Shammoth.

שׁמט *q* release, let go, drop; let go on one's own; remit.

ni be thrown down.

hi cause to release.

שְׁמִטָּה remission of debt.

שַׁמַּי *n. pers.* Shammai.

שְׁמִידָע *n. pers.* Shemida.

שְׁמִידָעִי *gent.* Shemidaite.

שָׁמַיִם heavens.

שְׁמִינִי eighth.

שָׁמִיר I thorn-bushes.

שָׁמִיר II diamond; emery; → *also* צִפֹּרֶן.

שָׁמִיר III *n. place* Shamir.

שְׁמִירָמוֹת *n. pers.* Shemiramoth.

שַׁמְלַי *n. pers.* Shamlai.

שׁמם *q* be without inhabitant, desolated; be deserted; shudder, be appalled.

ni be left without inhabitant, become desolate; be appalled.

poel pt. broken in spirit, stunned; devastator.

hi leave without inhabitant, desolated; agitate.

ho inf. desolation.

hitpo be astonished, perplexed, benumbed; *Eccles. 7.16* destroy oneself.

שָׁמֵם without inhabitant, desolated.

שְׁמָמָה desolation.

שִׁמָמָה dismay.

שִׁמָּמוֹן horror.

שׁמן *q* be/become fat.

hi make fat > make indifferent; grow fat.

שֶׁמֶן   olive-oil.

שָׁמָן*   fat.

שָׁמֵן   fat.

שְׁמֹנֶה   eight.

שׁמע   *q* hear; listen to, grant a favourable hearing; obey; understand; *Deut. 1.16* hear a case; *II Sam. 14.17* distinguish.

ni be heard, listened to, granted a favourable hearing, reported; be/become obedient.

pi summon.

hi cause to hear, proclaim, announce, summon; let oneself be heard.

שֵׁמַע I   sound.

שֶׁמַע II   *n. pers.* Shema.

שֵׁמַע   news, report; *w.* אֹזֶן hearsay.

שֹׁמַע*   report.

שָׁמָע   *n. pers.* Shama.

שֶׁמַע   *n. place* Shema.

שִׁמְעָא   *n. pers.* Shimea.

שִׁמְעָה   *n. pers.* Shimeah.

שְׁמָעָה   *n. pers.* Shemaah.

שְׁמָעָה   → שְׁמוּעָה.

שִׁמְעוֹן   *n. pers., n. peop.* Simeon.

שִׁמְעוֹנִי   → שִׁמְעֹנִי.

שִׁמְעִי   *n. pers.* Shimei; *gent.* Shimeite.

שְׁמַעְיָה(וּ)   *n. pers.* Shemaiah.

שִׁמְעֹנִי   *gent.* Simeonite.

שִׁמְעָת   *n. pers. f.* Shimeath.

שִׁמְעָתִי*   *gent.* Shimeathite.

שֶׁמֶץ   whisper.

שִׁמְצָה   laughing-stock?

שׁמר   *q* tend, guard; take care of, protect; store up, reserve; observe, heed, keep; keep guard; revere; *in conjunction with another verb* carefully, exactly.

ni be on one's guard; *Hos. 12.14* be protected.

pi venerate.

hitp be on one's guard.

שֶׁמֶר* I   sediment.

שֶׁמֶר II   *n. pers.* Shemer.

שֹׁמֵר   *n. pers. f.* Shomer.

שְׁמָרָה   guard.

שְׁמֻרָה*   eyelid.

שִׁמְרוֹן   *n. pers., n. place* Shimron.

שֹׁמְרוֹן   *n. place, n. terr.* Samaria.

שִׁמְרִי   *n. pers.* Shimri.

שְׁמַרְיָה(וּ)   *n. pers.* Shemariah.

שִׁמֻּרִים   vigil.

שִׁמְרָיְמוֹת   rd. *Q (II Chron. 17.8)*.

שִׁמְרִית   *n. pers. f.* Shimrith.

שָׁמְרֹן   → שִׁמְרוֹן.

שִׁמְרֹנִי   *gent.* Shimronite.

שֹׁמְרֹנִים   *n. peop.* Samaritans.

שִׁמְרָת   *n. pers.* Shimrath.

שֶׁמֶשׁ   sun; *Isa. 38.8* sun-dial; *Isa. 54.12; Ps. 84.12* shield.

שִׁמְשׁוֹן   *n. pers.* Samson.

שִׁמְשַׁי   *n. pers.* Shimshai.

שַׁמְשְׁרַי   *n. pers.* Shamsherai.

שֻׁמָתִי   *gent.* Shumathite.

שֵׁן   → בֵּית(־)שֵׁן.

שֵׁן   tooth; ivory; prong; crag.

שׁנא   *q* gleam.

     pi, pu → שׁנה.

שֵׁנָא   sleep.

שִׁנְאָב   *n. pers.* Shinab.

שִׁנְאָן   majesty.

שֶׁנְאַצַּר   *n. pers.* Shenazzar.

שׁנה   *q* change, be different; repeat; do a second time.

     ni be repeated.

     pi alter, pervert; pretend; change.

     pu change.

     hitp disguise oneself.

שָׁנָה   year.

שֵׁנָה   sleep.

שֶׁנְהַבִּים   ivory.

שָׁנִי   crimson.

שֵׁנִי   second.

שְׁנַיִם   two; twofold.

שְׁנִינָה   (cutting) ridicule, gibe.

שְׁנַמִּית   → שׁוּנַמִּית.

שׁנן   q sharpen.
pi impress.
hitp feel stabbed.

שׁנס   *pi* tuck up one's garments.

שִׁנְעָר   n. terr. Shinar.

שְׁנָת   sleep.

שׁסה   q plunder.
poel strip by plundering.

שׁסס   q plunder.
ni be plundered.

שׁסע   q be cloven.
pi tear, tear apart; *I Sam. 24.8* rebuke.

שֶׁסַע   cleft.

שׁסף   *pi* hew in pieces?

שׁעה   q regard, look; pay attention to.
hi look away.
hitp look about one.

שְׁעָטָה*   stamping.

שַׁעַטְנֵז   woven from two kinds of yarn.

שֹׁעַל*   hollow of the hand; handful.

שַׁעַלְבִים   n. place Shaalbim.

שַׁעֲלַבִּין   n. place Shaalabbin.

שַׁעַלְבֹנִי   gent. Shaalbonite.

שַׁעֲלִים   n. terr. Shaalim.

שׁען   *ni* support oneself, lean; rest.

I שׁעע   q be smeared, plastered up.
hi plaster up.
hitpalp be plastered up.

II שׁעע   *pilp* play, indulge; *pass. Isa. 66.12* be dandled.
hitpalp delight.

שַׁעַף   n. pers. Shaaph.

שׁער   q reckon.

I שַׁעַר   gate.

II *שָׁעַר measure.

שֹׁעָר* burst, bad.

שַׁעֲרוּר* horrible thing.

שַׁעֲרוּרִי* horrible thing.

שְׁעַרְיָה n. pers. Sheariah.

שַׁעֲרִים n. place Shaaraim.

שַׁעַשְׁגַּז n. pers. Shaashgaz.

שַׁעֲשׁוּעִים pleasure, delight.

שָׁפָה ni pt. bare.

pu be emaciated.

שְׁפוֹ n. pers. Shepho.

שְׁפוֹט judgment.

שְׁפוּפָם n. pers. Shephupham.

שְׁפוּפָן n. pers. Shephuphan.

שְׁפוֹת curds.

שִׁפְחָה female slave.

שָׁפַט q decide, settle; procure justice for; judge, punish; rule; pt. judge, ruler.

ni go to law; conduct a lawsuit; Isa. 66.16 execute judgment.

שֶׁפֶט* judgment.

שָׁפָט n. pers. Shaphat.

שְׁפַטְיָה(וּ) n. pers. Shephatiah.

שִׁפְטָן n. pers. Shiphtan.

I שְׁפִי bare hill; track.

II שְׁפִי n. pers. Shephi.

שְׁפִים → שַׁפָּם.

שְׁפִיפֹן species of snake horned snake?

שָׁפִיר n. place Shaphir.

שָׁפַךְ q pour, shed; vent, pour out; gush out; heap up.

ni be poured out, shed.

pu be shed, spilt; Ps. 73.2 steps > be brought down.

hitp Job 30.16 overflow; Lam. 2.12 be poured out; Lam. 4.1 lie scattered, strewn.

שֶׁפֶךְ heaping-up.

שִׁפְכָה urinary duct, male organ.

שָׁפֵל‎ *q* be/become low; sink, sink down; be humbled, be humble; *Eccles. 12.4* be muted.

hi bring down; throw down; abase, humble; *in conjunction with another verb* low down, deep down.

שֵׁפֶל‎ abasement.

שָׁפָל‎ low, deep; lowly; humble.

שִׁפְלָה‎ lowness.

שְׁפֵלָה‎ lowlands, foot-hills; *n. place* Shephelah.

שִׁפְלוּת‎ letting drop.

שָׁפָם‎ *n. pers.* Shapham.

שְׁפָם‎ *n. place* Shepham.

שֻׁפִּם‎ *n. pers.* Shuppim.

שֻׁפְמִי‎ *gent.* Shiphmite.

I שָׁפָן‎ rock-badger.

II שָׁפָן‎ *n. pers.* Shaphan.

שֶׁפַע‎ abundance.

שִׁפְעָה‎* superabundance, mass.

שִׁפְעִי‎ *n. pers.* Shiphi.

שׁפר‎° *q* be pleasing.

I שֶׁפֶר‎ antlers.

II שֶׁפֶר‎* *n. place* Shepher.

שֹׁפֶר‎ → שׁוֹפָר‎.

I שִׁפְרָה‎ being clear.

II שִׁפְרָה‎ *n. pers. f.* Shiphrah.

שַׁפְרִיר‎* royal pavilion?

שׁפת‎ *q* set, put; provide.

שְׁפַתַּיִם‎ *Ezek. 40.43* double hooks?; ledges?; *Ps. 68.14* sheepfolds?; pack-saddles?

שֶׁצֶף‎ outburst.

I שׁקד‎ *q* be vigilant, keep watch; lie in wait.

pu pt. in the shape of almond-blossom.

II שׁקד‎ *q Ps. 102.8* be wasted away.

שָׁקֵד‎ almond tree; almonds.

שׁקה‎ *ni rd. Q (Amos 8.8)*.

pu be moistened.

hi cause to drink, give to drink, water; *pt.* → *also* מַשְׁקֶה‎.

שִׁקּוּי drink; refreshment.

שִׁקּוּץ heathen image > abominable thing.

שׁקט q rest, enjoy peace; remain quiet, inactive.
hi make peace; remain quiet; enjoy peace.

שֶׁקֶט peace.

שׁקל q weigh; pay; *II Sam. 14.26* weigh.
ni be weighed.

שֶׁקֶל *unit of weight* shekel *(11.424 g)*.

שִׁקְמָה* sycamore tree.

שׁקע q sink, subside, abate.
ni Amos 8.8 Q sink.
hi Ezek. 32.14 let become clear; *Job 40.25* fasten down.

שְׁקַעֲרוּרָה* depression.

שׁקף *ni* look down.
hi look down.

שֶׁקֶף frame?

שְׁקֻפִים windows?

שׁקץ *pi* make abhorrent; abhor.

שֶׁקֶץ abhorrent thing.

שִׁקּוּץ → שִׁקּוּץ.

שׁקק q rush, attack suddenly; *Isa. 29.8; Ps. 107.9* parched.
hitpalp drive to and fro.

שׁקר q deal deceitfully.
pi deceive, cheat; deal falsely with; break *(faith, obligation)*.

שֶׁקֶר lie, fraud, deception; treacherously; *w.* לְ *also for nothing.*

שֹׁקֶת, שֶׁקֶת* watering-trough.

שֹׁר* navel-string; navel.

שָׁרָב scorching heat.

שֵׁרֵבְיָה *n. pers.* Sherebiah.

שַׁרְבִיט staff, sceptre.

שׁרה° q let loose.
pi free.

שָׂרָה* *Jer. 5.10 pl. of* שׁוּרָה.

שָׁרוּחֶן *n. place* Sharuhen.

שָׁרוֹן *n. terr.* Sharon.

שָׁרוֹנִי *gent.* Sharonite.

שְׁרוּקָה*   rd. שְׁרֵקֹת (*Jer. 18.16*).

שָׁרַי   n. pers. Sharai.

שִׁרְיָה   arrow-head.

שִׁרְיוֹן, שִׁרְיָן   coat of mail.

שָׁרִיר*   muscle.

שְׁרִירוּת   → שְׁרִרוּת.

שֵׁרִית   → שְׁאֵרִית.

שְׁרֵמוֹת   rd. Q (*Jer. 31.40*).

שָׁרַץ   q swarm; be innumerable.

שֶׁרֶץ   swarm; small animals.

שָׁרַק   q whistle.

שְׁרֵקָה   whistling.

שְׁרֵקָה*   flute-playing.

שָׁרָר   n. pers. Sharar.

שֹׁרֵר*   → שׁוֹרֵר.

שְׁרִרוּת   stubbornness.

שָׁרַשׁ   *pi* root out.

       pu be uprooted.

       poel strike root.

       poal be firmly rooted.

       hi take root.

שֶׁרֶשׁ   n. pers. Sheresh.

שֹׁרֶשׁ   root, root-stock, sucker; foundation, cause.

שָׁרָשׁוֹת   *pl. of* שַׁרְשְׁרָה.

שַׁרְשְׁרָה*   chain.

שָׁרַת   *pi* serve, assist; minister.

שָׁרֵת   cultic service.

שִׁשָׂה   → שׂשׂה.

I שֵׁשׁ   six.

II שֵׁשׁ   *Cant. 5.15; Esther 1.6* alabaster.

III שֵׁשׁ   linen.

שִׁשָּׂא   *pi* lead along.

שֵׁשְׁבַּצַּר   n. pers. Sheshbazzar.

שִׁשָּׂה   *pi* give the sixth part.

שָׁשַׁי   n. pers. Shashai.

שֵׁשַׁי   n. pers. Sheshai.

שִׁשִּׁי   rd. Q (*Ezek. 16.13*).

שִׁשִּׁי   sixth; sixth part, one-sixth.

שֵׁשַׁךְ *n. place* Sheshach.

שֵׁשָׁן *n. pers.* Sheshan.

שָׁשַׁק *n. pers.* Shashak.

שָׁשֵׁר red colour, vermilion.

I שֵׁת buttocks; *Ps. 11.3* foundation.

II שֵׁת *Num. 24.17* defiance.

III שֵׁת *n. pers.* Seth.

שתה *q* drink.

ni be drunk.

I שְׁתִי fabric.

II שְׁתִי *Eccles. 10.17* drinking.

שְׁתִיָּה drinking.

שָׁתִיל* cutting.

שְׁתַּיִם *f. of* שְׁנַיִם.

שׁתל *q* plant.

שֻׁתַלְחִי *gent.* Shuthelahite.

שׁתם *q pt. pass.* opened?

שׁתן *(hi) pt. iphtael of* שׁין.

°שׁתק *q* become calm.

שְׁתַר *n. pers.* Shethar.

שׁתת *q* set.

שָׁתֹת weaver?, rope-maker?

ת

תָּא guardroom.

I תאב *q* desire, long for.

II תאב *pi Amos 6.8* abhor.

תַּאֲבָה longing.

תאה *pi* mark, fix.

תְּאוֹ wild sheep?

תַּאֲוָה longing, eager desire, delight

תְּאוֹמִים → תּוֹאֲמָם.

תַּאֲלָה* curse.

תאם *hi* bear twins.

תֹּאֲמִים → תּוֹאֲמָם.

תַּאֲנָה* time of heat.

תְּאֵנָה fig-tree; fig.

תֹּאֲנָה   pretext, occasion.

תַּאֲנִיָּה   sorrow.

תְּאֻנִים   toil.

תַּאֲנַת שִׁלֹה   n. place Taanath-shiloh.

תאר   q bend round, turn.

    pi outline, sketch.

    pu extend?

תֹּאַר   form, fine appearance.

תַּאֲרֵעַ   n. pers. Tarea.

תְּאַשּׁוּר   cypress.

תֵּבָה   chest, ark.

תְּבוּאָה   produce.

תְּבוּנָה   insight, skill.

תְּבוּסָה*   trampling down > downfall.

תָּבוֹר   n. place Tabor.

תֵּבֵל   f. continent.

תֶּבֶל   vile interbreeding.

תֻּבַל   n. pers., n. peop. Tubal.

תַּבְלִית*   destruction.

תְּבַלֻּל   one who has a flaw.

תֶּבֶן   chopped straw.

תִּבְנִי   n. pers. Tibni.

תַּבְנִית   figure, pattern, likeness; model, plan; something like.

תַּבְעֵרָה   n. place Taberah.

תֵּבֵץ   n. place Thebez.

תָּבֹר   → תָּבוֹר.

תִּגְלַת פִּלְאֶסֶר,   n. pers. Tiglath-pileser.
תִּ׳ פִּלְנְאֶסֶר,
תִּ׳ פִּלְנֶסֶר,
תִּ׳ פִּלֶסֶר

תַּגְמוּל*   benefit.

תִּגְרָה°*   excitation.

תֹּגַרְמָה   n. pers., n. peop. Togarmah.

תִּדְהָר   ash-tree?

תַּדְמֹר   n. place Tadmor, Palmyra.

תִּדְעָל   n. pers. Tidal.

תֹּהוּ   waste, desert; nothingness; Isa. 29.21 empty plea; Isa. 45.19 to no purpose.

תְּהוֹם   primaeval deep, primaeval ocean, ocean flood.

תְּהֵלָה   error.

תְּהִלָּה   renown, glorious deed; praise, song of praise.

תַּהֲלֻכֹת   festal procession.

תַּהְפֻּכָה*   pl. perversity, perverse thing, intrigue.

תָּו   mark, sign.

תּוֹא   → תְּאוֹ.

תּוֹאֲמִם   twins; double.

תּוּבַל   → תֵּבֵל.

תּוּבַל קַיִן   n. pers. Tubal-cain.

תּוּבְנָה*   rd. Q (Job 26.12).

תּוּגָה   grief.

תּוֹגַרְמָה   → תֹּגַרְמָה.

תּוֹדָה   song of thanksgiving, thank-offering; confession; Neh. 12.31, 38,40 choir.

תוה I   pi make a mark.
        hi make a mark.

תוה II   hi grieve.

תּוֹחַ   n. pers. Toah.

תּוֹחֶלֶת   expectation, hope.

תָּוֶךְ   middle.

תּוֹכֵחָה   chastisement.

תּוֹכַחַת   correction, warning, remonstration; retort, contradiction; chastisement; reproof, reprimand.

תּוּפִּיִם   → תְּפִּיִם.

תּוֹלָד   n. place Tolad.

תּוֹלֵדוֹת*   descendants; story of the origin and development of > story, making, order of birth.

תִּוֹלוֹן   n. pers. rd. Q (I Chron. 4.20) Tilon.

תּוֹלָל*   tormentor?

תּוֹלָע I   red-dyed cloth.

תּוֹלָע II   n. pers. Tola.

תּוֹלֵעָה   maggot, worm; scale insect; w. שָׁנִי crimson cloth, crimson.

תּוֹלָעִי   gent. Tolaite.

תּוֹלַעַת   parallel form of תּוֹלֵעָה.

תּוֹמִיךְ   parallel form of pt. q תמך.

תּוֹמָם   → תּוֹאֲמִם.

תּוֹעֵבָה   abominable thing, abomination, abominable practice.

תּוֹעֵה confusion; perversion.

תּוֹעָפוֹת horns, summits; best.

תּוֹצָאוֹת exits; recesses, extremity; termination; *Ps. 68.21* escape; *Prov. 4.23* source.

תָּוְקְהַת *n. pers. rd. Q (II Chron. 34.22)* Tokhath.

תּוֹקְעִים striking hands.

תּוּר *q* spy out, explore, investigate; *Num. 15.39* go about.
hi send to spy out.

תּוּר I turn; pendant.

תּוּר II turtle-dove.

תּוֹרָה direction, instruction; law.

תּוֹשָׁב sojourner.

תּוּשִׁיָּה prospering, success; circumspection.

תּוֹתָח club, cudgel.

תזז *hi* break off.

תַּזְנֻת* unchaste behaviour; fornication.

תַּחְבֻּלוֹת deliberations; steering, wise direction.

תֹּחוּ *n. pers.* Tohu.

תַּחְכְּמֹנִי *gent.* Tahchemonite.

תַּחֲלֻאִים diseases.

תְּחִלָּה beginning.

תֹּחֶלֶת → תּוֹחֶלֶת.

תַּחְמָס *unclean bird* owl?

תַּחַן *n. pers.* Tahan.

תְּחִנָּה I supplication; mercy.

תְּחִנָּה II *n. pers.* Tehinnah.

תַּחֲנוּן* supplication.

תַּחֲנִי *gent.* Tahanite.

תַּחֲנֹתִי place of encampment?

תַּחְפַּנְחֵס, *n. place* Tahpanhes.
תְּחַפְנְחֵס

תַּחְפְּנֵ(י)ס *n. pers. f.* Tahpenes.

תַּחְרָא leather cuirass.

תַּחְרֵעַ *n. pers.* Tahrea.

תַּחַשׁ I porpoise.

תַּחַשׁ II *n. pers.* Tahash.

תַּחַת I place beneath; beneath, under; in place of, instead of, for.

תַּחַת II	*n. pers.*, *n. place* Tahath.
תַּחְתּוֹן	the lower.
תַּחְתִּי*	the lower, the lowest; depth.
תַּחְתִּים חׇדְשִׁי	*n. place* Tahtim-hodshi.
תִּיכוֹן, תִּיכֹן	middle.
תֵּימָא	*n. pers.*, *n. peop.*, *n. terr.* Tema.
תֵּימָן I	south, southern region; south wind.
תֵּימָן II	*n. pers.*, *n. peop.*, *n. terr.* Teman.
תֵּימָנִי	*gent.* Temanite.
תֵּימְנִי	*gent.* Temnite.
תִּימׇרה*	column.
תִּיצִי	*gent.* Tizite.
תִּירוֹשׁ	wine.
תִּירְיָא	*n. pers.* Tiria.
תִּירָס	*n. pers.* Tiras.
תִּירֹשׁ	→ תִּירוֹשׁ.
תַּיִשׁ	he-goat.
תֹּךְ°	oppression.
תכה	*pu unexplained.*
תְּכוּנָה	arrangement, fittings; *Job 23.3* abode.
תְּפִיִּים	poultry.
תְּכָכִים	*pl. of* תֹּךְ.
תׇּכְלָה	perfection.
תַּכְלִית	the utmost, extreme.
תְּכֵלֶת	violet-purple yarn/cloth.
תכן	*q* examine.
	ni be examined; be right, fair.
	pi fix securely; determine the measurement of.
	pu pt. counted out.
תֹּכֶן I	quantity, standard.
תֹּכֶן II	*n. place* Tochen.
תׇּכְנִית	example, model.
תַּכְרִיךְ°	cloak.
תֵּל	mound of ruins.
תלא	*q* hang; *Deut. 28.66 w.* לְ *and* מִנֶּגֶד be in uncertainty, danger.
תַּלְאֻבוֹת	fits of fever.
תֵּל אָבִיב	*n. place* Tel-abib.

תְּלָאָה   hardship, difficulty.

תְּלַאשָּׂר   *n. terr.* Telassar.

תִּלְבֹּשֶׁת   clothing.

תִּגְלַת פִּלְאֶסֶר,   → תִּגְלַת פִּלְאֶסֶר.
תִּ׳ פִּלְנֶסֶר

תלה   *q* hang.

     ni be hung up, hanged.

     pi hang.

תָּלוּל   towering.

תֶּלַח°   *n. pers.* Telah.

תֵּל חַרְשָׁא   *n. place* Tel-harsha.

תְּלִי*   sling for weapons *(quiver and arrows)*.

תלל   *hi* deceive, cheat.

     ho be deluded.

תֶּלֶם   furrow.

תַּלְמַי   *n. pers.* Talmai.

תַּלְמִיד   pupil.

תֵּל מֶלַח   *n. place* Tel-melah.

תְּלֻנּוֹת   murmuring.

תלע   *pu pt.* clothed in scarlet.

תַּלְפִּיּוֹת   courses of stones.

תְּלַאשָּׂר   → תְּלַאשָּׂר.

תַּלְתָּל*   date-cluster.

תָּם   whole, complete; godly, right, upright; *Gen. 25.27* quiet; *Cant. 5.2; 6.9 w. suffix* my all.

תֹּם   completeness, entirety; integrity, simplicity; *Job 21.23* full vigour; *pl.* → תֻּמִּים.

תֵּמָא   → תֵּימָא.

תמה   *q* be astonished, look in astonishment, be surprised.

     hitp gaze in astonishment.

תֻּמָּה*   integrity.

תִּמָּהוֹן   astonishment, confusion.

תַּמּוּז   *n. deity* Tammuz.

תְּמוֹל   yesterday, formerly.

תְּמוּנָה   form, likeness.

תְּמוּרָה   exchange, return for exchange, substitute.

תְּמוּתָה   death.

תֶּמַח   *n. pers.* Temah.

תָּמִיד   continually; continuity, regularity.

תָּמִים   complete; without blemish, faultless; perfect, blameless; whole; uprightly.

תֻּמִּים   *tog. w.* אוּרִים *lot for oracular consultation (decision in the affirmative).*

תמך   *q* take hold of, hold, hold fast.
     ni be held fast.

תְּמֹל   → תְּמוֹל.

תמם   *q* be complete, finished, completed, at an end; be used up, gone; be blameless, perfect.
     hi make ready, make up the full measure, finish; *Job 22.3* make blameless; *Ezek. 22.15* remove.
     hitp show oneself upright.

תֵּמָן   → I תֵּימָן.

תִּמְנָה   *n. place* Timnah.

תֵּמָנִי   → תֵּימָנִי.

תִּמְנִי   *gent.* Timnite.

תִּמְנָע, תִּמְנַע   *n. pers. f., n. peop.* Timna.

תֶּמֶס   dissolving.

I תָּמָר   date-palm.

II תָּמָר   *n. pr. f., n. place* Tamar.

I תֹּמֶר   palm.

II תֹּמֶר   scarecrow.

תִּמֹרָה   figure of palm-tree, as ornament.

תַּמְרוּק   rubbing, massage.

I תַּמְרוּרִים   bitterness.

II תַּמְרוּרִים   *Jer. 31.21* route-markers.

תַּן*   jackal.

תנה°   *q unexplained.*
     pi sing?
     hi unexplained.

תְּנוּאָה*   displeasure, cause of displeasure.

תְּנוּבָה   produce.

תְּנוּךְ   lobe of the ear.

תְּנוּמָה   slumber.

תְּנוּפָה   brandishing; consecration; wave-offering.

תַּנּוּר   oven.

תַּנְחוּמוֹת   consolation.

תַּנְחוּמִים   consolation.

תַּנְחֻמֶת *n. pers.* Tanhumeth.

תַּנִּים, תַּנִּין sea-monster, sea-dragon; serpent.

I תִּנְשֶׁמֶת *Lev. 11.30* chameleon.

II תִּנְשֶׁמֶת barn-owl.

תעב *ni* be abhorred.

    pi abhor; *Ezek. 16.25* make abhorrent.

    hi act abominably.

תעה *q* wander about, go astray; reel, be confused; *w.* מִן deviate.

    ni be deceived; reel.

    hi cause to wander about, mislead, lead astray; *Jer. 42.20* deceive oneself.

תֹּעוּ *n. pers.* Tou.

תְּעוּדָה confirmation.

תֹּעִי *n. pers.* Toi.

I תְּעָלָה trench, conduit, channel.

II תְּעָלָה growth of tissue *(over a wound)*.

תַּעֲלוּלִים caprice, ill-treatment.

תַּעְלֻם* *rd.* תַּעֲלֻמָה *(Job 28.11)*.

תַּעֲלֻמָה* hidden thing, secret.

תַּעֲנֻג ease, pleasure; *pl. also* pampering.

תַּעֲנִית* mortification, penance.

תַּעֲנַךְ *n. place* Taanach.

תעע *pilp* mock.

    „ *hitpalp* scoff.

תַּעֲצֻמוֹת abundant strength.

תַּעַר knife; sheath.

תַּעֲרוּבוֹת *w.* בֶּן hostage.

תַּעְתֻּעִים mockery.

תֹּף timbrel, tambourine.

תִּפְאֶרֶת adornment, ornament, splendour; glory, honour, distinction; pride.

I תַּפּוּחַ apple; apple-tree.

II תַּפּוּחַ *n. pers., n. place* Tappuah.

תְּפוּצָה* dispersion.

תְּפִינִים* *dub.*

תפל *hitp* *rd.* תִּתְפַּלָּל *(II Sam. 22.27)*.

I תָּפֵל whitewash.

II תְּפֵל   *Job 6.6* insipid thing.

תֹּפֶל   *n. place* Tophel.

תִּפְלָה   unseemliness; scandalous thing.

תְּפִלָּה   prayer.

תִּפְלֶצֶת*   horror.

תִּפְסַח   *n. place* Tiphsah.

תפף   *q* play the tambourine.

    poel beat.

תפר   *q* sew.

    pi tie together.

תפשׂ   *q* grasp, take hold of; manipulate, handle; capture; *Hab. 2.19*
    mount; *Prov. 30.9* take in vain.

    ni be seized, caught, captured, occupied.

    pi catch.

I תֹּפֶת   *Job 17.6* spitting.

II תֹּפֶת   *n. place* Topheth; place of sacrifice?

תָּפְתֶּה   *rd.* תָּפְתֹּה *(Isa. 30.33).*

I *תִּקְוָה   *Josh. 2.18,21* cord.

II תִּקְוָה   expectation, hope.

III תִּקְוָה   *n. pers.* Tikvah.

תְּקוּמָה   standing firm.

תְּקוֹמֵם*   adversary?

תָּקוֹעַ   *Ezek. 7.14* horn?

תְּקוֹעַ   *n. place* Tekoa.

תְּקוֹעִי   *gent.* Tekoite.

תְּקוּפָה*   turning-point, turn.

תַּקִּיף°   strong.

תקן°   *q* become straight.

    pi make straight; cast in suitable form.

תקע   *q* drive; pitch; clap; strike hands; thrust; blow.

    ni be blown; *Job 17.3* be guarantor.

תֶּקַע   blowing *(horn).*

תקף°   *q* overpower.

תֹּקֶף°   strength, power.

I תֹּר   → I תּוֹר.

II תֹּר   → II תּוֹר.

תְּרָאֵלָה   *n. place* Taralah.

תַּרְבּוּת new generation, brood.

תַּרְבִּית extra charge, usury.

תרגם *pt. pass.* translated.

תַּרְדֵּמָה deep sleep, stupor.

תִּרְהָקָה *n. pers.* Tirhakah.

תְּרוּמָה contribution.

תְּרוּמִיָּה contribution.

תְּרוּעָה alarm, alarm-signal; shout of joy.

תְּרוּפָה healing.

תִּרְזָה *species of tree.*

תֶּרַח *n. pers., n. place* Terah.

תִּרְחֲנָה *n. pers.* Tirhanah.

תָּרְמָה deceit.

תַּרְמוּת *rd. Q (Jer. 14.14).*

תַּרְמִית deceit.

תֹּרֶן signal-pole; mast.

תַּרְעֵלָה reeling.

תִּרְעָתִים *gent.?* Tirathites.

תְּרָפִים teraphim *(idol).*

תִּרְצָה *n. pr. f., n. place* Tirzah.

תֶּרֶשׁ *n. pers.* Teresh.

I תַּרְשִׁישׁ *precious stone.*

II תַּרְשִׁישׁ *n. pers., n. place, n. peop.* Tarshish.

תִּרְשָׁתָא governor.

תַּרְתָּן commander-in-chief.

תַּרְתָּק *n. deity* Tartak.

תְּשׁוּמֶת deposit?, joint property?

תְּשֻׁאָה* noise, shouting; crash.

תֹּשֵׁב → תּוֹשָׁב.

תִּשְׁבִּי *gent.* Tishbite.

תַּשְׁבֵּץ woven material.

תְּשׁוּבָה* return; reply, answer.

תְּשֻׁוָּה *rd.* תְּשֻׁאָה *(Job 30.22).*

תְּשׁוּעָה help, deliverance, salvation.

תְּשׁוּקָה* longing.

תְּשׁוּרָה gift ?

תְּשִׁיָה ← תּוּשִׁיָּה.

תְּשִׁיעִי ninth.

תֵּשַׁע nine.

תִּשְׁיעִי ← תְּשִׁיעִי.

Biblical Aramaic Part

א

אַב*   father, forefather.

אֵב*   fruit.

אבד   *pe* perish.
    ha put to death, destroy.
    ho be destroyed.

אֶבֶן   *f.* stone.

אִגְּרָא, אִגְּרָה   *f.* letter.

אֱדַיִן   then, thereupon.

אֲדָר   Adar *(name of a month, February/March)*.

אִדַּר*   threshing-floor.

אֲדַרְגָּזַר*   counsellor.

אַדְרַזְדָּא   *adv.* zealously.

אֶדְרָע   arm; force.

אזא   → אזה.

אַזְדָּא   declared.

אזה   *pe* heat.

אזל   *pe* go.

אָח*   brother.

אַחֲוָיָה*   *inf. ha of* חוה.

אֲחִידָה*   riddle.

אַחְמְתָא   *n. place* Ecbatana.

אַחַר*   after.

אַחֲרִי*   end.

אָחֳרִי   *f.* another.

אָחֲרֵין   *adv.* at last.

אָחֳרָן   another.

אֲחַשְׁדַּרְפַּן*   satrap.

אִילָן   tree.

אֵימְתָן*   terrible.

אִיתַי   there is/are.

אכל   *pe* eat, devour.

אַל   not.

אֵלֶּה   *rd. Q (Ezra 5.15)* these.

אֱלָהּ   God.

אֵלֶּה these.

אֲלוּ behold!

אִלֵּין these.

אִלֵּךְ these.

אִלֵּן → אִלֵּין.

אֲלַף thousand.

אַמָּה* cubit.

אֻמָּה nation.

אמן *ha* trust; *pt. pass.* trustworthy.

אמר *pe* say; command.

אִמַּר* lamb.

אֲנַבֵּה אֵב *w. suffix.*

אֲנָה I.

אִנּוּן, *f.* אִנִּין they; those.

אֱנוֹשׁ → אֱנָשׁ.

אֲנַחְנָא, we.
אֲנַחְנָה

אנס *pe* oppress.

אֲנַף* face.

אֱנָשׁ man; *coll.* men, mankind.

אַנְתְּ, אַנְתָּה you *(sg.)*.

אַנְתּוּן you *(pl.)*.

אֱסוּר bond, fetter.

אָסְנַפַּר *n. pers.* Osnappar.

אָסְפַּרְנָא *adv.* precisely, promptly.

אֱסָר interdict.

אָע wood.

אַף also.

אֲפַרְסָי* *gent.* Persian *or title of official.*

אֲפַרְסְכָי* *gent.* Persian *or title of official.*

אֲפַרְסַתְכָי* *title of official.*

אַפְּתֹם treasury?, finally?

אֶצְבַּע* finger; toe.

אַרְבַּע four.

אַרְגְּוָן* purple.

אֲרוּ behold!

אֹרַח* way.

אַרְיֵה lion.

אַרְיוֹךְ *n. pers.* Arioch.

אֲרִיךְ fitting, proper.

אַרְכֻּבָּה* knee.

אַרְכָה length, duration.

אַרְכְּוָי* *gent.* Archevite.

אֲרַע* earth.

אַרְעִי* bottom.

אֲרַק* earth.

אַרְתַּחְשַׁסְתְּא, *n. pers.* Artaxerxes.
אַרְתַּחְשַׁשְׂתְּא

אֹשׁ* foundation.

אֶשָּׁא fire.

אָשַׁף exorcist, sorcerer.

אֻשַּׁרְן* timber, panelling.

אֶשְׁתַּדּוּר revolt.

אֶשְׁתִּיו *pe pf. of* שתה *w.* א.

אָת* sign.

אתה *pe* come.
    ha bring; *pass.* be brought.

אַתּוּן* furnace.

אֲתַי → אִיתַי.

אֲתַר trace; place.

ב

בְּ in, at; with, by; from; over.

בְּאִישׁ* evil.

בְּאֵשׁ *pe w.* עַל it is displeasing to.

בָּאתַר after.

בָּבֶל *n. place* Babylon.

בַּבְלָי* *gent.* Babylonian.

בדר *pa* scatter.

בְּהִילוּ haste.

בהל *pa* frighten.
    hitpe hasten.
    hitpa be frightened.

בטל *pe* cease.
    pa stop, prevent; order to stop.

בֵּין between.

בִּינָה insight.

בִּירָה* fortress.

בַּיִת house.

בָּל heart, mind.

בלא *pa* wear out.

בֵּלְאשַׁצַּר *n. pers.* Belshazzar.

בְּלוֹ tax.

בֵּלְטְשַׁאצַּר *n. pers.* Belshazzar.

בֵּלְשַׁאצַּר *n. pers.* Belshazzar.

בנה *pe* build.

hitpe be built.

בִּנְיָן* building.

בִּנְיָן *pl. of* II בַּר.

בנס *pe* become irritated, be angry.

בעא, בעה *pe* seek, request.

pa seek.

בָּעוּ petition, prayer.

בְּעֵל owner, lord.

בִּקְעָה* plain.

בקר *pa* search, investigate.

hitpa be searched, investigated.

I בַּר* field.

II בַּר son; *also denotes membership of a group or class.*

I ברך *pe* kneel down.

II ברך *pe pt. pass.* blessed.

pa bless.

בְּרַךְ* knee.

בְּרַם but.

בְּשַׂר flesh.

בַּת* *liquid measure* bath *(between 22 and 45 l)*.

בָּתַר after.

 נ

נַב* back *or* side.

גֹּב pit.

גְּבוּרָה* might, power.

גְּבַר man.

גִּבָּר* strong man.

גִּדְבַר* treasurer.

נדד pe hew down.

גַּו,* גּוֹ(א)* interior.

גּוֹב → גֹּב.

גֵּוָה pride.

נוח ha stir up.

גִּזְבַּר* treasurer.

נזר pe pt. pl. astrologers, soothsayers.

itpe, hitpe break away, break loose.

גְּזֵרָה* decision, decree.

גִּיר* plaster.

גלא → נלה.

גַּלְגַּל* wheel.

גלה pe disclose, reveal.

ha deport.

גָּלוּ* deportation.

גְּלָל coll. w. אֶבֶן hewn stones.

נמר pe pt. pass. finished.

גְּנַז* treasure.

גַּף* wing.

גְּרַם* bone.

גְּשֵׁם* body.

ד

דָּא f. this.

דֹּב bear.

דבח pe sacrifice.

דְּבַח* sacrifice.

דבק pe hold together.

דִּבְרָה* matter.

דְּהַב gold.

דֶּהֱוָא rd. דִּי־הוּא (Ezra 4.9) that is.

דוק → דקק.

דוּר   *pe* dwell.

דּוּרָא   *n. terr.* Dura.

דּוֹשׁ   *pe* trample down.

דַּחֲוָה*   *dub.*

דחל   *pe* be afraid; *pt. pass.* frightful.
      pa frighten.

דִּי   *genitive particle; relative particle;* that, so that, in order that,
      because, for; *introduces direct speech.*

דִּין   *pe* judge.

דִּין   justice; judgment; court.

דַּיָּן*   judge.

דִּינָיֵא   *n. peop.?*

דָּךְ, *f.* דָּךְ   that.

דִּכֵּן   that.

דְּכַר*   ram.

דִּכְרוֹן*   record, edict.

דָּכְרָן*   annals.

דלק   *pe* burn.

דמה   *pe* be like, resemble.

דְּנָה   this.

דָּנִיֵּאל   *n. pers.* Daniel.

דקק   *pe* break in pieces.
      ha crush.

דָּר   generation.

דָּרְיָוֶשׁ   *n. pers.* Darius.

דְּרָע*   arm.

דָּת   order, law.

דֶּתֶא*   grass.

דְּתָבַר*   law official, judge.

ה

הֲ, הַ   *interrogative particle.*

הָא   look!

הֵא   as.

הַדָּבַר*   *high royal official.*

הַדָּם*   member, piece.

הֲדַר   *pa* glorify.

הֲדַר*   majesty.

הוּא   he; that.

הוָא, הוה   *pe* be; become; happen.

הִיא   she.

הֵיכַל   palace; temple.

הֲלַךְ   *pe* go, reach.

      pa walk about.

      ha rd. pa.

הֲלָךְ   *tax.*

הִמּוֹ, הִמּוֹן   *pl.* they, them.

הַמְוֹנְכָא   *rd. Q* necklace.

הֵן   if, whether.

הַנְזָקָה*   harm.

הַצְדָּא   → צְדָא.

הַרְהֹר*   fancies of a dream.

הִתְבְּהָלָה   haste.

הִתְנַדָּבוּ*   contribution.

ו

וְ, וּ   and, but, also.

ז

זְבַן   *pe* buy.

זְהִיר*   careful.

זוּד   *ha* act presumptuously.

זוּן   *hitpe* feed.

זוּעַ   *pe* tremble, quake.

זִיד   → זוּד.

זִיו*   brightness; *pl.* complexion.

זָכוּ   innocence.

זְכַרְיָה   *n. pers.* Zechariah.

זְמַן   *hitpe, hitpa* decide, make an agreement.

זְמַן, זְמָן   time; occurrence.

זְמָר* music for strings.

זַמָּר* singer.

זַן* kind.

זְעֵיר* small.

זְעִק *pe* cry.

זְקִף *pe pt. pass.* impaled.

זְרֻבָּבֶל *n. pers.* Zerubbabel.

זְרַע descendants.

ח

חֲבוּלָה offence.

חֲבַל *pa* hurt; destroy.

     hitpa be destroyed, perish.

חֲבָל hurt, damage.

חֲבַר* companion.

חַבְרָה* *pl.* the others.

חַגַּי *n. pers.* Haggai.

חַד one; -fold; *Dan. 2.35 w.* כְּ together.

חֲדֵה* breast.

חֶדְוָה joy.

חֲדַת new.

חוא, חוה *pa* inform.

     ha inform.

חִוָּר white.

חֲזָה *pe* see, perceive; *pt.* proper, usual.

חֱזוּ*, חֵזוּ* apparition, vision; *Dan. 7.20* appearance.

חֲזוֹת* sight > it was to be seen.

חֲטִי* sin.

חַטָּיָא sin-offering.

חַי living; *pl.* life.

חיה *pe* live.

     ha spare alive.

חֵיוָה beast; *coll.* animals.

חיט *pe or ha* repair?

חַיִל power, strength; army.

חַכִּים* wise, wise man.

חָכְמָה	wisdom.
חֵלֶם	dream.
חֲלַף	*pe* pass over.
חֲלָק	portion; lot.
חֵמָה	anger, rage.
חֲמַר	wine.
חִנְטָה*	wheat.
חֲנֻכָּה*	dedication.
חֲנַן	*pe* show mercy.
	hitpa make supplication.
חֲנַנְיָה	*n. pers.* Hananiah.
חַסִּיר	insignificant, of inferior value.
חֲסַן	*ha* take possession of, possess.
חֱסֵן*	power.
חֲסַף	clay.
חֲצַף	*ha pt.* severe.
חֲרַב	*ho* be destroyed, devastated.
חַרְטֹם	magician.
חֲרַךְ	*hitpa* be singed.
חֲרַץ*	hip.
חֲשַׁב	*pe* reckon, regard.
חֲשׁוֹךְ*	darkness.
חֲשַׁח	*pe* need.
חַשְׁחָה*	need.
חַשְׁחוּ*	need.
חֲשַׁל	*pe* crush.
חֲתַם	*pe* seal.

ט

טָאַב	*pe* be good.
טָב	good.
טַבָּח*	bodyguard.
טוּר	mountain.
טְוָת	fasting, in abstinence.
טִין*	clay.
טַל	dew.

טלל *ha* nest?

טעם *pa* give to eat.

טְעֵם understanding; order; advice, report; *Dan. 5.2* taste.

טְפַר* nail; claw.

טרד *pe* drive away.

טַרְפְּלָי* *gent.* Tarpelite *or class of officials.*

י

יבל *ha* bring.

    sa → סבל.

יַבֶּשֶׁה* earth.

יְגַר heap of stones.

יַד hand, paw; power.

ידא *ha* praise.

ידע *pe* know, be acquainted with, learn, perceive, understand; be known.

    ha tell; *Ezra 7.25* instruct.

יהב *pe* give; *Dan. 6.3* submit (report); *Ezra 5.16* lay (foundation).

    hitpe be given; *Ezra 6* be paid.

יְהוּד *n. peop.* Judaeans; *n. terr.* Judah.

יְהוּדָי* *gent.* Jew.

יוֹם day.

יוֹצָדָק *n. pers.* Jozadak.

יוב *ša* → שֵׁיזֵב.

יטב *pe* please.

יכל *pe* be able; overcome.

יַם* sea.

יסף *ho* be added.

יעט *itpa* take counsel together.

יָעֵט* adviser.

יצא *ša* → שֵׁיצִיא.

יצב *pa* discover exactly.

יַצִּיב reliable, certain; certainly!

יקד *pe* burn.

יְקֵדָה* burning.
יַקִּיר* difficult; illustrious.
יְקָר* honour, majesty.
יְרוּשְׁלֵם n. *place* Jerusalem.
יְרַח* month.
יַרְכָה* thigh.
יִשְׂרָאֵל n. *peop.* Israel.
יֵשׁוּעַ n. *pers.* Jeshua.
יָת* *accusative particle.*
יתב *pe* sit down; dwell.
     ha settle.
יַתִּיר extraordinary; *adv.* very, exceedingly.

כ

כְּ like, corresponding to, according to; about; *w. inf.* as soon as.
כִּדְבָה lie.
כָּה here.
כהל *pe* be able.
כָּהֵן* priest.
כַּוָּה* window.
כּוֹרֶשׁ n. *pers.* Cyrus.
כַּכַּר* *unit of weight* talent *(between 3,000 and 3,600 shekels, between 34 and 41 kg).*
כֹּל whole, every, all.
כלל *ša* complete.
     išt be completed.
כֵּן thus.
כְּנֵמָא thus.
כנשׁ *pe* assemble.
     hitpa assemble.
כְּנָת* associate, colleague.
כַּסְדָּי → כַּשְׂדָּי.
כְּסַף silver.
כְּעַן now.
כְּעֶנֶת and now.
כְּעֶת → כְּעֶנֶת.

כְּפַת *pe* be bound.

     pa bind.

כֹּר* *dry measure* corn *(between 220 and 450 l)*.

כַּרְבְּלָה* cap.

כרה *itpe* be troubled.

כָּרוֹז* herald.

כרז *ha* proclaim publicly.

כָּרְסֵא* seat, throne.

כַּשְׂדָּי *gent.* Chaldaean.

כתב *pe* write.

כְּתָב writing; document; prescription.

כֹּתַל wall.

ל

ל to, in order to, at, for, into, towards, that is, with regard to; *sign of the genitive, dative and accusative.*

לָא not.

לֵב* heart.

לְבַב heart.

לְבוּשׁ* garment.

לבש *pe* be clothed with.

     ha clothe.

לָה → לָא.

I לָהֵן therefore.

II לָהֵן unless, except; but, rather.

לֵוִי* *gent.* Levite.

לְוָת* with.

לְחֵם meal, banquet.

לְחֵנָה* concubine.

לֵילְי* night.

לִשָׁן tongue, language.

מ

מָה → מָא.

מָאָה hundred.

מֹאזְנָא* scales.

מֵאמַר word; order.

מָאן* vessel, utensil.

מְגִלָּה scroll.

מגר *pa* overthrow.

מַדְבַּח* altar.

מִדָּה tax, duty.

מְדוֹר* dwelling.

מָדַי *n. peop.* Medes.

מְדִינָה* province, city.

מְדֹר* → מְדוֹר*.

מָה what?, that which; *w.* כְּ how!; *w.* לְ lest.

מוֹת death.

מָזוֹן food.

מחא *pe* strike.

pa hinder.

hitpe be impaled *(on the stake)*.

מַחְלְקָה* division.

מטא *pe* reach, arrive at; come to; begin; *w.* עַל happen.

מִישָׁאֵל *n. pers.* Mishael.

מֵישַׁךְ *n. pers.* Meshach.

מלא *pe* fill.

hitpe be filled with.

מַלְאַךְ* angel.

מִלָּה word; matter, affair.

מלח *pe* eat *(salt)*.

מְלַח salt.

מֶלֶךְ king.

מְלַךְ* counsel.

מַלְכָּה* queen-mother.

מַלְכוּ sovereignty, kingship; kingdom; *Dan. 6.5* administration.

מלל *pa* speak.

מַן who?, whoever.

מִן from, of, since, in accordance with.

מְנֵא *unit of weight* mina *(50 shekels, 571.2 g)*.

מִנְדָּה → מִדָּה‎.

מַנְדַּע knowledge, understanding.

מנה *pe* number.

pa appoint, install.

מִנְחָה offering.

מִנְיָן number.

מַעֲבָד* work, deed.

מְעֵה* *pl.* belly, bowels.

מֶעָל* setting *(sun)*.

מָרֵא lord.

מְרַד rebellion.

מָרָד* rebellious.

מרט *pe* tear off.

מֹשֶׁה *n. pers.* Moses.

מְשַׁח oil.

מִשְׁכַּב* bed.

מִשְׁכַּן* dwelling.

מַשְׁרוֹ(ֹ)קִי* pipe.

מִשְׁתֵּי* banquet.

מַתְּנָה* gift.

נ

נבא *hitpa* appear as a prophet.

נְבוּאָה* prophecy.

נְבוּכַדְנֶצַּר *n. pers.* Nebuchadnezzar.

נְבִזְבָּה present.

נְבִיא* prophet.

נֶבְרְשָׁה* candlestick.

נגד *pe* flow.

נֶגֶד toward, in the direction of.

נְגַהּ* brightness.

נְגוֹ(א) *element of n. pers.* Abed-nego.

נדב *hitpa* volunteer; contribute; *Ezra 7.16 inf.* contribution.

נִדְבָּךְ course.

נדד *pe* flee.

נִדְנֶה sheath; body?

נְהִיר* *rd. Q (Dan. 2.22)* light.

נַהִירוּ illumination.

נְהַר stream; *frequently* Euphrates.

נוד *pe* flee.

נְוָלוּ heap of refuse, heap of ruins.

נוּר fire.

נזק *pe* suffer loss.

　　ha harm.

נְחָשׁ copper, bronze.

נחת *pe* descend.

　　ha deposit.

　　ho be deposed.

נטל *pe* raise up, raise.

נטר *pe* keep.

נִיחוֹחַ* incense offering.

נְכַס* treasure, money.

נְמַר panther.

נסח *hitpe* be pulled out.

נְסַךְ *pa* offer.

נְסַךְ* drink-offering.

נפל *pe* fall, fall down; fall to, be incumbent on.

נפק *pe* go out; *Dan. 2.13* be issued.

　　ha remove.

נִפְקָה* expense.

נִצְבָּה* hardness.

נצח *hitpa* distinguish oneself.

נצל *ha* save.

נְקֵא pure.

נקשׁ *pe* knock.

נשׂא *pe* take; carry away.

　　hitpa rise up.

נָשִׁין* wives.

נִשְׁמָה* breath of life.

נְשַׁר eagle.

נִשְׁתְּוָן* letter, decree.

נְתִין* temple slave.

נתן *pe* give.

נתר *aph* strip off.

ס

סַבְּכָא → שַׂבְּכָא.

סבל   *po* lay?, offer?

סבר   *pe* intend.

סגד   *pe* do homage.

סָגַן*   prefect, governor.

סגר   *pe* shut.

סוּמְפֹנְיָה   bagpipe?

סוף   *pe* be fulfilled.
    ha destroy.

סוֹף   end.

סלק   *pe* go up, come up.
    ha bring up.
    ho be hauled up.

סעד   *pa* support.

סְפַר   book.

סָפֵר   secretary.

סַרְבָּל*   trousers?

סָרֵךְ*   minister.

I סתר   *pa pt. pass.* that which is hidden.

II סתר   *pe* demolish.

ע

עבד   *pe* do, make; obey; commit, arrange.
    hitpe be made, carried out.

עֲבֵד   worshipper, slave, servant.

עֲבִידָה*   work, service; administration.

עֲבֵד נְגוֹ   *n. pers.* Abed-nego.

עֲבַר*   beyond.

עַד   up to; until.

עדה   *pe* go, come; pass away, be annulled.
    ha take away, depose.

עִדּוֹא   *n. pers.* Iddo.

עִדָּן   time; year.

עוֹד   still.

עֲוָיָה* offence.

עוֹף bird; *coll.* birds.

עוּר chaff.

עֵז* goat.

עִזְקָה* signet-ring.

עֶזְרָא *n. pers.* Ezra.

עֲזַרְיָה *n. pers.* Azariah.

עֵטָה counsel.

עַיִן* eye.

עִיר angel.

עַל on, over, against, to, concerning.

עֵלָּא above, over.

עִלָּה pretext.

עֲלָוָה* burnt offering.

עִלָּי* highest.

עִלִּי* upper room.

עֶלְיוֹן* the Most High.

עֲלַל *pe* go in.

   ha bring in.

   ho be brought in.

עָלַם remote time, eternity.

עֵלְמָי* *gent.* Elamite.

עֲלַע* rib.

עַם people.

עִם together with, at.

עַמִּיק* deep.

עֲמַר wool.

עַן* → פְּעַן.

ענה *pe* answer; begin.

עֲנֵה* wretched.

עֲנָיִן *pl. of* עֲנֵה.

עֲנָן* cloud.

עֲנַף* branch.

עֲנַשׁ fine.

עֲנָת* → פְּעֶנֶת.

עֳפִי* foliage.

עֲצִיב distressed.

עֲקַר *itpe* be torn out.

עִקַּר root-stock.
עָר* adversary.
ערב *pa* mix.
   hitpa mix.
עֲרָד* wild ass.
עַרְוָה* dishonour.
עֲשַׂב *coll.* herbage, grass.
עֲשַׂר ten.
עֶשְׂרִין twenty.
עֲשַׁת *pe* intend.
עֲתִיד* ready.
עַתִּיק old.

פ

פֻּם → פֻּם.
פֶּחָה governor.
פֶּחָר potter.
פְּטַיִשׁ* *rd. Q (Dan. 3.21)* article of clothing.
פלג *pe pt. pass.* divided.
פְּלַג half.
פְּלֻגָּה* division.
פלח *pe* serve.
פֻּלְחָן service, worship.
פֻּם mouth; opening.
פַּס palm, hand.
פְּסַנְטֵרִין zither.
פַּרְזֶל iron.
פרס *pe* be divided.
פְּרֵס *unit of weight* half-mina?, half-shekel?
פָּרַס *n. peop.* Persians; *n. terr.* Persia.
פַּרְסָי* *gent.* Persian.
פרק *pe* blot out.
פרשׁ *pa pt. pass.* made distinct.
פַּרְשֶׁגֶן copy.
פשׁר *pe* interpret.
   pa interpret.

פְּשַׁר   interpretation.

פִּתְגָם   word; edict.

פתח   *pe* open.

פְּתָי*   breadth.

צ

צבה   *pe* wish, desire.

צְבוּ   matter.

צבע   *pa* wet.

     hitpa be wet.

צַד   side.

צְדָא   true.

צְדָקָה   charity.

צַוַּאר*   neck.

צלה   *pa* pray.

צלח   *ha* prosper, make to prosper, make progress.

צְלֵם   statue.

צְפִיר*   he-goat.

צִפַּר*   bird.

ק

קבל   *pa* receive.

קֳבֵל   before, opposite, because of; *w.*-כָּל accordingly, thereupon.

קַדִּישׁ   holy.

קֳדָם   before; *w.* מִן before, on the part of.

קַדְמָה*   former time; *w.* מִן previously, before.

קַדְמָי*   first, former.

קום   *pe* stand up; stand; endure.

     pa establish, issue.

     ha set up, found; appoint; issue.

     ho be set up.

קטל   *pe* kill.

     pa kill.

     hitpe (hitpa) be killed.

קְטַר* knot > joint, difficult problem.

קַיִט summer.

קְיָם ordinance.

קַיָּם enduring.

קִיתָר(וֹ)ס rd. K zither.

קָל voice, sound.

קנא pe buy.

קצף pe become furious.

קְצַף anger.

קצץ pa hew off.

קְצָת end; part.

קרא pe call; read.

     hitpe be called.

קרב pe draw near, approach.

     pa offer.

     ha bring near, offer.

קְרָב war.

קִרְיָא, קִרְיָה city.

קֶרֶן horn.

קְרָץ* piece; w. אכל slander.

קְשֹׁט truth.

ר

רֵאשׁ head; beginning.

רַב great; head-, chief-.

רבה pe become great, grow.

     pa make great, elevate.

רִבּוֹ ten thousand.

רְבוּ greatness.

רְבִיעִי* fourth.

רַבְרְבָנִין* nobles, grandees.

רגז ha provoke to anger, anger.

רְגַז anger.

רְגַל* f. foot.

רגש ha come up running?, storm in?

רוּ* appearance.

רוּחַ wind; spirit.

רוּם *pe* raise oneself.
    pol praise.
    ha elevate.
    hitpol rise up.

רוּם* height.

רָז secret.

רְחוּם *n. pers.* Rehum.

רַחִיק* far.

רַחֲמִין compassion.

רחץ *hitpe* trust.

רֵיחַ smell.

רמה *pe* throw; set down; impose.
    hitpe be thrown.

רְעוּ* will.

רַעְיוֹן* thought.

רַעֲנַן flourishing.

רעע *pe* crush.
    pa crush.

רפס *pe* trample down.

רשׁם *pe* write.

שׂ

שָׂב* elder.

שַׂבְּכָא *triangular musical instrument.*

שׂנא *pe* become great.

שַׂגִּיא great; much, many; *adv.* very.

שָׂהֲדוּ* testimony.

שְׂטַר side.

שׂים *pe* place, lay; give; appoint; *Dan. 3.12; 6.14 w.* טְעֵם pay heed.
    hitpe be laid; be made, given.

שׂכל *hitpa* consider.

שָׂכְלְתָנוּ insight.

שׂנא *pe pt.* enemy.

שְׂעַר hair.

שׁ

שְׁאֵל   *pe* request, demand; ask.

שְׁאֵלָה*   question; matter.

שְׁאַלְתִּיאֵל   *n. pers.* Shealtiel.

שְׁאָר   rest, remainder.

שׁבח   *pa* praise.

שֵׁבֶט*   tribe.

שְׁבִיב*   flame.

שִׁבַע*   seven.

שׁבק   *pe* leave behind; leave, let alone.
hitpe be left.

יׁבשׁ   *hitpa* be perplexed.

שֵׁגַל*   concubine.

שׁדר   *hitpa* strive.

שַׁדְרַךְ   *n. pers.* Shadrach.

שׁוה   *pa rd. Q (Dan. 5.21)* make like.
hitpa be made into.

שׁוּר*   wall.

שׁוּשַׁנְכָי*   *gent.* of Susa.

שְׁחַת   *pe pt. pass.* corrupt, base; corruption.

שׁיזב   save.

שׁיציא   complete.

שׁכח   *ha* find; obtain.
hitpe be found; turn out to be.

שַׁכְלֵל   *ša of* כלל.

שׁכן   *pe* dwell.
pa cause to dwell.

שְׁלֵה   at ease, carefree.

שָׁלֵה   *rd. Q (Dan. 3.29)*.

שָׁלוּ   negligence; fault.

שַׁלְוָה*   happiness.

שׁלח   *pe* dispatch, send; *Ezra 6.12* dare.

שׁלט   *pe* rule; *Dan. 6.25* overpower.
ha make to rule.

שׁלְטֹן*   official.

שָׁלְטָן   dominion, power, realm.

שַׁלִּיט   powerful; official, ruler; *Ezra 7.24* it is permitted.

שְׁלֵם   *pe* be finished.

      ha deliver, abandon.

שְׁלָם   peace, prosperity.

שֻׁם   name.

שְׁמַד   *ha* annihilate.

שְׁמַיִן*   heavens.

שְׁמַם   *itpo* be overcome with fear.

שְׁמַע   *pe* hear.

      hitpa obey.

שָׁמְרַיִן   *n. place, n. terr.* Samaria.

שְׁמַשׁ   *pa* serve.

שְׁמַשׁ*   sun.

שִׁמְשַׁי   *n. pers.* Shimshai.

שֵׁן*   *f.* tooth.

שְׁנה   *pe* be different; be changed.

      pa change; *pt. pass.* different; *Dan. 3.28* transgress.

      ha change; transgress.

      itpa change.

שְׁנָה* I   year.

שְׁנָה* II   sleep.

שָׁעָה   short time, moment.

שְׁפַט   *pe pt.* judge.

שַׁפִּיר   beautiful.

שְׁפַל   *ha* bring low.

שְׁפַל   lowly.

שְׁפַר   *pe* please.

שְׁפַרְפָּר*   dawn.

שָׁק*   lower leg.

שְׁרה   *pe* loosen; dwell.

      pa begin.

      hitpa be loosened.

שֹׁרֶשׁ*   root.

שְׁרשׁוּ   *rd. Q (Ezra 7.26)* banishment, exclusion.

שֵׁשְׁבַּצַּר   *n. pers.* Sheshbazzar.

שֵׁת   six.

שָׁתָה *pe* drink.
שִׁתִּין sixty.
שְׁתַר בּוֹזְנַי *n. pers.* Shethar-bozenai.

ת

תבר *pe pt. pass.* brittle.
תְּדִיר* duration; *w.* בְּ continually.
תוב *pe* return.
    ha return, send back; answer.
תוה *pe* be astonished, be frightened.
תּוֹר* ox, bull.
תְּחוֹת under.
תְּלַג snow.
תְּלִיתָי third.
תְּלָת three.
תַּלְתָּא, תַּלְתִּי triumvir?
תְּלָתִין thirty.
תְּמַהּ* wonder.
תַּמָּה there.
תִּנְיָן* second.
תִּנְיָנוּת a second time.
תִּפְתָּי* police official.
תַּקִּיף* strong, mighty.
תקל *pe* weigh.
תְּקֵל *unit of weight* shekel (*11.424 g*).
תקן *ho* be re-established.
תקף *pe* be/become strong; grow hard.
    pa enforce.
תְּקֹף* might.
תְּקָף might.
תְּרֵין two.
תְּרַע door; court.
תָּרָע* door-keeper.
תַּרְתֵּין *f.* two.
תַּתְּנַי *n. pers.* Tattenai.